Welcome to

THE EVERYTHING® DOG BREED GUIDES

AS THE OWNER of a particular type of dog—or someone who is thinking about adopting one—you probably have some questions about that dog breed that can't be answered anywhere else. In particular, you want to know what breed-specific health issues and behavioral traits might arise as you plan for the future with your beloved canine family member.

THE EVERYTHING® DOG BREED GUIDES give you clear-cut answers to all your pressing questions. These authoritative books give you all you need to know about identifying common characteristics; choosing the right puppy or adult dog; coping with personality quirks; instilling obedience; and raising your pet in a healthy, positive environment.

THE EVERYTHING® DOG BREED GUIDES are an extension of the bestselling EVERYTHING® series in the pets category, which include *The Everything® Dog Book* and *The Everything® Dog Training and Tricks Book*. These authoritative, family-friendly books are specially designed to be one-stop guides for anyone looking to explore a specific breed in depth.

THE

EVERYTHING®

Labrador Retriever Book

Dear Reader:

It's not surprising that you're interested in a Labrador Retriever. These handsome, intelligent, fun-loving dogs have been the most popular dog breed in America for more than ten years. That doesn't mean they're right for everyone, though. It's important to learn about the Lab's quirks and characteristics before committing yourself to a lifetime with the breed. That's where I come in.

As a lifelong dog lover and writer who specializes in the subject of dogs, it's my goal to help people find out which dog is right for them. Labs have many advantages: They're large (but not too large), versatile, and smart. Nonetheless, life with a Lab can be overwhelming if you're not prepared. That's why I've written *The Everything® Labrador Retriever Book*. In it, you'll find Lab-specific tips about choosing a puppy, training, health, exercise, and more. It will help you learn all you can about the breed before taking one home. Happy hunting!

Kim Campbell Thornton

THE EVERYTHING® LABRADOR RETRIEVER BOOK

A complete guide to raising, training, and caring for your Lab

Kim Campbell Thornton

Adams Media
Avon, Massachusetts

Dedication:

To Terri Albert's Tank, who helped me explore the Labrador character.

Publishing Director: Gary M. Krebs
Managing Editor: Kate McBride
Copy Chief: Laura MacLaughlin
Acquisitions Editor: Bethany Brown
Development Editor: Patrycja Pasek-Gradziuk
Production Editor: Jamie Wielgus

Production Director: Susan Beale
Production Manager: Michelle Roy Kelly
Series Designers: Daria Perreault and John Paulhus
Cover Design: Paul Beatrice, Frank Rivera
Layout and Graphics: Colleen Cunningham
Rachael Eiben, Michelle Roy Kelly, John Paulhus,
Daria Perreault, Erin Ring

Published by Adams Media, a division of F+W Media, Inc.
57 Littlefield Street, Avon, MA 02322 U.S.A.
www.adamsmedia.com
ISBN 13: 978-1-59337-048-0
ISBN 10: 1-59337-048-2

Printed in the United States of America.

20 19 18 17 16 15 14 13

Library of Congress Cataloging-in-Publication Data
Thornton, Kim Campbell.
The everything Labrador retriever book / Kim Campbell Thornton.
p. cm.
(Everything series book)
ISBN 1-59337-048-2
1. Labrador retriever. I. Title. II. Series: Everything series.

SF429.L3T496 2004
636.752'7–dc22

2003023145

Cover photo ©Kaelson, Carol J. / Animals Animals / Earth Scenes
Interior photographs courtesy of Karen Hocker Photography

This book is available at quantity discounts for bulk purchases.
For information, call 1-800-289-0963.

General Appearance and Personality

The Labrador Retriever is known for his people-friendly personality; short, dense coat; and otterlike tail.

Size and Weight

Height at withers (shoulder): 21½ to 24½ inches
Weight: 55 to 80 pounds

Eyes

Labs are known for their kind and unique eyes. Eye color is usually brown in black and yellow Labs, and brown or hazel in chocolate Labs.

Body

According to the American Kennel Club, "the Labrador should be short-coupled, with good spring of ribs tapering to a moderately wide chest. Correct chest conformation will result in tapering between the front legs that allows unrestricted forelimb movement. Loins should be short, wide, and strong; extending to well developed, powerful hindquarters."

Coat

The coat is one of the Lab's most recognizable features. It should be short, straight, and very dense. Labs have a soft, weather-resistant undercoat for protection from the elements. A Lab's coat colors are black, yellow, and chocolate.

Acknowledgments

My thanks go to the many Labrador Retriever owners who shared their love for and knowledge of their dogs: Terri Albert; Cheri Bush; Margie Dykstra; Doris Engbertson; Evie Glodic; Bonny Georgia Griffith; Deb Hamele; Susan Lennon and Harley and Ralph; Susan McCullough and Allie; Wendy McNaughton; Sara Malchow; Laura Michaels; Dianne Mullikin; Elizabeth Pannill, DVM; Anna Schloff; Judith Stoddard; and Dranda Whaley.

• • •

Contents

Introduction

▶SINCE THE TIME THAT PEOPLE DOMESTICATED DOGS some 15,000 or more years ago, the genus *Canis familiaris* has evolved into more than 300 varieties. Over the millennia, people have developed dogs to perform tasks ranging from hunting to herding to retrieving. Some breeds are multitaskers, capable of doing many different types of work. The Labrador Retriever is one such breed.

When many of us think of dogs, it's the Lab that often comes to mind. The Labrador Retriever is not one of the oldest breeds of dogs, but it is arguably the most popular and versatile member of the canine family. From their beginnings as fishermen's helpers, they have gone on to become retrievers without equal; guide dogs; assistance dogs; drug-, arson-, and bomb-sniffing dogs; therapy dogs; search-and-rescue dogs; and—of course—family friends. Many of us know at least one person who has a Lab.

Always ready for a game of fetch, willing and able to learn anything you can teach, a friend to all the world, the Lab is everything you could want in a dog. That said, he's often more dog than many people are ready for. It takes a special person to live successfully with a Lab, someone who's active, fun-loving, and caring. Labs are definitely trainable and willing to please, but without guidance they can run amok and make life miserable for their caregivers.

The Everything® Labrador Retriever Book will help you recognize and understand the Lab's needs in life so you can decide whether this is really the right breed for you. In this book, you'll learn about the Lab's history and how he became the dog he is today. You'll also find tips on housetraining, manners, socialization, health issues, dog sports, and dealing with behavior problems. This book will guide you through all phases of your Lab's life, from puppyhood to old age. Ⓔ

Meet the Labrador Retriever

WHEN MANY PEOPLE THINK OF DOGS, the image they hold in their heads is that of a Labrador Retriever. This classic sporting dog boasts qualities that make it a favorite of families, athletes, hunters—anyone, in fact, who enjoys a dog with great energy, a sense of humor, and a true love of people. The Lab excels at every kind of job dogs can do, and when he's done working, he's ready to play. Small wonder then that the Labrador is the most popular dog in America.

It's not often that a dog's name says exactly what it does, but that's so in the case of the retriever.

Labrador's Fetching Personality

Labs will fetch anything, anytime, anywhere. You throw something and it will come—back to you in the mouth of the Lab. It's this strong desire to retrieve, as well as versatility, that makes the Lab such a desirable companion in the home with children, in the field, and in the working world.

Other characteristics that distinguish the Labrador are his friendly temperament and loving nature. Some people complain that the Lab is *too* friendly. Often Labs will bark a warning if strangers come to the door, but most are happy to let intruders in and then helpfully point out the valuables. This is a breed that's easygoing and laidback, yet works hard to please the people it loves.

The Labrador Retriever ranks number one in American Kennel Club (AKC) registrations. In 2002, the AKC registered 154,616 Labs. That's 98,492 more than the second most popular breed—Golden Retrievers. The Lab has held the number-one position for several years, and its popularity shows no sign of flagging.

How the Lab Got His Name

If you went strictly by the breed's name, you would be justified in assuming that the Lab originated in the province of Labrador, on Canada's northeastern coast. It's not quite that simple, though. Breed historians offer a number of possibilities for how the Lab acquired its moniker.

One theory is that the name comes from *labrador,* the Spanish word for "farm worker" (surely appropriate for this hard-working breed) or from the *cani di castro laboreiro,* the dogs of Portuguese fishermen. As early as the fifteenth century, Spanish and Portuguese fishermen were known to troll the cod-filled waters of the Grand Banks, southeast of Labrador and the neighboring Newfoundland region. Fishermen often brought along water dogs to help them pull in their nets, retrieve objects, rescue people who fell overboard, or even to swim messages from boat to boat. When heavy fog descended, the dogs' barks helped warn away other nearby boats. Another theory is that the Lab is descended from the Pyrenean (France) mountain dog, brought to the Labrador-Newfoundland area by Basque shepherds.

The Lab's Early History

What is known, however, is that by the beginning of the eighteenth century, there were a number of dogs referred to as Lesser

Newfoundlands, St. John's Newfoundlands (in reference to the town of St. John's in Newfoundland), or simply St. John's dogs. Where does the Labrador reference come in? As noted above, it may have been a Spanish or Portuguese term for the dogs, or it may have been a way to distinguish these dogs from others found in the Newfoundland region.

The first published reference to the Labrador was in Colonel Peter Hawker's *Instructions to Young Sportsmen, In All That Relates to Guns and Shooting,* in 1814.

Sportsmen Discover the Lab Prototype

Colonel Peter Hawker, a well-known sportsman who visited Newfoundland in 1814, described the St. John's Newfoundland dog as having an excellent sense of smell, flexibility in the field, and speed. In Hawker's diary, he says of the St. John's dog that it is:

> oftener black than of another colour and scarcely bigger than a pointer. He is made rather long in head and nose; pretty deep in the chest; very fine in the legs; has short or smooth hair, does not carry his tail so much curled (unlike the ordinary Newfoundland [dog], which had a rough coat and a tail that curled over its back), and is extremely quick and active in running and swimming . . . The St. John's breed of these dogs is chiefly used on their native coast by fishermen. Their sense of smelling is scarcely to be credited. Their discrimination of scent . . . appears almost impossible . . . For finding wounded game of every description, there is not his equal in the canine race; and he is a sine qua non in the general pursuit of waterfowl.

The Water Dogs

The dog's hunting abilities were noted even earlier, in 1662, when W. E. Cormack, traveling through Newfoundland, observed some small water dogs. Of them, he wrote that they were "admirably trained as retrievers in fowling and are otherwise useful. The smooth or shorthaired dog is preferred because in frosty weather, the longhaired kind become encumbered with ice on coming out of the water."

Cousin to the Newfoundland?

The Labrador Retriever and the Newfoundland may well descend from the same ancestor. One of the speculations about the Newfoundland's heritage is that he descends from Great Pyrenees dogs brought to Newfoundland by Basque fishermen, and as noted above, a similar supposition is made about the Labrador's beginnings. The Newfoundland is much larger than the Lab (which is why the Lab was originally known as the Lesser Newfoundland or Little Newfoundland) and has a long, heavy coat.

Development in England

Being a seafaring dog, the Little Newfoundland eventually made its way to England. It is believed that the Englishmen, who settled the St. John's area of Newfoundland, brought these dogs to England through the port of Poole in the county of Dorset. And it wasn't long before they came to the attention of the second Earl of Malmesbury, who thought they would be perfect for the hunting on his estate, which was surrounded by swampy lands. He called the dogs Little Newfoundlanders, and in 1822 arranged to import more of them.

The dogs that probably contributed the most to the development of the modern Labrador Retriever were Buccleuch's Ned, Buccleuch's Avon, A. C. Butter's Peter of Faskally, and Major Portal's Flapper.

A Noble Breeding Program

Carrying on the family tradition, the third earl began a serious breeding program. It was he who affixed the name Labrador to the breed. In an 1887 letter to a friend, he wrote: "We always call mine Labrador dogs, and I have kept the breed as pure as I could from the first I had from Poole, at that time carrying on a brisk trade with Newfoundland. The real breed may be known by its close coat, which turns the water off like oil and, above all, a tail like an otter." The earl gave the dogs to many of his friends, and they rapidly spread throughout England, becoming known as peerless swimmers and efficient retrievers.

Working Toward Consistency

As yet, however, the breed had little consistency in type. Historical factors came into play that changed this, though. The first was a high tax on dogs in Newfoundland, followed by the introduction of the British quarantine law, both of which effectively put a halt to imports of the dogs. English breeders turned their attention to perfecting the breed, keeping written records of pedigrees (a line of ancestors or lineage), and entering the dogs in the newly popular dog shows. They drew up a breed standard (a written description of what the breed should be), and England's Kennel Club officially recognized the Labrador Retriever—by that name—in 1903.

Back to the Americas

American sportsmen were eager to bring the Labrador to their own shores to retrieve upland game and waterfowl—from mourning doves and quail to wild turkeys, ducks, and geese. There's some dispute over which Labrador should get the honor of being the first registered with the American Kennel Club. The AKC cites Brocklehirst Floss in 1917, while the Labrador Retriever Club names Brocklehirst Nell, also in 1917. Yet another source claims the title of first for Virginia Vennie, in 1914.

Essential

Dogs that resemble Labradors have appeared in works of art for centuries. Paintings from the fifteenth and sixteenth centuries by Italian artists DiCosimo and Titian and the Spanish artist Velasquez portray gun dogs that look much like the Labrador Retriever.

A Club for American Labradors

The breed's main advocate in the United States was Franklin B. Lord, who imported Labradors from Lorna Howe of England's Banchory Kennels. Lord wrote a column on the breed for the AKC's magazine, the *Gazette,* and was instrumental in the founding of the Labrador Retriever Club in 1931. Two years later, Boli of Blake became the first Labrador to earn an American championship. From the late 1920s through the 1930s, many Labradors were imported to this country from England, and they were the foundation of the American Labrador.

A Lab Goes to the White House

The breed's popularity continued through the twentieth century. A Lab even took over the White House in December 1997, when President Bill Clinton received a three-month-old chocolate Lab. He named the pup Buddy, after a favorite uncle who had bred and trained dogs. Buddy was the first Labrador to live in the White House.

Labrador Needs

When you look at his history, it's easy to see how and why the Labrador has become such a favorite among dog lovers. That relationship goes both ways, though. In return for his fun-loving companionship, the Labrador has certain needs of his own. Besides regular meals and a sturdy roof over his head, he needs plenty of exercise, consistent training, and interaction with his family. The Lab that's provided with all these things can't help but become your best friend.

▲ **These four black Labs are all related.**

Exercise

Labs are sporting dogs. For almost 200 years, they've been bred to work all day in the field under any conditions. Not surprisingly, they enjoy activity, whether it be work or play. A Lab will be happy to play fetch for hours on end, to work on perfecting his obedience commands, or to go walking, hiking, jogging, or bicycling with you, or to train for agility, flyball, or other dog sports. Remember that they are hard-wired to be companion hunting dogs, retrieving over all kinds of terrain and in water, in close contact with people.

This is one of the biggest areas of caution when it comes to choosing a Lab over another breed. These dogs need a lot of exercise, mental stimulation, and human contact. Expect to play with, train, or exercise your Lab at least three or four times daily, for at least fifteen to thirty minutes at a time.

Exercise Time Requirements

After puppyhood and up to five years of age, the typical play/exercise requirements for a Lab are a thirty- to forty-five-minute walk in the morning, a fifteen- to thirty-minute play period at lunchtime, and a forty-five- to sixty-minute walk before dinner with short potty breaks in the evening. If you have a fenced yard or access to a dog park, off-leash play can be spent retrieving, playing with other dogs, or practicing training commands. Swimming is also a favorite Lab sport.

The Labrador Retriever has a high activity level. This can be disconcerting to the person who's expecting a dog to relax with while watching ESPN or *Survivor.* The Lab will be happy to watch television with you, but only after hours of exercise and play.

Even older Labs need vigorous play and extended walks a couple of times a day to stay on an even keel. When their exercise needs are met, they're more content to sleep during the day while the family is at work or school. When their exercise needs aren't met, they can turn into demanding, stubborn, naughty dogs. They have strong personalities and won't be placated by anything else—except, perhaps, food. One of the most common reasons people give when they take a Lab to the animal shelter is "I didn't realize he would need so much exercise, and I didn't have time to give it to him." To fully experience the Lab's wonderfully goofy, biddable, loving personality, be prepared to give him the exercise and human contact he craves.

Training

Because they've been bred to work closely with people, Labs are highly trainable. They watch their people closely and soak up what's wanted of them—like those paper towels you see advertised on television. The Lab, indeed, is the "quicker picker-upper" of the dog world. Begin training early, on the first day you bring him home. By the time he's enrolled in puppy kindergarten–at ten to twelve weeks of age–he'll be more than ready to shine in class, eager to show off his sit, down, and come skills, plus whatever else you've been teaching him. Continue his training throughout his life so he doesn't get bored or forget what he's learned.

▲ **This chocolate Lab gets some big air as she launches herself into the pond.**

Companionship

Most important, your Lab needs lots of love and attention. He's a people-pleasing, people-loving dog, and his greatest joy in life–besides fetching that ball–is spending time with his family. By giving your Lab plenty of exercise and training, you'll mold a dog that has an acceptable indoor activity level and nice manners, both of which are the foundation of a good housedog. Your Lab should live in the house. Of course he needs a yard to play in, but for meals, bedtime, and just enjoying life, he should be indoors with the rest of the family. Ⓔ

Chapter 2
The Labrador Defined

FROM THE FIRST DOMESTICATED CANINE 15,000 or more years ago, dogs have evolved into an incredible variety of shapes, sizes, and temperaments. Over the millennia, people have developed them to perform tasks ranging from hunting to herding to retrieving. Along the way, we have also set down guidelines as to how each type of dog should look and act. Here, you'll learn about the Labrador's appearance, temperament, and working ability.

The Labrador Retriever Breed Standard

If you look in a dictionary, you'll see that the Labrador Retriever is described as a compact, strongly built retriever having a short dense black, yellow, or chocolate coat. That's certainly the breed in a nutshell, but there's a lot more to know about what a Lab should look like, how he should be built, and how he should move and act. For that, you need to know what the breed standard says.

The American Kennel Club (AKC) breed standard is a picture in words that describes what the perfect dog in each breed should look like, detailing the physical and mental qualities that make a particular breed good at what it does–in this case, retrieving. Of course, there is no such thing as a perfect dog, but the standard gives breeders something to strive for. The standard also ensures that the Lab looks like a Lab instead of a Golden Retriever, a Chesapeake Bay Retriever, or a Curly-Coated Retriever.

Founded in 1884, the American Kennel Club (AKC) is a registry that certifies a particular dog and its progenitors as purebreds. Besides maintaining a registry of purebred dogs, the AKC sponsors events, such as conformation shows and field trials, and promotes responsible dog ownership.

Defining Characteristics

When you look at a Lab, you should see a strongly built, medium-sized dog that is sound and athletic, with a stocky, muscular body. The well-built Labrador can hunt and retrieve waterfowl and upland game for hours on end under difficult conditions, and his character and quality are good enough that he can compete in the show ring, as well as be a family companion. Ideally neither too leggy nor too squat, adult males weigh 65 to 80 pounds and stand 22.5 to 24.5 inches at the withers (shoulder); females weigh 55 to 70 pounds and stand 21.5 to 23.5 inches. The characteristics that distinguish the Lab from other retrievers—and other dogs in general—are a short, dense, weather-resistant coat; otter tail; clean-cut head with broad back skull and moderate stop; and kind, friendly eyes.

There are three distinct types of Labrador Retrievers. The English type is a square-faced, thick-set dog with the Lab's distinctive otter tail. The American show dog type is taller and thinner with a longer face. The field trial type, bred strictly for working ability, can look like the English or American show type or may fall somewhere in between.

The Lab in the Show Ring

When Lab experts look at dogs in the show ring, they want to see dogs with overall balance: a good-looking head; good reach of neck; well-angulated shoulders; strong bone; tight, round feet; a solid topline; good depth through the ribcage; a thick, dense coat; and a fat otter tail. A well-built Lab is slightly longer than tall. And boy can he move! The following overview of the Lab standard will help you understand what's meant by some of these terms.

Head First

The Lab's clean-cut head has the appearance of a finely chiseled piece of sculpture. The skull and foreface are on parallel planes of almost equal length. A slightly pronounced brow defines the "stop" (discussed in the sidebar), and the skull is not in a straight line with the nose. A broad back skull ensures that there's plenty of room for brains—something the Lab has in abundance. The wide nose has well-developed nostrils for taking in scents. The nose should be black on black or yellow Labs and brown on chocolate Labs. It's okay if the nose color fades to a lighter shade, but a pink nose or one without any pigment (coloration) at all would be a disqualification in the show ring.

The stop is the indentation between the eyes where the nasal bones and cranium meet. The topline is the back. A round foot, also known as a cat foot, is compact with well-arched toes that are bunched tightly together.

The jaws are powerful, allowing the Lab to retrieve a bird as large as a wild goose. A scissors-bite (one in which the outer side of the lower incisors touches the inner side of the upper incisors) and correct neck construction are what give the breed its famous "soft mouth," the ability to carry its quarry so tenderly that it leaves not a single toothmark. Teeth should be strong, and the dog should have all forty-two of them.

Framing the face are pendant, or hanging, ears that are set slightly above eye level. If you were to draw them across the Lab's face, they would reach only as far as the inside of the eye.

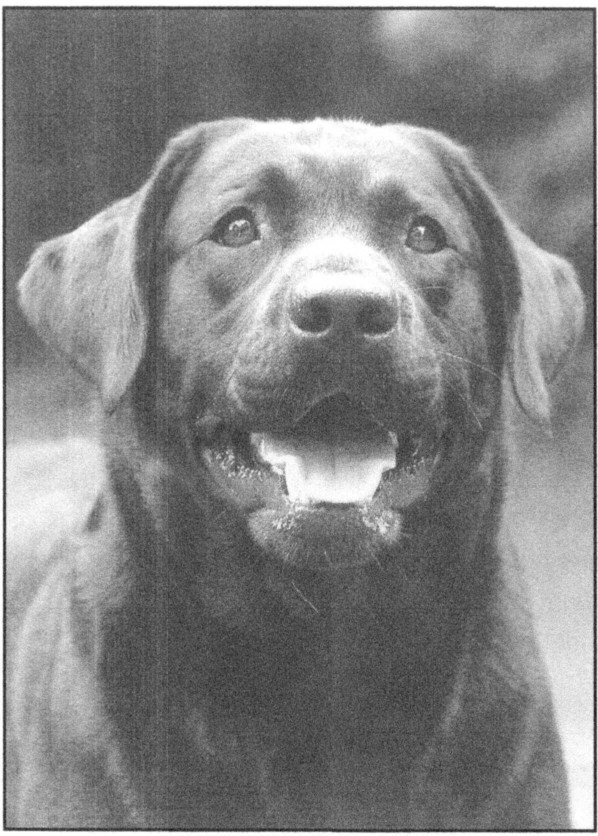

◀ **A three-year-old male black Lab.**

Kind, friendly eyes embody the Lab's intelligent, alert, and friendly temperament. Neither protruding nor deep-set, the eyes are of medium size and placed well apart. In black or brown Labs they should be brown—the color of burnt sugar—with black eye rims. Chocolate Labs may have brown or hazel eyes with brown eye rims. Black or yellow eyes can give the Lab a harsh expression that's not typical of the breed.

Body Beautiful

The Lab's strong, muscular neck rises from the shoulders with a moderate arch. It should be just long enough to allow the Lab to retrieve game easily. A proper Lab neck is free of throatiness, defined as loose skin beneath the throat. A short, thick neck—also known as a ewe neck—is not desirable.

The shoulders need to have correct angulation if the Lab is to move properly. The standard says the shoulders should be well laid back, long and sloping. This means they should form an approximately ninety-degree angle with the upper foreleg. When the angulation is correct, the dog can move its front legs easily with strong forward reach. Ideally, the length of the shoulder blade should equal the length of the upper foreleg.

▲ A two-year old black male shows off the breed's conformation standard.

A strong back allows the Labrador to work tirelessly all day. From the shoulders to the pelvic girdle, the back is level, whether the dog is standing or moving. A sloping back indicates too much angulation in the rear legs. Flexibility in the loin—the area between the ribs and the pelvic girdle—gives the Lab the athleticism that marks him as a sporting dog. A short loin with long ribbing allows good movement.

The underline is also straight, without much tuck-up, or waist, at the loin. Wide and strong, the loin joins with the powerful rear end to give the Lab an efficient, driving gait. The rump is nice and round, with short thigh muscles. The ribs curve out to make room for the heart and lungs.

From the side, the Lab's forechest should look well developed but not exaggerated. A chest that's too narrow gives the appearance of hollowness between the front legs. One that's too wide would give the Lab the look of a Bulldog. The correct chest tapers between the front legs so the dog can move without restriction.

Leg Work and Movement

Front legs are straight with strong but not excessive bone. Viewed from the side, the elbows should be directly beneath the withers, close to the ribs without being loose. Labs that are "out at the elbows" can't move freely. Strong, muscular hind legs have well-turned stifles (knees) and strong, short hocks (heels). The knee shouldn't slip out of place when the dog is moving or standing (a condition known as luxating patella). Labs with short, heavy-boned legs aren't typical.

Thick pads and well-arched toes support and protect the strong, compact feet in much the same way as good athletic shoes or hiking boots. Dewclaws, the additional toenails that are positioned up on the inside of the leg, may be removed if the breeder chooses. This is a minor procedure that's usually done with newborn pups, although dewclaws can also be removed at a later age, during any other routine surgery, such as spaying or neutering.

Economy of movement best describes the Labrador's gait, or the way he moves. Gait is the pattern of footsteps at various rates of speed, with each pattern distinguished by a particular rhythm and footfall. With elbows held neatly to the body, the Labrador moves straight ahead without pacing or weaving, covering plenty of distance with a long, smooth stride. From behind, it looks as if the hind legs are moving as nearly as possible in a parallel line with the front legs.

Coat and Color

One of the distinctive features of the Lab is his short, straight, dense coat of black, yellow, or chocolate. The double coat–a short, hard outer layer over a soft, warm undercoat–protects this avid water dog from cold, damp conditions as well as all types of ground cover and brush. It's acceptable for a Lab's coat to be slightly wavy down the back, but woolly, silky, or slick coats don't properly shed water, let alone the burrs and mud that this dog encounters in a typical day of playing or working hard.

▲ A spectrum of Lab colors: a five-year-old yellow female, an eight-year-old chocolate female, and a seven-year-old black female.

It was once said that Labradors come in only three colors: "black, black, and black." It's agreed, now, however, that good Labs come in all of the three accepted colors. Black Labs are solid black and should not have any brindle or tan markings. A small white spot on the chest is permissible but not desirable in the show ring. Yellow Labs come in varying shades, from pale cream to fox red. There's no such thing as a white Lab, although some yellow Labs are so creamy as to appear white. The shades of yellow may vary on the ears, back, and belly. The chocolate Lab also varies in color, ranging from light milk chocolate to the deep, shiny richness of the best Belgian chocolate.

Tail End

The otter tail is another distinctive physical characteristic of the Labrador. This type of tail is thick at the base, round and tapering toward the tip. It's of medium length and should extend no further than the hock.

The coat wraps thickly around the tail, giving it an unusual rounded appearance. The hair is parted or divided on the underside, with no feathering. The bottom of the tail should look flat, with the hairs interlacing to produce the flat appearance.

When a Lab is out of coat (a dog is said to be out of coat during seasonal sheds), the bottom of the tail may not wrap all the way from the tip to the base, but the last 2 or 3 inches at the base should always wrap.

When a Lab is swimming or moving, the tail is carried straight out from the body, never too high or too low. The tail completes the Lab's balanced look by giving the dog a flowing line from the top of the head to the tip of the tail.

Pet, Show Dog, or Hunter?

One of the many virtues of the Lab is his adaptability. Although the Labs started out as field dogs whose only job was to retrieve, they have since proven themselves in a number of areas. In addition to their popularity in the home, show ring, and field, Labs have found work as guide or assistance dogs, search-and-rescue dogs, arson detection dogs, therapy dogs, and more. Find out what the Lab can do and which aspects of this breed are right for you.

Whether you want your Lab to be a family friend, show dog, or hunter (or all three!), the standard will help you understand which characteristics are most important for each job. For instance, if your Lab will be a pet or hunting dog, it doesn't matter if he has black or yellow eyes, but in the show ring eyes of those colors would count against him.

The versatile Labrador Retriever is capable of fulfilling the roles of pet, show dog, and hunter. Nonetheless, what you want in a dog will determine the type of Lab you look for. The qualities a companion dog needs vary depending on family lifestyle and the presence or absence of children. And like many hunting breeds, the Lab's temperament and appearance can vary, depending on whether he's been bred for the show ring or the field. Decide what you want in a Lab before you start looking at puppies.

Family Friend

A Labrador that's going to be a family companion should have a calm, stable temperament. He should come from parents that have this same temperament and who have health certifications indicating healthy hips, elbows, hearts, and eyes. Ideally, the parents have both proven themselves to be good examples of the breed by earning a championship in the show ring. Your family dog is a big investment, and you should want to get the most for your money.

Show Dog

Show Labs, besides having the potential for excellent conformation have a charisma that's obvious even in puppyhood. Dog show judges often say that the dogs they choose were "asking for the win," and it's this level of appeal that can help ensure a show dog's career. If you want to show your Lab, choose a pup with no obvious disqualifications and only minor faults. Light eyes and a slightly pink nose aren't going to cut it in the show ring. Naturally, the parents should have the same health certifications you would expect if you were buying a pet puppy, and they should have proven themselves in the show ring by earning a championship.

Conformation is the form and structure of a dog as defined by the breed standard. A conformation show is a competitive event where dogs compete in several classes at various levels to determine the one that most closely meets the breed standard. Dogs that earn the required number of points and combinations of points are awarded the title of champion.

Retriever Par Excellence

Labs from field or performance bloodlines are bred to have high energy levels that will carry them through an exhausting day at a field trial. This is great if you want a dog to hunt or compete with, but it's maybe not so great if you simply want a family companion. Dogs from show lines are usually bred to be somewhat calmer, but that doesn't mean they can't hunt or compete in field trials. Just be aware of the potential differences in activity levels if you're considering pups from two different litters—one bred for field work and one for show. If you want to hunt or field trial your Lab, look for a pup that's built to do the work it was bred for. Structural and movement faults will be a problem in the field, because the dog won't be able to work all day, run as fast, or carry game properly. Again, require health certifications and proof that the parents have earned field championships.

Alert!

Faults are weaknesses that can cost a dog points in the show ring or field. They can be structural (for instance, a wedge-shaped head or misaligned teeth), or cosmetic (such as black or yellow eyes or ears that are too short, too long, or too large). Disqualifications are serious flaws that make a Lab ineligible for show or field competition (like eye rims or nose lacking in any pigment).

The Working Lab

The Labrador also makes an incredible working dog. Although you may not need him for any of these purposes, it's good to know just how smart your dog can be. That way you won't underestimate him or what he's capable of.

Assistance Dog

Assistance dogs help people with disabilities by pulling wheelchairs, picking things up, carrying items, pushing doors open, switching lights on and off, and performing many other tasks. And, of course, they also provide companionship. Labs have a number of qualities that make them superb assistance dogs.

Foremost, of course, are their strong aptitude for retrieving, their ability to learn quickly, and their friendly, stable temperament. A Lab that goes into service work may be asked to pick up an item as small as a paper clip or as large as a pair of crutches. The variety of work involved in being an assistance dog is appealing to the hard-working Lab.

The Lab's easygoing temperament is a plus as well. Labs rarely have aggression issues. They take in stride the many different sights, sounds, and people that assistance dogs encounter without letting them get in the way of their work.

Besides being strong and hardworking, Labs have another advantage: Their short coat requires little grooming–a good brushing once a week will keep it healthy. And they're large enough to be useful, but not so large that they can't fit beneath the table in a fine restaurant–or McDonald's, for that matter. All of these traits and attributes combined make the Lab a desirable and successful assistance dog.

Guide Dog

Guide dogs learn to take people who can't see on their daily rounds, helping them to navigate stairs, doorways, and traffic. Guide dogs require many of the same attributes as assistance dogs. They must be quick to learn and eager to please.

Often, guide dogs are bred to be smaller than the average Lab. The smaller size gives them two advantages. They're less conspicuous, and they fit more easily on public transportation or beneath tables.

Service dogs must learn eighty or more commands. These include pushing elevator buttons, summoning help, retrieving objects such as the telephone or the television remote control, and retrieving food from the refrigerator (without eating it).

Both guide and assistance dogs usually come from special breeding programs, although some programs accept donations from breeders or pet homes. Not every Lab has the right stuff to become an assistance or guide dog. Each is carefully tested as a puppy to make sure he has the right personality and aptitudes for this important work. For instance, Labs that are overly dominant or overly submissive don't work well. Additionally, service dogs must have a low prey drive, to be able to sublimate their desire to chase a bird while pulling a wheelchair or guiding someone across a busy street.

Search-and-Rescue Dog

These highly trained dogs and their handlers seek and find hundreds of missing people every year. They also help rescue people trapped after catastrophic events, such as the collapse of the World Trade Center, earthquakes, and avalanches. Search-and-rescue (SAR) dogs can specialize in any of the following kinds of search:

- **Wilderness searches:** Seeking missing persons in forested or other wild areas
- **Water searches:** Sniffing out the scent of drowning victims, which rises to the surface of the water
- **Urban searches:** Following an individual scent in a highly populated area
- **Avalanche work:** Searching for people buried beneath snow
- **Disaster searches:** Looking for victims of earthquakes, hurricanes, fires, among other disasters

Among the attributes that make Labs good SAR dogs are their exquisite sense of smell, size, strength and stamina, swimming ability (for water search dogs), and that easy-care coat.

Detector Dog

The Labrador's ability to differentiate one odor from another is one of the factors that makes him such a superb working dog. Labs have found employment with the FBI as chemical explosives dogs, with the U.S. Customs Service as drug-sniffing dogs, and with fire departments or insurance companies as arson detectors.

The FBI's chemical explosives dogs are trained to sniff out different explosive chemicals. During their extensive training, the dogs learn to identify approximately 19,000 different combinations of explosives.

The U.S. Customs Service Canine Enforcement Program uses Labradors, among other breeds, to find drugs, currency, and other contraband being smuggled across the border. Labs considered for the program must be one to three years old with an outgoing, curious personality, as well as the ability to remain calm and focused in the face of crowds, loud noises, or chaotic situations. A passion for retrieving is a must—a trait the Lab has in abundance.

If you could remove the sensory membranes that line the inside of a dog's nose and stretch them out flat, their total surface area would be greater than the total surface area of the dog's body.

Arson dogs are trained to detect the presence of accelerants and ignitable liquids, such as gasoline or paint thinner, that are often used to set fires. When the dog locates an accelerant, he touches the area with his nose. Once again, the Lab's highly sensitive nose is what makes him ideal for this type of work. His personable nature, calm demeanor, and quiet manners also make him the dog of choice for arson detection work.

Therapy Dog

Studies show that simply petting a dog can lower blood pressure. A visit from a dog to patients at nursing homes and hospitals can raise spirits and soothe agitation. Not surprisingly, the good-natured Lab is a popular therapy dog. He enjoys meeting people and loves getting petted. His trainability allows him to perform entertaining tricks, such as "Speak" or "Shake hands," when he's making his rounds.

Therapy dogs, or facility dogs (as they're sometimes called), receive training from organizations such as Therapy Dog International, the Delta Society Pet Partners, and Love on a Leash. They don't need formal obedience training, but they are expected to have certain skills. These include being able to meet strangers in a friendly manner, sit politely for petting, walk nicely on a leash, walk through crowds, be comfortable around walkers and crutches, and get along well with other dogs. Therapy work is a great way to spread the Lab love around.

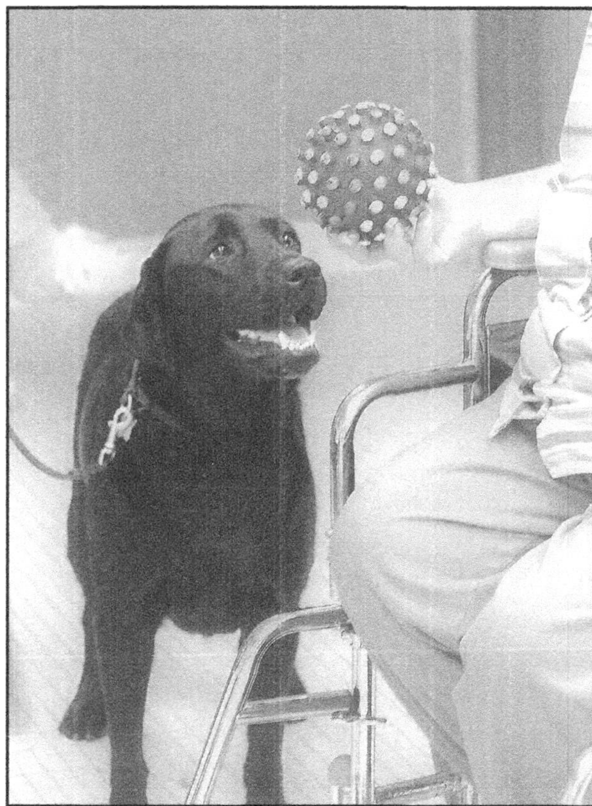

◀ **Labs make great therapy dogs. Here, a twenty-month-old female black Lab assists with physical therapy.**

Understanding the Labrador Character

It is believed the Labrador Retriever is always smiling with a twinkle in his eye. He's been described as loving the world. A Labrador with ideal temperament is 100-percent unflappable. No matter what's going on around him, he's cool, calm, and collected–unless, of course, he's being called on to play ball with the kids or show his talents in the field, when he can let loose with his natural exuberance. The loving Lab tolerates and forgives toddlers that pull his tail and tug on his ears in an effort to stand up. That doesn't mean, however, that he should be expected to put up with those things. The ever-patient Lab should be protected from mistreatment, however innocent the intent might be.

The Lab's very best qualities are that he's intelligent and easy to train. On the flip side, he likes to be busy, especially in puppyhood. This is not a couch-potato dog that will be content to lie around all day, at least not until he's older. While a mature Lab is more laid back, the Lab puppy or adolescent that's not occupied with play, training, or work will turn to chewing, barking, and digging to keep himself entertained.

The ideal Lab is kind, outgoing, and willing to please. He's never aggressive toward people or other animals. Any sign of aggression or shyness is not typical of the breed and should not be excused, either in the show ring or in the home.

As a watchdog, the Labrador is neither the most territorial nor the least territorial of dogs. As befits his easygoing personality, he falls somewhere in between. A Lab will usually bark if the doorbell rings or even if he hears someone walk up to the door. He'll gauge your reaction to a stranger before deciding how to act. Once he's given the signal that someone is okay, he turns into a wiggling bundle of joy at the opportunity of having someone new to pet him.

Well-bred Labs with good temperaments usually get along just fine with other dogs and cats. Family birds might need to watch their tail feathers, though. A Lab will sit and stare at a bird in a cage all day long, just waiting for his big chance to retrieve it. Other pets a Lab might drool over are hamsters or guinea pigs.

The breed's most outstanding quality, without a doubt, is its adaptability and versatility. With training, the Lab can do just about anything you ask, short of typing your novel or giving a speech. Because of his love for people, the Lab is receptive to training, eager to "do for" and please its person. That's one of the reasons the breed makes such a great guide or assistance dog.

Chapter 

Looking for a Labrador Retriever

YOU'VE EVALUATED YOUR LIFESTYLE and come to the conclusion that you have the energy, time, and patience to live happily with a Labrador Retriever. You know what activities you want to do with the dog, and you've studied the breed standard, so you understand what you're looking for in a Lab. Your children are sturdy enough to enjoy playing with a rambunctious Lab and old enough to take on simple dog care under supervision. All you have to do now is consider where to get the Labrador of your dreams.

Looking in All the Right Places

When you're ready to get your Lab, you have a number of choices when it comes to deciding where to acquire your new dog. You can purchase a Lab from a breeder or adopt one from an animal shelter or a rescue group. Each source has advantages and disadvantages. Take a look at the possibilities so you can make the decision that's right for you.

The Reputable Breeder

Anyone can breed two Labs and sell the puppies. They don't have to have a license or know anything about dogs. Ideally, however, you'll buy your Lab from a hobby breeder (also referred to as a reputable or responsible breeder). This is someone who has been involved with Labs for several years—showing their dogs in conformation classes, field trialing them, or participating in obedience trials. In this book, Appendix B provides solid guidelines for finding a reputable breeder.

This breeder should belong to the national Labrador Retriever Club, as well as to local all-breed or specialty dog clubs. Hobby breeders study pedigrees carefully, looking to find the best matches for their dogs' strengths and weaknesses. Before breeding, they take their dogs to the veterinarian for health screenings to rule out such heritable conditions as hip or elbow dysplasia, eye problems, and heart disease.

A good breeder can be the source for a first-rate Lab puppy or a well-adjusted older Lab that has retired from breeding or the show ring. It's your job to sort out breeders who are just out for a buck from the committed breeders who are dedicated to the breed's well-being.

Breeder Advantages

There are many advantages of buying from a reputable breeder. You can meet the mother and sometimes the father if he's in the same locale. (Females are often shipped long distances to be bred with the right male.) Even if the father isn't in the area, the breeder may have photos or videos of him. You may also be able to meet other relatives of the puppies you're considering buying. This is important because it gives you a good idea of what your Lab will be like as an adult.

Breeders can also become mentors. They're there to answer questions as your Lab goes through adolescence—always a trying time—and if you want to show your dog, they can guide you through the process. If you live in the same area as the breeder, he or she may board your dog while you're traveling, allowing him to stay in a familiar place and giving you peace of mind that he's being well cared for. And if there's ever a reason you can't keep your Lab, a true reputable breeder will insist on taking the dog back to keep him or find another home for him.

Breeder Disadvantages

What are the disadvantages of buying from a reputable breeder? Sometimes they can be hard to find. It takes patience and persistence to find the one that's right for you. But if you want to get your money's worth, a hobby breeder is the way to go. You will know that your new pup has been raised in a home by a knowledgeable breeder, who has bred high-quality dogs and provided her pups with proper nutrition, veterinary care, and early socialization.

A reputable breeder's main priority is that his or her puppies go to a good home where they'll be loved all their lives. Be wary of a breeder who seems anxious to get rid of puppies or who pressures you to take one of his or her puppies.

Labrador Rescue Organizations

What if you want a Lab, but you like the idea of giving a home to a dog in need? A Labrador rescue group can give you the best of both worlds. The Labrador Retriever Club supports rescue efforts by maintaining a list of people nationwide who help place lost or abandoned Labradors.

What You'll Find from Rescue Groups

As with the Labs found in shelters, these are usually dogs six months or older. In most cases, before they're placed, they are spayed or neutered, vaccinated, checked for heartworm disease, and tattooed or microchipped. Sometimes the Labs in rescue have behavior problems—such as fence jumping, digging, or barking—but the rescue group can help you find training to resolve the problem. Labs adopted from breed rescue groups usually go on to become wonderful family companions.

Breed Rescue Advantages and Drawbacks

Adoption from a Labrador rescue group has several advantages. Generally, people involved in breed rescue are committed to the welfare of the Labs they work with and try hard to match people with the right dog. They follow up with new owners after the adoption, offering advice and counseling as needed.

Before you decide that breed rescue sounds like an inexpensive way to get a Lab, be aware of the disadvantages. Puppies are rarely available through breed rescue groups. This is true even with popular breeds, such as Labrador Retrievers. People whose Labs have puppies usually know that an ad in the newspaper will sell the puppies.

The Labrador Retriever Club maintains a national emergency fund to help care for Labs that are abandoned in multiple numbers after the shutdown of a puppy mill or that need help in the event of a natural disaster, such as a flood or tornado. It helps pay for immediate care needs, such as vaccinations, health checks, or short-term boarding.

Be aware, too, that the heritage of a puppy or dog adopted through a breed rescue group is rarely known—and if it is, it's usually not of very high quality. Generally speaking, the people who surrender a Lab to a rescue program are not the people who have carefully selected a breeder. Furthermore, you don't have the advantage of being able to see the health clearances on the parents. Severe hip dysplasia or other congenital or hereditary problems may not appear for some time.

Finding a Breed Rescue Group

To find a Labrador rescue group in your area, contact the Labrador Retriever Club (as listed in Appendix A). You can also go to your favorite search engine and type in "Labrador breed rescue and [your state]." When you find a Lab rescue group, ask for literature on the program, such as a brochure or newsletter. Take a look at the adoption contract; it should state that the program will accept the return of the dog for any reason if you are unable to keep it. Another requirement should be that all dogs placed are spayed or neutered first, with exceptions only for age or medical conditions.

The Breed Rescue Process

Adopting from a breed-rescue group isn't as simple as going in, picking the dog you want, and writing a check for it. Like reputable breeders, breed rescue volunteers are interested in what you bring to a dog's life and care. They want to place each dog in the best possible home, and this requires a period of evaluation that takes time. The wait is influenced by the number of dogs available and the number of other equally or sometimes more suitable applicants.

Rescue programs vary in what they require for adoption. Some insist on a fenced yard (often with prohibitions on electronic fences), as well as an appreciation of the amount of exercise a Lab needs. All look for a realistic lifestyle for good dog care. Expect to be asked whether you have time for a dog, which is understandable when you consider that a major reason Labs are surrendered to rescue programs is a lack of time to care for and exercise the dog properly.

You'll be asked to fill out an application first. Most groups require and check references, ideally from a veterinarian and a trainer. Many groups also schedule home visits, so they can evaluate the environment where the Lab will be living, as well as your experience with and readiness for a Lab. Adoption fees usually range from $150 to $300. That's a pretty good deal, considering what you get: a spayed or neutered dog with current vaccinations and a health check.

Truthfully provide all the information requested by the rescue group about yourself and your home. Be willing to permit the home visit, and don't be offended by what may seem to be personal questions. Just as you want a good Lab, the rescue group wants good homes for its dogs.

Animal Shelters and Humane Societies

Believe it or not, you can find a nice Labrador Retriever in an animal shelter or humane society. Sometimes puppies are turned in to shelters when the family that bred them hasn't been able to sell them. Other times, adolescent or older Labs are given up because their caregivers decided they didn't have time for them. If you are considering getting an older Lab, or you like the idea of giving a home to a dog that really needs one, but there's not a Lab rescue group in your area, the shelter can be a great place to look. Expect to find Labs between six and eighteen months of age, although there might be some that are younger or older.

Types of Shelters

No two animal shelters are alike, and there is no such thing as a centrally organized Society for the Prevention of Cruelty to Animals (SPCA) or humane society that oversees local organizations. You can look for a Lab at a municipal animal shelter—one that's funded by tax dollars and user fees. Municipal shelters enforce animal control ordinances, license dogs, and quarantine animals that have recently bitten someone. They identify stray pets and return them to their owners when possible. Progressive municipal shelters with adequate budgets may offer such services as animal placement, community education, and vaccination clinics.

Your town may also have one or more privately funded non-profit animal shelters. Those with open admissions take any animal brought to them. So-called "no-kill" shelters pick and choose which animals they'll accept, based on species, age, health, adopt-ability, and availability of kennel space. Often these shelters send out newsletters or have Web sites listing the types of dogs they have available.

If your local shelter doesn't have any Labs available, check out *www.petfinder.com*. Rescue groups and animal shelters post descriptions there of animals that need homes, and potential adopters can search the site by breed, area, and other parameters.

Shelter Advantages and Drawbacks

The greatest advantage of adopting a Lab from a shelter is that warm, fuzzy feeling you get from giving a needy dog a good home. Another advantage is the variety of services provided by some shelters. You may go home with a Lab that has been health-checked, spayed or neutered, and vaccinated. He may even be housetrained or know basic obedience skills. Some shelters offer training classes and behavioral counseling so the two of you can get off to a good start.

The disadvantage—if you can call it that—to adopting from a shelter is that most of them don't provide instant gratification. Like breeders and Lab rescue groups, many shelters nowadays have a rigorous screening process. They want to make sure that the dogs they place go to forever homes, not temporary housing. While it might seem onerous, think of it as a benefit to the dog rather than as a hoop you must jump through.

Sometimes, however, the only place to adopt a dog is an understaffed, overburdened city shelter. Be aware that adopting from a shelter where the staff does not have the time or resources to evaluate each animal entails an element of risk. It's one thing to take home a Lab with an unknown history that has been evaluated by a trained shelter employee. It's quite another to take home a Lab without knowing anything at all about him. Nonetheless, this risk can usually be overcome by working with a trainer or behaviorist after the adoption.

Looking in All the Wrong Places

Because Labs are so popular, many people breed them just to make a fast buck. Sure, it's easy to get a Lab from these people, but the thing to consider is that you get what you pay for. These breeders usually don't start out with high-quality Labs, and they don't do the pedigree searches and health screening that hobby breeders do. With this in mind, here are some places to avoid when looking for that perfect Lab pup.

Just because a dog is registered with the AKC or another association doesn't guarantee that he's of high quality. Registries provide documentation based on what the breeder tells them, so take time to find a breeder whom you feel answers all your questions honestly.

The Lab Next Door

Not every breeder is a hobby breeder knowledgeable about and committed to the Labrador breed. So-called "backyard breeders" are usually pet owners looking to get a little money back on the purchase price of their dog. They're often unfamiliar with a breed's health problems and don't do any health checks before mating the dog with another that may or may not have health or temperament problems. They usually advertise their pups in the newspaper, unlike hobby breeders, who often have a waiting list before they ever breed a litter. Tipoffs that someone is a backyard breeder include use of the word "thoroughbred" to describe the pups (instead of purebred), failure to screen buyers carefully, or letting the pups go before seven or eight weeks of age.

Run of the Mill

Commercial breeders, often referred to as puppy mills, produce puppies on a large scale and wholesale them to pet stores. Their pups are not raised in the home but in kennels, which may or may not be well kept. Because the numbers of pups they produce is so great, these breeders are not able to give the dogs much human attention during their early formative weeks, when they should be learning to love people.

How much does a Lab puppy cost?

Whether you buy from a hobby breeder, a backyard breeder, or a pet store, you can expect to pay anywhere from $400 to $800 for your Lab puppy. The price can vary depending on what part of the country you're in, whether you're buying a male or female, and whether you want a pet-quality or show-quality dog.

Commercial breeders don't usually sell directly to the public, although there are some exceptions. These people may also have three or more breeds and always have litters available. Hobby breeders breed once a year or sometimes only once every two years. Their goal is to improve the breed, not to make money. If any breeder can't show proof of involvement with the breed–Labrador Retriever Club membership, conformation and field championships on their breeding stock, health screening for the breed's genetic problems—walk away. Puppy millers and backyard breeders don't do these things.

How Much Is That Puppy in the Window?

Without a doubt, a pet store is the most convenient place to find a Lab puppy, but perhaps it's not the best place. At a pet store, you can't meet the parents or other relatives, and you have no way of knowing the conditions in which the pup was raised, or whether the parents were screened for health problems. However, it's not necessarily always bad to get a Lab from a pet store. Some pet supply stores don't sell pups themselves, but instead team up with a local animal shelter or breed rescue group to offer pets for adoption. This is a win-win situation. Pups get the visibility from being on display, and the adoption group can still screen adopters before letting the pup go.

To Your Lab's Good Health

Is there anything else you should consider before getting a Lab? Absolutely! Like all breeds, Labs are prone to certain genetic health problems, diseases that are passed from parents to pups. These include orthopedic problems, eye problems, heart disease, and epilepsy, which are covered in greater detail in Chapter 18. Find out more about the Lab's propensity for these conditions so you know exactly what you're getting into and—when possible—how to avoid them.

Don't assume that these things are important only for show dogs. Even if your Lab is simply going to enjoy life as a pet, you deserve a dog that's healthy and problem-free. In any case, run, don't walk, from a breeder who claims to produce dogs without any health problems whatsoever. Every breeder—even the best, most conscientious one—runs into hereditary health problems with his or her dogs at one time or another.

Choosing a Labrador Retriever

EVEN THOUGH ALL LABS can be great dogs, you don't want to rush out and buy the very first one you see. There are a number of things to consider before you decide which pup to get. First, you'll want to decide whether your Lab will be a pet, show dog, hunting dog, or all three. You need to consider your preferences regarding a puppy or an adult dog, whether you want a male or a female, and how the dog might interact with your children or other pets. Finally, you need to be aware of all the details involved in getting a puppy, from choosing the one with the right personality and temperament for your lifestyle, to understanding all the papers that come with a pup, to knowing the right age to bring him home.

Know What You Want

As you learned in Chapter 1, the Lab is a versatile dog that shines in many areas, but there can be marked differences in structure, retrieving ability, and birdiness in Labs that are bred for different things. Show dogs are bred with the aim of producing a dog with perfect conformation. Field dogs are bred strictly for working ability, not looks. However, either type can make a good companion dog as long as your personality and lifestyle are compatible with the Lab's high energy level and love of fun.

Many people who compete in conformation say their dogs are every bit as good in the field as hunting-type Labs, while people who breed for field competition often say their Labs have more stamina and better retrieving skills. Whatever the case, it's hoped that the latest revisions to the breed standard will bring the two types closer together.

In a perfect world, there would be no substantial difference among Labs bred for conformation, field trials, or as companions. A Lab from a responsible breeder with a high-quality breeding program should be able to perform all three jobs without batting an eye.

Many Labrador breeders aim for versatility in their dogs, and they produce Labs that meet the breed standard and maintain the retrieving skills for which the breed is famous. Nonetheless, some breeders place more emphasis on form than function, and vice versa. Know which type you're dealing with and meet the breeder's adult dogs before you take a pup home.

Show Sense

Labs that are bred primarily to be show dogs tend to have more laidback temperaments than those bred to be hard-driving field dogs. If you think you want to show your Lab—but might enjoy trying field trials or hunt tests—you're better off getting a Lab from show lines. These dogs have the looks required for the show ring (shorter legs, heavier bones, and a broader head), but in most cases they haven't lost the nose and retrieving ability that make them stars in the field.

Performance Plus

Look for a Lab from field lines if performance is your main interest and you don't plan to show your dog. These dogs have the high energy levels, drive to retrieve, and conformation (longer legs, leaner body, and a more narrow skull) necessary to compete and succeed in difficult, day-long field trials. Whether you're looking for a show or field dog, ask what titles the pup's parents have earned. Reputable breeders prove their dogs' qualities in the show ring or field.

Companion First

What if your Lab's main job will be as a family companion? The laidback Lab from show lines will best suit your needs. He will still have plenty of energy to play with kids, but he will be less likely to run you off your feet.

Puppy Versus Adult

Of course you're going to get a puppy! Aren't you? Well, it's definitely something to think about. Puppies have their charms, no doubt about it, but adult dogs have advantages you might not have considered. Consider your lifestyle, and go over the pros and cons with your family before making a decision.

Labs don't start settling down into the calmness of adulthood until they're two or three years old. Your Lab may look grown up, but he'll act like a puppy for quite some time.

Puppies: Sugar, Spice, Naughty, Nice

Many people believe that the number-one advantage to a puppy is the cuteness factor. Arguably, there's nothing more lovable on earth. There's also nothing more maddening. Raising a puppy is a full-time job, comparable to having a curious toddler in the home. If you have young children, you may take a puppy in stride, or he may push you over the edge.

Puppies require constant supervision to ensure that they don't pee or poop on your new carpet, chew the drywall, or gnaw on the cords beneath your desk. They need to go out for potty breaks every two to four hours, and they must eat more frequently than an adult dog. They have a nonstop supply of energy.

On the upside, getting a puppy gives you the opportunity to mold your Lab into the dog of your dreams. If you want to have the greatest amount of influence over your Lab's development into adulthood, it's best to get one that's seven to ten weeks old. Also, you have more control over the outcome of your dog's behavior if you start training and socialization at an early age. It's much easier to teach a puppy than it is an adolescent.

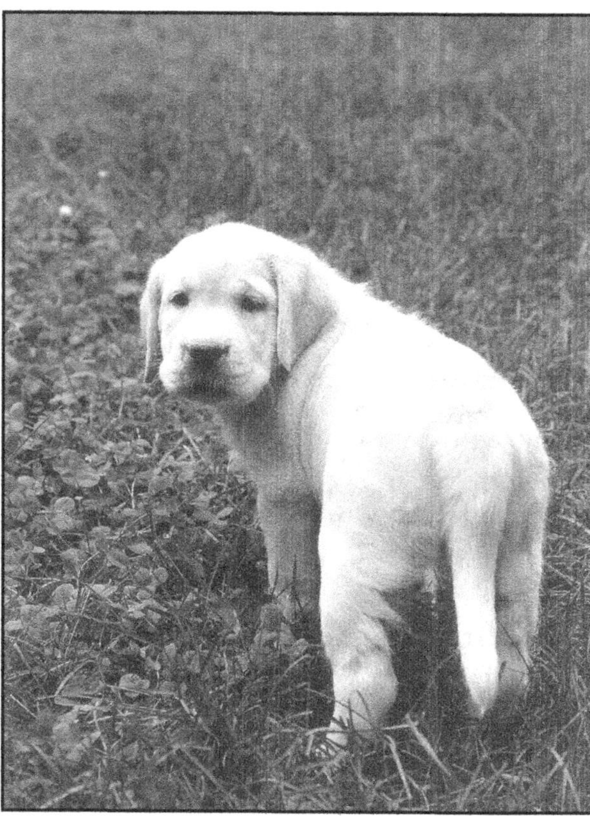

◀ **A male seven-week-old yellow Lab puppy.**

Adults: What You See Is What You Get

It might not have occurred to you to adopt an adult Labrador Retriever, but once you consider the advantages, you'll see that the idea has a lot of appeal. First, there are no surprises with an adult Lab. You know exactly what you're getting as far as size, conformation, and temperament. This can be especially beneficial if you're in the market for a show dog or field prospect.

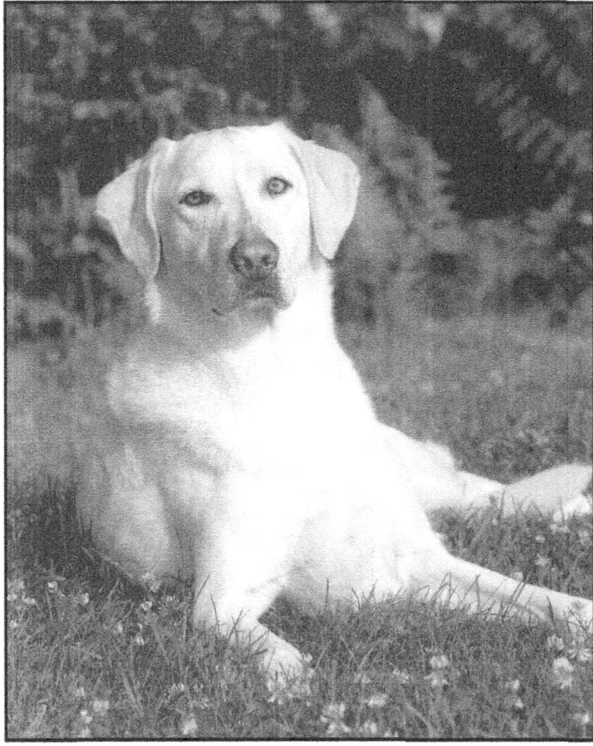

◀ A 4½-year-old female yellow Lab.

With respect to family life, an adult Lab may already be familiar with household routines. He may be housetrained or have some obedience training. This is a big advantage for people who aren't home during the day to provide the adjustment period that a puppy needs. Older dogs are generally past the destructive chewing stage, and they tend to be somewhat less active than puppies. These dogs may be more content to sleep the day away while you're at work, as long as they get attention and exercise when you're home.

An adult Lab requires fewer initial veterinary visits and vaccinations than a puppy. Usually, by the time a dog reaches maturity, any health problems he may have are evident. Adopting an older Lab allows you to choose one that you know is healthy or at least to be aware of the health problems your new dog has rather than being surprised by them.

Consider an older dog as well if you have kids. Adult Labs have often "been there, done that" when it comes to interacting with children. They know that children move suddenly and sometimes pull tails, and they're calm enough to take it all in stride, unlike a puppy that's still learning the ropes of family life.

All you need to win a Lab's heart is a good throwing arm and a steady supply of treats. If you can pass up the pleasures of puppyhood for the joy of building a relationship with a Lab that has retired from the show ring or whose first home didn't work out, then an adult dog is a good choice for you.

The Art of Compromise

Your kids want a puppy, but you think an older dog sounds like less work. Consider compromising by selecting an adolescent Lab that's six or seven months old. A dog this age is still full of puppy fire and brimstone, but his bladder capacity is greater and he needs meals only twice a day, instead of three or four times. He's young enough to be highly adaptable, and he has a longer attention span than a young pup. On the downside, he's just going into adolescence, which is always a trying time, but you'd have to face it at some point if you got a younger puppy.

Where do you find this adolescent dog? Often, breeders keep several pups to "run on," in the hope that they'll develop into good show prospects.

Male or Female?

When it comes to gender, many people want female dogs. They have a reputation for being easier to handle and "cleaner," as far as not marking in the house. There can be some surprising differences between the sexes, however, so don't automatically rule out one over the other.

In personality, male Labs tend to be sweeter, believe it or not. They're often mama's boys that will stick close to the woman of the house. Don't be surprised if your male puppy grows up to be a big sweetheart that wants to sit on your lap and give you a big slobbery kiss every morning before he goes about his business of supervising the household.

On the downside, males will lift a leg and urinate on just about anything inside or outside the home. It takes training and patience to redirect or control this habit. Neutering helps too and has the added benefit of protecting your Lab from testicular cancer, prostate disease, and perianal adenomas, or growths around the anus that are testosterone-dependent.

Without careful supervision, a female will escape in search of a male to meet her sexual needs. Spaying eliminates these concerns, and spaying a female before her first season greatly reduces her chances of developing breast cancer.

Females can be independent. When it comes to relating to other dogs in the household, they are often the leaders of the group. They tend to be more protective and may well be the first to bark at anything unusual. Calmer and quieter than males, a female Lab is a good choice if you have younger children that she can nurture.

Be aware that unless a female is spayed, she will go into season—sometimes referred to as "heat"—twice a year, for about three weeks each time. During this hormone-driven period, you can expect her to spend a lot of time licking her swollen genitals and enthusiastically humping anyone or anything she can find. You'll need to protect your carpet and furniture from her bloody discharge, which can range from light to heavy.

One Lab or Two?

If one Lab is fun, just think how entertaining two could be! People often decide to get two Labs at the same time, and there is some method to their madness. Because they're sporting dogs, bred to work companionably with other dogs, Labs tend to be social, enjoying the company of other dogs. Two Labs can play with each other, releasing some of the energy that you would otherwise have to deal with. They can keep each other company during the day while you're at work and the kids are at school, and they'll be less likely to develop separation anxiety.

What is a brace?
People who show or hunt their dogs often use special terminology when they refer to them. A brace is a pair of dogs. If you attend a Labrador specialty show, you may see a brace class—two Labs being shown together, tails wagging in unison.

The Downside of Multiple Labs

Before you decide that getting two Labs is a great idea, however, bear in mind that there are also disadvantages to consider. Two Labs can be twice as destructive as one. They shed twice as much as one, and while they will certainly keep each other company, they will also egg each other on, reducing your peace of mind and quiet time. You might think they'll nap and play at the same time, but if they take turns, you won't get any time off from supervising them.

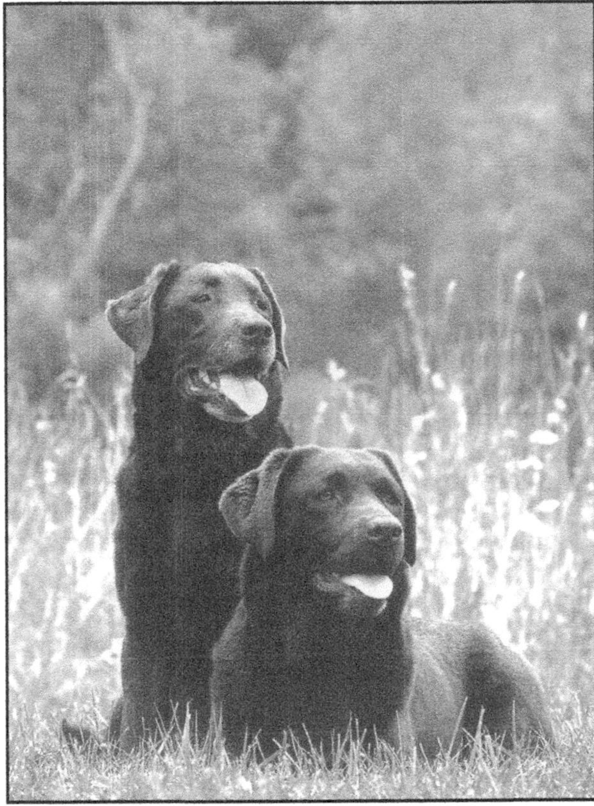

◀ A pair of female chocolate Labs: a five-year-old and a 2½-year-old.

If you get two puppies at the same time, they may bond more closely with each other than with family members. Labs are big, strong dogs, and it can be difficult to handle two of them on leash at the same time, unless you have a spouse or friend who's willing to help walk them. And it's a hassle to housetrain two pups at once. There's an economic drawback as well: You'll have greater expenses for equipment, food, toys, training, and veterinary care.

Making It Work

Two pups at the same time might not be easy, but it's not impossible. Just know that it will take a greater amount of dedication to civilize them than it would a single pup. The biggest danger to guard against is becoming so overwhelmed that the puppies end up keeping each other company all the time. It's important to take the time to bond with them, play with them, and train them, together and separately. Each puppy should have a primary caregiver in the family, and the two should not spend 100 percent of their time together.

You may have heard that it's not a good idea to get two puppies from the same litter or to get two of the same sex. In most cases, however, it doesn't matter whether they're from the same litter or of the same or opposite sex. They are going to bond with each other regardless. The work involved is more related to the pups' age than to their gender or relationship.

Labs and Children

Labs love children. There's no doubt that the two were made for each other. The important thing to realize, however, is that Labs are highly active dogs, especially as puppies. It's not unusual for them to inadvertently knock children down in play.

Before you get a Lab, consider whether your child is old enough to interact with a rambunctious dog. Labs are great as far as being patient with a toddler's roaming hands, but they're a bit on the large side for a child of this age to play comfortably with them. You may be better off waiting until your child is at least six years old and capable of standing up to this breed's sometimes rough—but never mean—play.

Labs and Other Pets

Easygoing Labs have a reputation for getting along well with other pets. In large part, that's because they're hunting dogs and must work and play well with other dogs. Aggression should never be part of a Lab's temperament. In groups, however, Labs do play rough with each other. If you have a smaller dog, be sure to supervise play so the little one doesn't get injured.

Much of your cat's relationship with a Lab will depend on the cat itself. Cats that stand up for themselves usually rule the roost, while cats that turn tail and run are likely to get chased. Keep your Lab on lead when you introduce the two so you can control his reaction.

Can your Lab get along with cats, ferrets, rabbits, and other small, furry pets? In most cases, the answer is yes. There are always exceptions, but usually if a Lab is introduced to cats and other pets in puppyhood, they can learn to live happily together.

Adult Labs can also learn to live with noncanine pets, but you will need to provide a supervised introduction and give them time to get to know one another. Just to be on the safe side, it's best to keep such small pets as hamsters, gerbils, guinea pigs, and birds well out of reach. Teach your Lab to "look but don't touch."

Puppy Primer

Choosing the puppy that's right for you and your family can be the most difficult part of purchasing a Labrador. All puppies are cute, but each one has its own individual personality that sets it apart from the others. In predicting a puppy's adult personality and temperament, you'll want to consider activity level, interactions with littermates, and reaction to people, as well as the breeder's own observations and recommendations. By taking all of this information into account, you'll be much more likely to make an appropriate choice.

▲ A seven-week-old black Lab puppy.

Your first look at the puppies will probably come when they are six or seven weeks old. By that time they'll have had their first vaccinations and will be less at risk of infection from outside sources. You'll no doubt be swept away by their cuteness at first, but don't forget to examine them carefully for clues to their behavior, temperament, and health.

No Shy Labs!

Avoid puppies that appear to be shy around people. Remember that shyness is a serious fault that should not be excused, according to the Labrador Retriever breed standard. Shy puppies can seem appealing because of their vulnerability, but this trait is difficult if not impossible to overcome. There's no point in having a Lab if it's going to run away from everyone who approaches it.

On the other hand, be careful not to confuse caution with shyness. Some puppies approach people without hesitation, while others like to take a little more time to scope things out. This type of caution isn't necessarily a bad thing. A cautious pup will eventually approach you on his own terms, but the shy pup must be coaxed out of a corner or even picked up because he won't come.

Look at the Adults, Too

Don't forget to pay attention to the breeder's adult dogs. Their temperament is a good indicator of what the puppies' temperaments will be. The mother's influence is especially strong. A shy mother is almost sure to produce shy puppies unless the breeder has worked hard to socialize them from day one.

Lab Personality Tests

To help gauge a puppy's personality and temperament, you can perform some simple tests that are unscientific but useful in deciding which pup is right for you. They can help you evaluate such factors as dominance and submissiveness, trust in people, willingness to follow, and sensitivity to touch and sound. Ask the breeder's permission before performing your test. She may want to supervise, or she may have suggestions of her own. These same tests apply if you're adopting a Lab puppy from an animal shelter.

Temperament is such an integral part of a Labrador that most breeders won't tolerate anything other than a sweet, loving dog. Reputable breeders can't afford to produce aggressive dogs—not only because it's a surefire excusal from the show ring or field, but also because it's bad for the breed's reputation as a whole.

People-Friendly and Personable?

Sit down and see if a particular puppy will come to you. Your Lab should be people-oriented. As the pup approaches, is he excited or a little submissive? A confident pup moves with ears up and tail wagging.

Offer a treat. A Lab with good training potential will come forward to take it. Speak softly, and see if the pup is interested in listening to you. A puppy that sticks around to be with you rather than running off to be with the other dogs is a good choice.

Play with the puppy for a couple of minutes to help put him at ease. Throw a ball, or offer him a toy. When you take the toy away, does he give it up willingly or try to hang onto it? A possessive Lab isn't typical. Toss the toy and see how the puppy reacts. Does he run after it and pounce on it or proceed in a more methodical and straightforward fashion? His actions are a clue to his future personality.

Likes Being Touched and Held?

Once the pup has relaxed a bit, check to see how he feels about being touched. Gently run your hands over his body. Does he flinch when you touch him or welcome the contact? You want a dog that's comfortable being handled. Pick up his feet, look in his ears, and examine his teeth. Next, pick the puppy up. Being held is stressful for puppies, so it's a good test of how a pup responds to stress. See if he struggles and squirms or relaxes into your arms.

Some puppies struggle a bit when you hold them and then relax. Choose one that's able to calm down in a reasonable amount of time. A Lab that's unable to control its fear or desire to be in charge may be headed for future behavior problems.

Open to New Experiences?

Still holding the puppy, walk away from the mother and littermates. Does the puppy show alarm at being separated from them, or does he settle down and enjoy the ride? It's normal for a puppy to be a little uneasy in this situation, but if he trusts people, he should eventually relax. You may find that a previously bold puppy becomes a little apprehensive, or a quiet one gains confidence and shows more curiosity.

Willing to Follow?

Set the puppy down and walk away from him. Does the puppy follow you with a little encouragement? A nice Lab with a moderate temperament will come without a lot of wild behavior, such as barking or running in circles.

Sensible about Sound?

To test for noise shyness, wait until the pup's not watching you, then clap your hands or drop something that will make a loud noise. A frightened puppy will run away, while a confident one will ignore the sound or come over to investigate. That's the one you want. A Lab that's fearful of loud noises isn't much use in the field. As a pet he's likely to develop a fear of thunderstorms, loud jets, or other common noises.

The Breeder's Advice

By the time you start looking at puppies, the breeders you meet with have been observing their litters for at least six weeks. They know each puppy's personality and temperament. Tell the breeder exactly what you're looking for in a Lab. Chances are she will match you up with the perfect puppy. It might not be the puppy you were thinking of, but you'll be surprised to find that he is indeed just what you wanted.

Just as important as temperament and personality is good health. You don't want to take home a sickly puppy. Look at puppies closely for signs of good—or poor—health. The first thing you might notice is energy level. Healthy puppies are active, moving easily on strong legs. They might be sleepy just after they've eaten, so try to arrange your visit before mealtime. Healthy puppies also have bright eyes, clean ears, pink gums, white teeth, and shiny coats. Avoid puppies with runny eyes or ears that smell bad. Look at the gums. If they're pale, not pink, the puppy may have internal parasites, such as roundworms.

Labrador puppies love everyone and bond well with a new family at any age, but they need at least seven weeks with their mother and littermates to learn what they need to know about interacting with other dogs.

Other obvious signs of poor health are dull fur and loose stools. A dull coat and a pooched-out stomach that looks like a beer belly are signs of internal parasite infestation. Evidence of diarrhea in the yard or kennel area is another red flag. Healthy puppies have small, firm stools. While each of these may be a sign of a treatable condition, they also signal a breeder who's not responsible.

Ask if the puppies have been dewormed and vaccinated. By six to eight weeks of age, the pups should have been vaccinated at least once for distemper and parvovirus. In some areas where the incidence of parvo is high, two vaccinations may have been given.

Choosing an Adult Lab

Whether you're choosing an adult Lab from a shelter, Lab rescue group, or breeder, many of the same temperament tests suggested above for use with puppies can also help you choose an adult Lab that will be a good fit for your family and lifestyle. Of course, you can't pick up a grown Lab to see how he reacts to being carried, but you can see if he'll willingly roll over for a tummy rub, a good sign of trust in and submissiveness toward people. The most important thing is to spend time getting to know the dog.

At a shelter, ask if you can take the dog out of the kennel. Most shelters have a yard or a room where you can interact with the dog you're considering. The way a dog behaves in his kennel is very different from the way he behaves in a less restricted situation. Spend a little time talking to the dog, walking him on a leash, and playing with him.

Avoid the discredited "alpha roll," which involves pinning a dog by the throat and staring at it. The alpha roll is not only dangerous to you, it's detrimental to a dog's mental health and well-being.

Some things to look for include whether the dog makes eye contact with you, whether he seems glad to be in your company, and whether he responds when you speak to or move toward him. A Lab that shows no interest in you is going to be a tougher act than one who immediately seeks your affection, gives you his paw, or nuzzles you. Any sign that a dog wants to interact with you is positive. Choose a dog whose style of playing or interacting with you is one that you find pleasurable and that the dog seems to enjoy as well.

▲ A ten-year-old chocolate Lab.

Take note of the dog's activity level. This will be affected by circumstances, such as whether the dog has been out of his kennel recently, or has just eaten or is about to eat. Nonetheless, you can usually tell if a dog seems to have a lot of frenetic energy or a more mellow personality. If he is a very active dog, be honest with yourself about your ability and desire to walk him several times a day or channel his energy through dog sports so he doesn't become destructive. See if the dog knows any commands, such as "Sit," "Down," or "Fetch." Put a leash on him and take him for a walk. Lots of dogs pull. Find out before you adopt one whether you're able to control him.

If possible, bring everyone in the family to meet the dog. Many shelters require this before they'll complete an adoption. That's because the way a dog interacts with adults may be different from how he interacts with children. If you have another dog in the home, it can even be a good idea to bring him along so you can make sure the two will get along. (Call to arrange this beforehand.) The neutral setting of the shelter is a great place to introduce them. All of these interactions are important sources of information about how the dog might behave in your home.

Finally, ask yourself whether this is a dog you would enjoy having in your home and in your life. If the answer is yes, you're ready to take your new friend home. Give him time to adjust to his new surroundings and provide him with firm, consistent rules and lots of love. In a few months, you'll wonder how you ever did without him. Ⓔ

Preparing for Your New Labrador Retriever

FEW EVENTS IN LIFE ARE MORE MEMORABLE than the first day with a new puppy or dog. By being prepared beforehand with the appropriate equipment and food, not to mention a completely Lab-proofed home, you'll enjoy the day even more. What follows is a guide to the necessary preparation and get-acquainted period with your new dog, from ways you can make your home and Lab safe from each other to the supplies you'll need—especially if you're a first-time dog owner.

Family Affair

Who will care for your new Lab? The kids, who have been begging for a dog for months and promising that they'll do all the work involved in caring for it? Or the parents, who are ultimately responsible for the dog's welfare? The answer is that everyone needs to be involved in your Lab's care and training. Even if he's being acquired for a specific family member, he'll be interacting with everyone, and all family members should know how to treat him properly.

As the adults, it's your job to ensure that your new Lab gets plenty of exercise, eats right, learns his manners, and stays groomed and well cared for. The kids—depending on their ages—certainly can and should participate in his care, but it's a well-known fact that children have short attention spans and need constant nagging when it comes to dog care. It's great to involve the kids in the dog's care, but an adult needs to ensure that meals are given on time, water dishes are kept filled and refreshed daily, and grooming is done. The dog shouldn't suffer because of a child's forgetfulness or activity schedule.

If you get a Lab for the kids, it should be because you want and will enjoy having a dog too. It's not fair to the dog to rely on youngsters' promises to take care of it and then to get rid of the dog when they don't follow through.

Decisions you as the parent must make include where the dog will sleep, whether it's allowed on the furniture, and who is responsible for the various elements of dog care: feeding, training, grooming, and so on. To help keep things running smoothly, make a Lab-care checklist with everyone's responsibilities and post it in a prominent area, such as on the refrigerator or by the front door. That way, no one can say "I forgot" or "I didn't know it was my turn." Include the following items on your checklist:

- **Mealtime:** As a rule, schedule three meals daily for puppies, switching to two meals daily at four months of age.
- **Potty time:** Puppies need to go out as soon as they wake up, after every meal, after playtime, and just before bedtime. Your Lab should have an opportunity to relieve himself every two to four hours.
- **Playtime:** Start with ten-minute walks, gradually increasing the distance as your Lab matures. Free play in the backyard is fine, too, but limit jumping until the dog is eighteen to twenty-four months old.
- **Grooming:** A weekly brushing will keep your Lab's coat shiny and healthy.

- **Training:** Training classes usually meet weekly, but your Lab puppy needs daily practice in two or three five- to ten-minute sessions.
- **Health:** Note any upcoming veterinary visits for booster shots or exams, as well as who's responsible for taking the dog to the vet.

Children who are at least six years old can perform such tasks as feeding the dog, keeping its water dish filled, and brushing the dog. Children who are ten and older can be responsible for taking the puppy out first thing in the morning and last thing at night if the dog sleeps in their room. They can also attend training class with an adult and learn how to handle the dog. The whole family should take turns at home practicing commands so the dog will understand that he should respond to every family member.

Puppy (and Dog) Proofing Your Home

The first thing you need to know about living with a Lab is that these dogs are curious. Thanks to their superb sense of smell, they are natural-born explorers and can sniff out trouble—in the form of garbage to raid and lovely leather shoes to chew—quicker than you can say "Oh, no!" Labs learn about the world mainly by putting things in their mouth. They discover what things are good to eat or gnaw on for entertainment. It takes only a second for a Lab to decide that the end table would make a good chew toy, or that it would be an awful lot of fun to shred the magazine lying on the coffee table.

That Lab puppy may look sweet and innocent, but the amount of damage it can do in only a short amount of time boggles the mind. The Lab will redecorate your new baseboards with tooth marks, chew the runner off your favorite rocking chair, eat the pretty towels in your guest bath, spread trash throughout the house, and generally wreak more havoc than you ever imagined. If it's within reach, your Lab puppy will go on a seek-and-destroy mission in his attempt to discover more about his new surroundings. So before you bring that puppy (or adult dog) home, take steps to protect your home by putting things you value—or that would be dangerous to a dog—well out of reach. Do this in every room of your house.

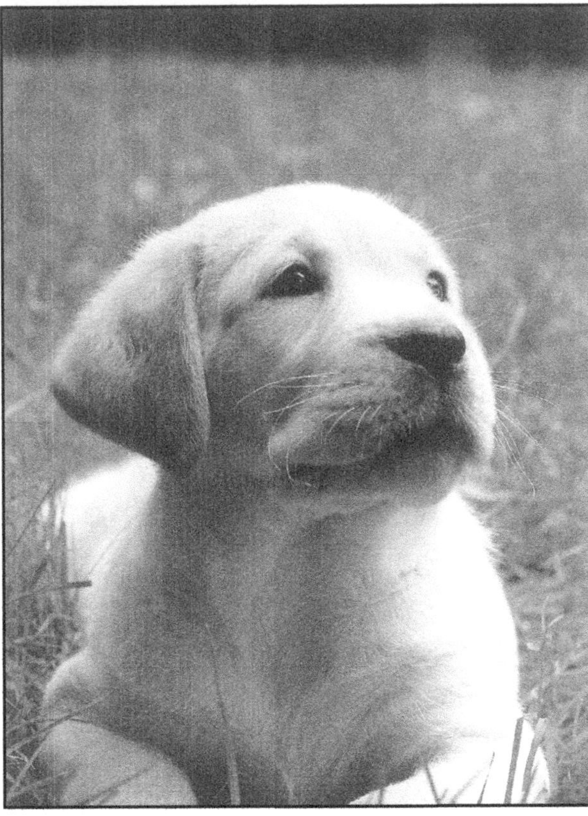

◀ This seven-week-old male yellow puppy is ready to play.

Living Room, Family Room, and Home Office

Check first for dangling cords from lamps, televisions, stereos, computers, and any other electrical appliances in the room. Wrap cords with tough plastic cable ties and place them out of reach if possible. Otherwise, coat them with Bitter Apple paste to repel a taste-testing Lab. Lots of Labs completely ignore the taste of Bitter Apple spray, but the paste seems to do a good job of putting them off. It can also be a good idea to place something solid in front of an outlet with a plugged-in cord, such as a chair or a small but heavy chest.

If your kids are used to doing their homework on the floor, remind them not to leave papers lying around. Labs were probably the original cause of the excuse "The dog ate my homework." Other things to keep out of reach that might be found in these rooms are toys, knickknacks, glass frames, photo albums, sewing materials, pens and pencils, books, cameras—you name it. Protect furniture legs by wrapping them in aluminum foil—not pleasant to bite down on—or coating them in Bitter Apple paste.

How long does it take before your Lab can be left on his own in the home?
Some Labs might be trustworthy at three years of age, while others never outgrow puppy mischief and must always be supervised or confined to a safe place when you're not there.

A number of common houseplants can cause toxic reactions if they're eaten, ranging from mouth irritation or upset stomach to respiratory problems or even death. Most dogs love nibbling on green things and digging in dirt, so put plants out of reach (even if they're not toxic). Plants that are known to be toxic include the following:

- Asparagus fern
- Boston ivy
- Caladium
- Calla lily
- Dieffenbachia (dumb cane)
- Elephant's ear
- Mother-in-law plant
- Philodendron
- Pothos

Check with your veterinarian or a local poison control center for a more complete list.

Bedrooms

Hang up clothes, and put shoes in the closet. Once a puppy has chewed up a favorite or expensive item of clothing, your children and spouse may finally become motivated not to leave things lying around. Keep the closet door closed, especially if that's where your laundry hamper is. Labs love to chew on items that bear the scent of their people, and dirty clothes are their favorites.

Be aware that your Lab is smart and perfectly capable of thinking up and carrying out a plan to achieve a particular goal, such as getting into the trash. It's important to try to think like a dog when you're puppyproofing.

Do you have things stored under the bed? Your puppy will crawl under there to go exploring. Consider putting storage boxes out of reach until your Lab is safely past the chewing stage or too big to get under the bed.

If you have a waterbed, keep your Lab's nails trimmed short, and don't let the dog stay in the bedroom unsupervised. Labs have been known to puncture waterbeds and then play in the resulting pool until their caregivers came home to discover the mess. They are water dogs, after all.

Kitchen and Bathroom

Child locks on kitchen and bathroom cabinets will help keep your Lab from getting into stored food, cleansers, cosmetics, paper towels and toilet paper, toothpaste, and other house essentials. Place trash cans behind closed doors or out of reach, or cover them with securely locking lids. Perhaps the top of the refrigerator can be a good temporary place for a trash can. Put dishtowels out of reach. Your Lab won't hesitate to eat that dangling piece of cloth, which could then cause a gastrointestinal obstruction that will require surgery to remove.

In the bathroom, keep toilet lids closed so that your Lab doesn't drink out of the toilet or climb up on the rim and fall in. Any self-respecting Lab will see dangling toilet paper as an invitation to grab and run. Don't leave a long piece hanging from the roll after use. Unplug and put away blow dryers and curling irons after use so your Lab doesn't pull them down on his head or electrocute himself by chewing on them.

Basement, Attic, and Garage

All kinds of things are stored in your house basement or attic—from old clothes and toys to poisons and traps for pests. It's best to deny your Lab access to these areas. If that's not possible, place dangerous or special items out of your pet's reach.

Many garages contain chemical hazards such as antifreeze, cleansers, fertilizer, glue, paint, pesticides, strippers, and turpentine. Sharp-edged tools can also pose a threat. Dogs have been known to bleed to death in the garage before they were found. Clean up antifreeze drips or oil spots, and place chemicals on high shelves or inside locked cabinets. Automatic garage doors can also be dangerous. Be sure you know where your puppy is before you close the door. Dogs can get caught beneath them and crushed.

Lots of dogs enjoy snacking out of the cat's litter box. If your cat's litter box is in the garage, consider getting a covered litter box or placing the box in an area that's perhaps accessible to the cat but not the dog. Try placing the box behind a baby gate and cutting a small hole in the bottom. Your cat will be able to slip through, but the dog won't fit.

Yard

For a Labrador, your yard is crying out for exploration, but it's full of dangers you may be unaware of. Before you turn your Lab loose in the yard, check for and remove any poisonous plants and bait left out for pests, as well as tools or other hazards that are lying around. Repair or board up holes in fences that a puppy could wiggle through, fix broken locks so gates close securely, and sand down sharp or pointed edges along fencing.

The bulbs, leaves, or berries of a number of plants commonly found in yards can cause gastrointestinal upset, irritation, respiratory problems, skin reactions, and even death if they're eaten. Remove them or make sure your Lab can't get to them. Plants that can be toxic include the following:

- Azalea
- Chinaberry
- Daffodil/buttercup
- Jasmine
- Lupine
- Monkeypod
- Privet
- Tomato vine
- Wisteria
- Yew tree

Labs love water. If you have a pool or spa, keep it securely covered if you're not there to supervise. If the pool or spa is enclosed by a fence, make sure the gate latches securely. Don't leave the pool sweep going if you're not there. Your Lab will try to retrieve it.

▲ Labs don't care if it's a pond or a pool, they just love to swim and will dive right in.

Fence off garden areas so your Lab doesn't snack on your tomatoes and strawberries. Try surrounding garden areas with chicken wire, a picket fence, or bamboo crisscross edging. These may not survive a rampaging Labrador, but they can help fend him off.

Your Lab's Safe Place

Because he's a member of your family, your Lab will be spending most of his time indoors with you. That's how he learns to live politely in the home. Until he's civilized, however, you'll need to have a safe place where you can leave him when you're not there to supervise, secure in the knowledge that he won't be able to do any (or much) damage.

A suitable safe place usually has a tile or linoleum floor, so it's easy to clean up accidents. It doesn't contain much furniture or anything else that can be chewed. Common choices for safe rooms are the kitchen, bathroom, laundry room, or garage. A crate is another option you should consider.

A crate is an essential piece of equipment for any Lab caregiver, as it serves as your Lab's bed, his safe place, and as a housetraining tool. Dogs are den animals, so they are comfortable curling up inside a crate when it's bedtime or for a nap when you can't be around to watch them.

If you choose a safe spot such as the kitchen, laundry room, or bathroom, use a baby gate to block the doorway. That way your Lab can still see everything that's going on. A closed door will only encourage him to whine, bang, and maybe even chew his way out. If you're concerned that your Lab will chew on cabinetry or baseboards in the same room, put him inside a puppy playpen—also referred to as an x-pen—so that he can't get to those areas.

A dog-proofed garage can also be a good place to let your Lab stay unsupervised. Some people turn part of the garage into a complete dog room, with carpeted floor, crate, grooming table, bed, and toys. A dog door leading to the yard lets your Lab play outside when he wants.

Where Will Your Labrador Sleep?

To help your Lab feel like a member of the family, let him sleep indoors. By putting his crate in your bedroom at night, you'll be providing him with quality time, even though all of you are asleep. This is especially important if the dog is home alone during the day. Sleeping in the same room with his caregivers is a great way for him to bond with them.

Should your Lab sleep in the bed with you? Probably not. A puppy is small, and you run the risk of rolling over onto it during the night. A puppy may also wet the bed–not fun to clean up in the wee hours of the morning. Sleeping in the bed can also give big ideas to a Lab with a dominant personality. He might start to think that he's in charge, not you. For this reason, most trainers advise against letting a dog sleep in the bed.

A Lab who spends all his time indoors won't get enough exercise and will be grumpy and destructive. A Lab who's left outside all the time won't be able to bond with his family and learn how to behave nicely in the house. Your job, as a Lab caregiver, is to create a balance between the two that's happy for all involved.

An Inside or Outside Dog?

In the best of all worlds, your Lab will spend part of his day in the house, socializing with his fellow family members, and part of his day playing outside–barking at squirrels, chasing birds, splashing in the baby pool you've filled up for him–all the things Labs love best. Make sure you provide him with the balance he needs. After all, there's not much point in having a fun and companionable dog like a Lab if you're not going to spend any time with him, or if you don't provide him with enough exercise and outdoor play.

Doghouses and Dog Runs

Your Lab should have a safe room in your home, and he should also have certain forms of shelter in the yard. A doghouse, a dog run, and a fenced yard will all help keep your Lab safe. Together, they protect him from the elements–sun, rain, snow–from getting into trouble, and from running away.

Doghouses come in all shapes, sizes, and styles. You can buy one made of wood or high-impact plastics at any pet or home supply store, or you can design and build one of your own creation. Besides being sturdy–so your Lab doesn't chew it up–a doghouse should be large enough for him to stand up and turn around inside.

If your Lab has a digging problem–and many do–consider buying or building a dog run so your Lab has a secure place to play where he can't damage your yard. A dog run should be at least 6 feet high and 12 feet long to allow for plenty of sniffing area. Make it as big as you can so your Lab has lots of room to play. A cover provides shelter from sun and rain. Place a doghouse in the run so your Lab has a nice place to nap.

Fenced Yards

Make sure your fence is high enough to confine your Lab. Some are jumpers, so you'll need a fence that's at least 6 feet high. Labs can chew through the bottom of chain link, so the best choice is a solid fence made of wood or stucco–anything the dog can't see through. Thorny shrubs or roses planted against the fence can serve as an additional barrier. Consider burying wire hardware cloth along the bottom edge of the fence to make it more difficult for the Lab to dig there.

What about underground electronic fences? This type of fence requires that you train your dog to stay behind its borders. The dog must wear a special collar, which delivers a shock if the dog crosses the line, so to speak.

Essential

To help discourage dog thieves, place a sign on your fence or dog run noting that your dog is tattooed and microchipped. Thieves are less likely to steal a dog that's easily identifiable.

Most trainers don't recommend the use of electronic fences, and many consider them cruel. Electronic fences have other disadvantages. Your Lab can still run across the boundary if he sees a squirrel or bird that he simply must chase, and he may then be unwilling to risk another shock by returning to the yard. Nor will an electronic fence keep other dogs or animals out of your yard. A solid fence is a better choice.

Necessary Dog Supplies

You've made your home safe for–and from–your Lab. It's almost time to bring him home, but first you need a few supplies. Necessary items include a collar, tag, and leash; food and water dishes; food; a crate; and grooming supplies.

Collars and Tags

You can choose from a dizzying array of collars at the pet supply store. They come in leather, nylon, and chain, as well as every color and pattern you could imagine. The collar you choose should be attractive, to please you; sturdy, to survive being worn by your Lab; and functional, to help you control your dog.

The first thing you want to look for in a collar is a buckle. A buckle is adjustable, so the collar can grow with your Lab. Your dog should never wear a choke (chain) collar for everyday use. It can all too easily get hung up on something and strangle the dog. A flat buckle collar in leather is a classic look for a classic-looking dog, such as the Lab. If you prefer something with a little more pizzazz, look for a decorative nylon buckle collar.

Because Labs are big dogs and tend to be pullers, you might want to consider a martingale collar for use in training class. A martingale collar has a double loop design that gently tightens around the neck when the leash is taut and loosens when the leash is slack. It has no buckles or snaps, but slips on over the dog's head and can be adjusted for comfort. The advantage of a martingale over a choke collar is that it provides even pressure to the neck rather than pulling at the throat. The dog can't slip out of this type of collar, and it's a good training tool for preventing pulling. Martingales can be made of nylon, chain, or nylon and chain. Don't choose a martingale as your Lab's everyday collar. Take it off when you end your training session or walk, and replace it with his regular collar.

Of course, your Lab's everyday collar needs an identification tag. Tags can be made of metal or plastic, and they come in a variety of shapes (bones, shamrocks, round) and colors. You can purchase a tag from a machine at your local pet supply store and have it engraved right then and there. There's only so much information you can fit on a tag, so only include the most important: your name and phone number. You might also want to include an additional phone number, such as that of your office or your vet's office.

Some dog experts recommend putting only your name on the tag, rather than your dog's name. Learning a dog's name by looking at its collar can make it easier for a thief to lure your dog away.

Leashes

Like collars, leashes come in leather, nylon, and chain. Leather leashes look good and are long-lasting, but your Lab will love to chew on one–so keep it out of reach when it's not being used. A nylon leash is also durable and can be chosen to match your dog's collar. It probably doesn't smell quite as good as leather to a Lab, but it's still chewable.

Chain leashes are heavier than leather or nylon and they can be clunky-sounding. You probably wouldn't want to use one for a puppy—too heavy—but if your Lab is a puller, a chain leash might be useful in restraining him. Chain is also unlikely to fall apart if your Lab decides to chew on it.

What about an extendible leash? These extend out up to 16 feet and allow your Lab a greater degree of freedom than the typical 4- or 6-foot leash. A brake in the handle allows you to lock the leash at a given length, or to stop the line from reeling out if you need to haul your dog back to you.

The advantage of an extendible leash is the freedom it offers the dog. You'll quickly learn to hit the brake fast if you need to stop your dog. A disadvantage is that some communities limit the length of a dog's leash, so it's possible you could be fined for letting the leash all the way out. The extendible leashes are also not permissible in the show or obedience ring. Consider having an extendible leash for "fun" time and a regular leash for "work" time.

Crate

Your Lab's crate should be just large enough for him to stand up and turn around in. This provides a cozy feel and—in the case of a puppy—ensures that there's not so much room that he can eliminate in one corner and sleep in the other. That's important, because the crate serves not only as your Lab's bed, but also as a housetraining device, which we'll discuss further in Chapter 7.

Two types of crates are available. Airline-style crates have solid sides and are made of hard plastic. These are a good choice if you know your Lab will be traveling by air at some point in his life. Plastic crates are usually sized from 100 (small) to 500 (giant). The appropriate size crate for an adult Lab is usually a 400 or a 500.

Wire crates give the dog a better view of what's going on around him. They're nice for hot climates because they allow more of a breeze to enter the crate, and they can be covered on chilly nights. A cover also gives a wire crate more of a denlike quality. A good size for a Lab would be 19 inches by 24 inches, or 24 inches by 36 inches. You can use the smaller size in the car and the larger size in the house.

Crate your Lab when he's riding in the car. Not only does this keep him safe in case of an accident, it also keeps him from chewing through the seatbelts and the door. Yes, Labs have been known to do that very thing!

No matter which style you choose, you're probably best off buying a large crate that comes with a divider so you can add space as the puppy grows. You'll probably want to put some kind of bedding in the crate to make it soft and comfortable for your new Lab. Just be aware that it's likely to get chewed up quickly. Use old blankets or towels that you don't mind having ruined instead of an expensive bed. Another good option is artificial lamb's wool, which Labs seem less likely to chew.

Food and Feeding Supplies

For your Lab's intestinal comfort, start by feeding him the same diet the breeder gives. This will prevent any vomiting or diarrhea that could result from a too rapid change in diet. If you plan to feed your puppy (or adult dog) a different brand, choose a high-quality food that's specially formulated for puppies. Make the switch over a seven- to ten-day period by gradually adding the new food to the old diet. Ask the breeder what she's feeding, and make sure you have enough to last for two weeks.

Besides food, the food and water dishes are sure to be one of your Lab's favorite items. Dishes can be made of metal, ceramic, or plastic—and all can be put in the dishwasher, which is a plus. Wash your Lab's food bowls daily so they don't become encrusted with food. You wouldn't want to eat off grungy dishes, and neither does your Lab.

Toys

Some people might consider toys nonessentials, but Labs are playful, energetic dogs. They need rough, tough toys that can stand up to their play and keep them entertained. Toys that Labs might not destroy immediately include Kongs, Nylabones, Giggle balls and Buster cubes, tennis balls, and stuffed toys that squeak or make other noises.

Kongs are great because they can be stuffed with peanut butter or liver sausage and dog biscuits. Freeze the stuffed Kong and then give it to your Lab. He'll spend hours trying to work all the yummy stuff out of the hole. Kongs last a long time, but they can eventually be chewed up. Giggle Balls, Buster Cubes, and similar toys have holes into which dry dog food or small biscuits can be placed. As the dog rolls the ball (which makes a giggling sound as it moves) or pushes the cube, food falls out. Some people keep their dogs occupied for some time by putting a meal's worth of kibble in this type of toy.

What grooming supplies should Labs have?
Fortunately, it doesn't take much to keep a Lab looking his best. A curry brush and nail trimmers are all you need at first. As your Lab grows, you might want to add some more specialized tools, such as a shedding blade and a toothbrush.

Labs love retrieving tennis balls and field bumpers (oblong plastic training devices for field dogs). You can buy plain old tennis balls for your Lab, or choose one of the many tennis ball toys with attached ropes or handles for throwing ease. Look for field bumpers in pet-supply catalogs or hunting supply stores. Many Labs also cherish stuffed animals–they sleep with them, carry them around, and offer them to guests. A very large stuffed animal—as big as or bigger than the puppy—can give him something to snuggle with in his crate and help fill up the empty space.

Choosing a Veterinarian

The veterinarian is your partner in caring for your Lab. If you've never had a dog before, choosing the right veterinarian should be one of the most important items on your to-do list before bringing your puppy home. Also, by selecting a veterinarian in advance, you can avoid the need to find someone in a hurry if your Lab becomes unexpectedly ill. And, of course, you'll want to have your new puppy or dog examined first thing to make sure he's healthy.

How to Find a Veterinarian

Word of mouth is one of the best ways to find a veterinarian. A referral from someone you trust is a good start. If you have friends, neighbors, or coworkers with Labs, ask them where they go and if they're satisfied with the treatment their dog receives. The breeder can also recommend someone if you're buying your puppy locally.

Another source for finding a veterinarian is the American Animal Hospital Association (AAHA). The AAHA performs inspections and provides references to veterinary hospitals that meet its standards in such areas as anesthesia, dental cleaning, medical recordkeeping, and surgery.

The Yellow Pages are also a good resource. A veterinarian's ad can tell you whether the clinic is close enough to your home for convenience and whether the veterinarian offers any special services, such as boarding, grooming, or twenty-four-hour emergency care.

How to Choose the Right Veterinarian

When you have the names of a few veterinarians, set up an appointment to meet them and tour their clinics. Try to interview several veterinarians to make sure you find one you like. It's important that you share the same health care philosophy. Veterinary issues that might be important to you include how often vaccinations are administered, the type of diet your Lab eats, or the use of alternative therapies.

The hospital tour and a meeting with the veterinarian and staff will help you make the right decision. Not every hospital, even if it's a good one, is going to suit everyone. It's important to find a hospital that suits your needs, provides the level of care you want, and that has the attitude you want in the veterinarian and staff. Questions you might want to ask during the interview include the following:

Most veterinarians have the title of DVM, Doctor of Veterinary Medicine. Veterinarians who graduate from the University of Pennsylvania School of Veterinary Medicine bear the title VMD, Veterinary Medical Doctor.

- What are your charges for office visits, vaccinations, parasite preventives, and spay/neuter surgery?
- What forms of payment do you accept? Can I pay a large bill over time?
- What are your office hours?
- Do you have overnight facilities for boarding, treatment, or observation? Is someone there twenty-four hours a day?
- What's the procedure if my Lab has an emergency in the middle of the night or on a Sunday?
- Are you affiliated with the AAHA?
- Approximately what percentage of your clinic's patients are dogs? Of those, how many are Labs?

During the clinic tour, pay attention to the surroundings. The clinic should be clean and odor free. Make notes on what you like or dislike so you can make comparisons with other clinics you visit. Once you make a decision, you can set up an appointment for your new Lab's first visit.

Bringing Your Labrador Home

THE BIG DAY HAS ARRIVED! It's time to bring your new puppy or dog home. You can help this event go smoothly by planning when and how to introduce your Lab to his new surroundings. This includes getting a complete information packet from the breeder, shelter, or rescue group, and scheduling a trip to the veterinarian for a health check.

Plan Ahead and Take Time Off

Introducing a dog to a new home and family shouldn't be done haphazardly. If you can take time off from work to get the dog settled into his new home, you have a better chance of starting him off on the right paw as far as housetraining and learning house rules. A week is ideal, but even a long weekend will help you start this new relationship off on a solid foundation.

Avoid the Holidays

Great, you may be thinking. I'll bring him home over the Christmas holidays when I have time off anyway. Not a good idea. The hectic holiday season is not the best time to bring a new dog into the home. There's too much going on–food cooking, relatives visiting, packages and decorations just waiting to be attacked by an excited dog. Wait until you can focus on the dog instead of the festivities.

Anticipation

Rather than bringing your new dog home during the holiday season or in the middle of a birthday party, give the promise of a dog instead: a box containing a collar, leash, and a copy of this book. The time to bring the dog home is when the excitement is over. That way you can focus on supervising and teaching him from the very first day.

Picking Your Lab Up from the Breeder

If the breeder is within driving distance, you'll want to fetch the puppy yourself instead of having him shipped. Pack the car with a crate for him to ride in on the way back. It's fun for a passenger to cuddle a puppy, but inside the crate is the safest place for a squirmy and no doubt confused Lab pup. Bring along his new collar, tags, and leash as well. A chew toy will keep him occupied on the ride home.

Ask for an item that has the scent of mom and littermates on it. This can be a towel or T-shirt that you've provided in advance. The familiar scent will help calm your puppy during his first few days with you.

When you arrive at the breeder's home, take notes on the puppy's feeding schedule, amount fed, and sleeping habits. Ask if he has any experience with potty training or knows any basic commands, such as "Sit." These same questions apply if you're adopting an adult dog. You can teach your new Lab better and faster the more you know about his behavior.

Before you leave the breeder's home, put the puppy's new collar and tag on. The breeder should provide you with a puppy package as well. The following list details items the packet should include:

- AKC papers (blue slip) and pedigree
- Vaccination records
- Copy of parents' health certificates
- Sales contract

Some breeders also include such items as brochures on pet health insurance, breed club membership information, breed history information, a book on the breed, or a small bag of the food the dog has been eating.

Having Your Puppy Shipped

If your puppy must be shipped by air, confirm with the breeder that he's sending the puppy on a morning flight (a cooler time of day) and on as direct a flight as possible–preferably one that's nonstop. Be aware that some airlines won't ship dogs during the heat of the summer. Also, there's no need for the puppy to be tranquilized since at altitude, drugs can do more harm than good.

The ideal situation would be for you or the breeder to find someone who can take the puppy in the cabin in a carrier that fits beneath the seat and deliver him to you at the airport. If that's not possible, call ahead to the airport to find out exactly where you can pick the dog up. Be there on time so he doesn't have to wait in a noisy, unfamiliar place.

When you pick up your Lab at the airport, make sure to put on his collar, tags, and leash right away and hustle him outside so he can relieve himself.

Visiting the Veterinarian

If possible, your next stop should be the veterinary clinic. It's a good idea to make sure your new dog has a clean bill of health before you become so attached to him that you can't give him up. At the very least, schedule a health check within forty-eight hours of acquiring the dog.

This first visit to the veterinarian should be a friendly one. Ask for a physical exam only. This allows your puppy to gain a positive first impression of the veterinarian, staff, and clinic as a whole. Praise and a treat will reinforce his conception of the vet clinic as a good place to go. Save painful vaccinations for another trip.

Starting a Medical History

On this first visit, be prepared to complete a form detailing your Lab's age, sex, color, and so on. The veterinarian will fill in the dog's weight and other notes on his condition. This information will become the foundation of your Lab's medical history. Don't forget to add the vaccination and deworming records from the breeder to the dog's new file.

Other information that will help the veterinarian evaluate your dog includes where you acquired it (from a breeder or from a shelter, for instance). Knowing where the dog came from can help the veterinarian determine what types of things to look for.

What the Exam Will Cover

The first physical exam will involve listening to the dog's heart and lungs with a stethoscope to check for early heart disease. The vet will also examine such things as eye condition (no signs of disease or infection) and range of motion in the limbs (which might suggest loose hips, for example). A stool sample, if the dog is obliging enough, allows the vet to check for parasite infestation.

Arriving Home

When you get home, walk the puppy around outside first and give him an opportunity to relieve himself. He'll be excited and nervous, so this probably won't take long. Praise him when he performs: "Good go potty!" The sooner he starts learning this phrase, the better.

Supervising Starts Now

Take him inside on leash. Until you're sure he's reliably housetrained and knows the house rules (which will take a minimum of several months), your new Lab should never be allowed the run of the house. He should be on leash, confined to his safe place or crate, in a fenced yard or dog run, in someone's lap, or under a watchful eye. Use baby gates to prevent wandering.

Alert!

Your Lab's crate is his safe place, where he can go when he wants to rest. Teach the kids that they aren't to bother him when he's in his crate or to climb inside the crate with him.

Spend plenty of time playing with and interacting with your new dog these first few days. Your attention will help distract him from missing his mom and littermates. Take him out every couple of hours so he has plenty of opportunities to learn that "outside" is where he needs to go potty. Start teaching simple commands, such as "Sit" or "Come." And play, play, play.

Meeting the Family and Neighbors

This is a big day for your new dog. He's undoubtedly bewitched, bothered, and bewildered by all the new sights, sounds, smells, and people he's encountering. Give him a break, and don't overwhelm him with new experiences all in one day.

Ask neighbors to refrain from bringing their own dogs over to meet the pup. It's important for him to get to know the neighborhood dogs, but right now his immature immune system needs to be protected. Check with your veterinarian to see what age is appropriate for dog-to-dog meetings. Usually it's advisable to wait until the pup is twelve weeks old.

Rules for Kids

If you have children, they'll most likely want to show off their new friend. That's fine, but make a rule that only one or two friends at a time can come over to play with the new pup. Keep a lid on loud squealing, poking, and prodding. It's okay for the kids to throw a ball for the puppy to fetch—he'll love it—but rule out dressing the dog up in baby clothes or carrying him around dangling beneath their arms. It's all too easy for a child to drop and injure a squirmy pup, even one as sturdy as a Lab.

Even if you don't have children, your Lab is likely to encounter them in everyday life. Be aware of any children who may be approaching so you can control any interactions. Hold a toddler's or young child's hand to guide her strokes, and suggest that children ask their parents' permission before petting your dog. Explain that dogs have very sensitive ears, so it's not nice to scream around them.

Teach your children to never hit the dog. Many young children like being the dog's "boss" and think it's their job to yell at or hit the puppy if he does something wrong. Explain very clearly that it's never okay to hit the dog.

Nap Time

After half an hour of play, your new dog will probably be ready to rest. Walk him around to see if he'll go potty again, then put him in his crate. Give him a treat before you close the door, and tell him he's a good dog. Your puppy will probably be ready to leave his crate after a short nap. Keep an eye on him, and when he wakes up, take him for another potty break.

Meeting Other Pets

Bringing your Lab into a home with other pets involves diplomatic skills worthy of Colin Powell. They all need to learn to live together amiably—or at least neutrally. It's your job to help them deal effectively with conflicts. A proper introduction will help keep tensions to a minimum and allow all pets to develop cordial relationships.

Remember that animals like routine and structure. Begin introductions slowly, rather than just throwing everyone together and hoping they all get along. The way you introduce them depends on which species are involved.

Dog Pals

Labs are the original buddy dogs. They get along with everyone, especially other dogs. Nonetheless, it's a good idea to introduce them on neutral territory, such as a nearby park or a neighbor's yard. It may help smooth the initial relationship, and it certainly can't hurt.

As a rule, an adult dog is more likely to welcome a puppy than a dog of its own age. Nonetheless, if your first dog is very old and you're bringing a puppy home, be sure the older dog has a place he can escape to when puppy play becomes too rambunctious.

With each dog on a slack leash, let them sniff and circle each other. This is an essential part of the dog greeting ritual. Let them take their time. A puppy may show deference to an older dog by rolling over on its back. When they seem to be getting along, walk them home. This gives them more time to adjust to each other's presence.

Sometimes a meeting on neutral territory isn't possible. If that's the case, be sure your other dog is confined when you first come home. Let the new dog sniff around the yard on leash to get the scent of the other dog. Then put the new dog in his crate or in the dog run. Let your other dog out so it can visit through the crate or kennel bars. Once they've had a few minutes to get used to each other's presence, you can let the newcomer out for a nose-to-tail meeting.

When it's time to go in the house, take the new dog in on leash. You want him under your control until you're sure how he's going to behave. He should spend the first day on leash at your side (or in his crate) so you can supervise the dogs' interactions.

Feline Friends Not Foes

Introductions between dogs and cats should always start with the dog on leash. This is especially true with a puppy, who might not know to be respectful of a cat's claws. A smart Lab will approach a cat somewhat cautiously. Praise the dog, and give a treat if he ignores the cat or proffers a gentle sniff. Use the leash to restrain him if he lunges at the cat.

Cats that stand their ground are likely to fare well with a new dog and may even rule over the dog with an iron paw. Cats that turn tail and run, however, may instigate a never-ending game of chase, with themselves as the prey.

Another way—probably the best way—to introduce dogs and cats is for one of them to be in a crate. This allows them to see and smell each other first before venturing a closer inspection. Schedule a cage-free meeting—again with the dog on leash—after an energetic play session. A tired Lab might be less likely to lunge at kitty. Remember that it can take a couple of weeks for cats and dogs to become used to each other. Be sure the cat has a place to go where it can escape the dog, such as a room with a baby gate or a tall cat tree.

Other Pets

Labs are intrigued by birds. They'll spend hours staring at a bird in a cage, figuratively—or literally—licking their chops. They are bird dogs, after all. One way you might be able to break your Lab of this habit is to allow him to stick his nose through the cage bars. A nip from a parrot's beak is painful and may teach your Lab to keep a wise distance from the bird. Don't try this with a large parrot, such as a macaw; its powerful beak could do some serious damage.

Rabbits, guinea pigs, hamsters, and other pocket pets may also rouse a Lab's prey drive. With careful supervision, Labs can learn to get along with these small pets. No matter how well they seem to get along, however, they should never be left alone together unless the smaller pet is in a cage that's safely out of reach.

Naming Your Lab

Choosing the right name for your Lab is an important step. You want a name that sounds good and is easy to call. Your Lab's registered name might be a mouthful—O'Henry's Lord Tobias Liberty, for instance—but for his "call name"—the one you use every day—stick to short names of one or two syllables, such as Toby or Hank.

Avoid choosing a name such as Moe or Beau, which could be confused with the word "No." You don't want your Lab to think you're correcting him when what you really want is for him to come to you.

There are lots of good ways to choose a suitable name for your Lab. You can base it on color, appearance, or personality, or on heritage and historical associations. You can even look through a baby name book or one of the many pet name books.

A black or chocolate Lab might be named for its color associations. Kahlua, Java, Godiva, Nestlé, Hershey, Kona, Mocha, Fudge, and Snickers are all good names for Labs of these colors.

Lots of Labs are named for their behavior or appearance. They carry such monikers as Chase, Crash, and Tank. A look in a name book will help you find other names that suit your Lab. For instance, you might name a yellow Lab Boyd, which means "yellow-haired." The name Nigel means "dark or black." Have fun picking the perfect name for your dog.

The First Few Nights

After a busy first day, it's finally bedtime. Take the dog out to go potty one last time. Praise him, and give a treat when he performs. Then, put him in his crate. If it's located in your bedroom, he'll feel more comfortable knowing that you're nearby. Having the crate in the bedroom also allows you to take him out first thing in the morning (or in the middle of the night if necessary) so he doesn't have an accident.

Don't take your puppy out of the crate to comfort him if he cries or whines. That simply teaches him that making noise gets him out of there. Instead, say "Shh" or "Quiet" so he knows you're there.

Some puppies settle down and sleep through the night right away. If you get one of those, give yourself a pat on the back. More likely, your pup will cry or whine the first few nights. Grit your teeth and ignore it. He'll fall asleep eventually.

Housetraining

HOUSETRAINING IS THE MOST IMPORTANT lesson your Lab needs to learn, second only to an instant response to the "Come!" command. Without an understanding of where it's okay to relieve himself, he can never be a full-fledged member of your household. The keys to successful housetraining are using a crate, establishing a routine, observing elimination behavior, understanding dog physiology, consistent positive reinforcement, and plenty of patience.

Crates and Housetraining

What does a crate have to do with housetraining? Plenty! For starters, it prevents your Lab from having accidents in the house. Dogs are den animals, and their instinct is never to soil their den—in this case, the crate. Putting your Lab in his crate when you aren't there to supervise keeps him from having an accident on your carpet.

Crates Aren't Cruel

You might worry that putting your Lab in a cage is cruel. Nothing could be farther from the truth. Your Lab will appreciate having a place where he can relax and feel safe. What's cruel is not protecting him from making mistakes and then punishing him when he does something wrong. Teaching your Lab through positive means–by showing him what you want and preventing him from doing the wrong thing–is much more effective than yelling at him after he makes a mistake.

To help make the crate special for your dog, make it a happy place. Besides sleeping in the crate at night, he can eat his meals in there, too. Every time you put your Lab in his crate, give him a treat and say "Crate!" "Place!" or "Bed!" in a happy tone of voice. Pretty soon, all you'll have to do is call "Crate!"–or the word of your choice–and your Lab will scramble to go to his bed so he can get that yummy snack.

Use the Crate Responsibly

Except for nighttime, your Lab should never spend more than four hours at a time in his crate. For one thing, he needs plenty of opportunities to exercise. Plus, if he's left in his crate too long, he'll have an accident inside it, which defeats the purpose of crate-training.

If you are gone for longer than the four hours, leave your Lab in his safe room instead. Open his crate, put a couple of chew toys in it, as well as food and water dishes in one part of the room. Cover the floor with papers, so that any accidents will be easy to clean up. If you find that your Lab consistently potties in a certain area, you can gradually take up the papers, leaving them only in the favored potty spot.

The crate is not meant to be a place for punishment. Never put your dog in the crate in an angry fashion. You want it to be a safe, secure place for him.

Establishing a Routine

It's easy to predict when puppies will need to go to the bathroom. You can count on a potty trip first thing in the morning when they wake up, after eating and drinking, and after an energetic play session. Use this knowledge to set up a housetraining schedule that will reduce or eliminate accidents in your home.

Stick to the Schedule

By taking your Lab out at set times, he will learn when and where it's okay to go potty. A timer or alarm clock can help you remember to take the dog out at specific intervals. A good rule of thumb is to base the frequency of trips on the dog's age in months. A two-month-old puppy might need to go out every two hours, a three-month-old every three hours. Remember, though, that each dog is different and may need to go out more or less frequently.

Escort Service

One of the reasons for having your dog sleep in a crate in your bedroom is so you can hear when he needs to go out in the morning. Take him out of the crate, escort him to the door, and put a leash on him. Walk him outside and let him sniff around. When he performs, give lots of praise in a happy tone of voice: "Good go potty!" or whatever phrase you choose to use. Popular alternative phrases include "Do your business" and "Get busy."

A Lab puppy's holding capacity varies. Some need trips outside every hour on the hour, while others can make it for two or three hours. Sample schedules that you see in books are just that—samples! You need to determine your own schedule based on your dog's needs.

Why take him outside on leash? Because you need to make sure he really does potty, and you need to be there to praise him when he does. Too often, people put their dogs out in the backyard and just assume that they've eliminated. The dog comes in and immediately potties on the carpet, earning himself a scolding he doesn't understand. Your Lab doesn't know why he's outside, so you need to be there to "explain" it to him by praising his actions.

Be Consistent

If your dog doesn't eliminate after ten or fifteen minutes, take him inside and put him in his crate. Try again in half an hour. Follow the same routine after every meal, after playtime, and before bedtime. Try to take the dog to the same spot every time. The lingering scent will prompt him to go there again. Spend some time playing with him before you go back inside.

Change the routine only if your pup needs to go out in the middle of the night. As soon as he potties, take him back inside and put him in his crate instead of giving him the usual playtime. You don't want him to start demanding playtime at 2:00 A.M.

Part of your Lab's routine should be eating his meals at the same time every day. If you know when he has eaten, you can better predict when he'll need to eliminate. On the other hand, if you leave food out all the time for him, you won't have any idea that he ate just before you got home from work and needs to go out now!

Be sure everyone in the family uses the same phrase when telling the dog to eliminate. You don't want to confuse him.

Feed breakfast after he eliminates in the morning. Space all meals about six hours apart. So if breakfast is at 6:00 A.M., lunch will be at noon, and dinner at 6:00 P.M. Most puppies will need to potty half an hour to an hour after eating. Start by taking your dog out ten minutes after he eats. If he doesn't do anything, continue taking him out at ten-minute intervals until he performs. This will help you figure out how soon after eating he needs to pee and poop.

Elimination Association

Pay attention to the way your Lab behaves before starting to eliminate. Some dogs circle, whine, or sniff first. Others assume a particular expression. Know the signals so you can hurry your dog outside when you see them. Get his attention and say, "Do you want to go out?" Don't wait "just until the next commercial." By then it will probably be too late.

After the dog eliminates, you can spend some time playing with him outdoors or indoors. It's just like studying: homework first, then play. When playtime is over, put him in his crate for a nap. When it's time for him to come out, take him outside first to go potty.

Depending on what they're exposed to in puppyhood, dogs can develop potty preferences for certain surfaces, such as grass, gravel, or concrete. Try to expose your puppy to different surfaces, so he doesn't balk when faced with going on concrete instead of grass.

Your Lab puppy needs to go out every one to three hours to relieve himself. He will learn fastest if you stick to a given schedule instead of just taking him out whenever you think of it or whenever it's most convenient for you. If you're not home during the day, arrange for a neighbor or a pet sitter to come by and take him out at the appropriate time.

You can also teach your puppy to alert you when he needs to go out. To do this, hang a bell on the doorknob and ring it before you open the door to take him out. Many dogs learn quickly to ring the bell when they need to go out.

Sometimes you may find a puddle or pile right in front of the door. This is a good thing! It means your dog tried to potty as close to the outdoors as he could get. He just didn't have anyone to open the door for him. Of course, you shouldn't praise your dog if you catch him eliminating in front of the door, but you should acknowledge to yourself that he's trying.

Paper Training

Teaching a puppy to go on papers inside the house has certain benefits. People who live in condos or high-rises without access to a yard can find it easier to use this method. It's also great for anyone who acquires a puppy in the winter and doesn't want to venture outside and stand around shivering eight times a day. That said, many trainers see dogs that find it difficult to make the transition from paper training to going outside. If you have access to a yard, it's best to skip paper training altogether.

How to Paper Train

To paper train a dog, place papers in the area where you want the dog to go. When your dog shows signs of needing to eliminate—circling, sniffing, whining—take him to the papers. If he moves off them, put him back. When he performs, praise him.

Help your puppy remember what the papers are for by using a sponge to capture some of the urine. Use it to scent a clean set of papers. The next time you take your dog to the papers, he'll smell the urine and be prompted to go again.

Paper Training Alternative

Besides paper, you may also want to try using housetraining pads. Available at pet supply stores, these pads are specially scented to attract a dog and encourage urination and defecation. The benefit is that their water-resistant backing makes them easier to clean up than papers. The drawback—besides expense—is that these pads may or may not work. Some dogs use them for their stated purpose, while others just chew them up.

Accidents Happen

No matter how careful you are, accidents are bound to happen. That's just the way it is with puppies. If you catch your Lab in the act, it's okay to say "Aaagh! Outside," but avoid using the N-word ("No") or saying "Bad dog!" It's the place he chose that's bad, not the act itself. Anger and punishment only increase stress and fear, not to mention a greater likelihood of more accidents.

If you find a puddle or pile after the fact, simply clean it up. It's too late to scold. Never use the long-discredited practices of rubbing the dog's nose in the mess or swatting him with a newspaper. That only teaches a dog that you're a big bully who attacks him for what is, after all, perfectly natural behavior.

Clean-up Supplies

Keep a good enzymatic cleanser on hand for puppy clean-up. These products contain enzymes that break down organic debris and waste. Products that do a good job include Resolve carpet cleaner, OdorMute, and Nature's Miracle. Look for them at your grocery store or pet supply store. Before using any such product, test an inconspicuous area of the carpet (or other fabric surface) first to make sure it's colorfast.

Avoid using any cleansers that contain ammonia. It's one of the components of urine, and the scent of it will draw your puppy back to the same spot. Stick to cleansers made specifically for cleaning up pet accidents.

How to Clean Up After Your Dog

When you find a puddle, use an old towel to soak up as much of the wetness as possible. Then saturate the area with the cleanser of your choice. Lay a clean towel on the spot and cover it with some heavy books or another heavy item. This helps wick the moisture out of the carpet.

For a pile of poop, use a plastic bag or a towel to pick up as much of the mess as possible. Spray the area with the cleanser and use a clean towel to blot up any remaining stool. Then follow the steps described above. When the area dries, it should be odor-free.

Keep lots of old towels or rags on hand. You're going to need them. Dump used towels in a pail in the laundry room and wash them in hot water so they'll be ready for the next accident.

How Long Does Housetraining Take?

It's important to remember that your Lab is still a baby in many ways. Just as it takes months to toilet-train a toddler, it also takes months to reliably housetrain a dog. Be patient during this process. Yelling at your dog when you find an accident only teaches him to sneak around and find secret places to potty. He may even avoid peeing or pooping in front of you at all, which really slows down the process.

Remember, too, that until he's at least six months old, your Lab isn't physiologically capable of controlling his bladder or sphincter for long periods. The muscle control just isn't there yet, and it's not something that can be hurried along. That's why you need a crate and a schedule.

Never assume that your Lab is fully housetrained until he's been reliable in the house for months without an accident. He may have occasional setbacks until he's a year old. If that occurs, make sure you still have him on a regular schedule. See if there are changes you can make to give him more opportunities to go outside when he needs to.

Housetraining an Adult Lab

The same techniques you'd use with a puppy are effective with adult dogs. The advantage is that an adult dog doesn't have to go out as often. The main thing he needs to learn is where you want him to go.

A schedule is still important, simply to give your new Lab some structure in his new life. Dogs appreciate routine. Going out, eating, and playing at set times will help him adjust more quickly to living in your home. You can also crate-train an adult Lab. Use the same techniques described for crate-training puppies. Again, a crate will keep your dog out of trouble and in your good graces.

Housetraining Problems

Puppies who came from an environment where they were accustomed to eliminating in a cage are often difficult to housetrain—so crate-training doesn't always work with them. Sometimes, they wait to eliminate until they're put in a crate, because that's all they've ever done. Working with this puppy requires an extra dose of patience, as well as some creative thinking.

One way to teach a dog to potty outside is to reward the action in a way he'll remember. Take a clicker and some treats outside with you. As the dog urinates or defecates, click. When he's finished, give him a treat. He'll soon be very anxious to potty for you when you go outside.

Provide Extra Supervision

If you're faced with a puppy who doesn't understand that he's not supposed to potty in his crate, try keeping him leashed by your side all the time. That way you'll be right there if he shows signs of needing to go out. Take him out as often as possible until he potties outside, and then heap praise on him.

Be Persistent

If he potties in his crate at night, take him outside just before bedtime and try to get him to go. If he doesn't go the first time, take him out again in half an hour. Even if you have to go out several times, do your best to get him to go potty before you put him in his crate for the night.

Don't give up! It can take months before something clicks inside this puppy's brain and he realizes that outside is the place to go. By learning his schedule and understanding his body language, you can help teach him what you want.

Relapses in Housetraining

What do you do if your Lab suddenly starts having accidents in the house after months of being reliable? The first step is to take him to the veterinarian. Many health problems, such as bladder infections, cause housetraining lapses. A physical exam and possibly a urinalysis or fecal exam can rule out any health problems.

If your Lab gets a clean bill of health, study the circumstances surrounding the accidents. Has your routine changed? Is there a new pet or baby in the home? Insecurity can cause housetraining problems. Make any reasonable changes you can to help your Lab feel more comfortable, such as providing extra playtime or giving additional attention. You may need to go back to a strict routine of going out at specific times and confining him as needed until he's back on track.

Housetraining takes time. If your Lab is having lots of accidents, review your schedule to see where you might be going wrong. Take him out more often, and don't forget to crate him or put him in his safe room when you can't watch him. Patience and a positive attitude will get you successfully over the housetraining hurdle.

Basic Nutrition

IT'S THE RARE LAB THAT DOESN'T LOVE TO EAT. While your Lab will most likely be happy to eat whatever you set in front of him, you'll want to be a little more discriminating. The quality of dog foods available ranges from barely-qualifies-as-food to good-enough-to-eat-myself. To figure out which food is best for your Lab, it helps to know some nutrition basics.

Vital Nutrients

Nutrients are substances that promote growth, provide energy, and help the body perform metabolic functions, such as maintaining and synthesizing tissues and regulating temperature. The nutrients a dog needs to maintain life and health are protein, carbohydrates, fats, vitamins, minerals, and water. These nutrients are found in meats, grains, fruits, and vegetables. A balanced diet supplies all the nutrients a dog needs.

Protein

Proteins are the building blocks of enzymes and hormones. The body uses proteins to create protective and structural tissues, such as skin, hair, nails, cartilage, ligaments, and tendons. Proteins carry oxygen and iron to the tissues and form the antibodies the immune system uses to fight disease.

The units that make up proteins are called amino acids. They are important in tissue growth and repair. Without amino acids, your Lab's body couldn't function. These multifunctional units can be used directly for energy or stored as fat or glycogen for later use as energy.

Providing high-quality nutrients in the correct amounts is one of the best ways to ensure that a puppy leads a long and healthy life. Each nutrient plays a pivotal role in the way the body functions.

Sources of protein are meat, grains, or a combination of the two. Common meat proteins you might see listed on a dog food label are beef, chicken meal, and meat by-products. The quality of animal protein varies, ranging from poor to excellent. For instance, the protein quality of chicken depends on whether the food contains chicken meat and skin, or chicken feathers, bones, heads, and feet. Bones and feathers are made up of collagen, a protein that isn't easily digested, so they aren't a good source of protein.

Nutritional deficiencies in dogs can manifest themselves in all kinds of ways, including chronic ear infections, loose stools, scratching, a dull coat, or dry, flaky skin.

The protein quality of grain doesn't vary as much as that of meat. Grain proteins aren't as good as high-quality sources of animal protein, but they're better than low-quality sources of animal protein. Plant protein ingredients include corn gluten meal, ground whole brown rice, and soybean meal.

Fat

Fats, also known as lipids, provide energy and make food taste good. Fat pads vital organs, protecting them from injury, and serves as insulation, helping the body conserve heat. Among other things, the body uses fats to help transmit nerve impulses and transport nutrients. The essential fatty acids in fats contain the fat-soluble vitamins A, D, E, and K. All are essential for a number of bodily functions, such as gastric acid secretion, inflammation control, and muscle contraction.

Animal fats and vegetable oils are the sources of fat in dog foods. If a single type of fat is used in a food–chicken fat, for example–it must be described that way on the ingredient label. Otherwise, you'll see the general term "animal fat."

Besides providing the most concentrated form of energy of all the nutrients, fat is also highly digestible. Despite these advantages, high-fat foods taste so good that dogs–especially Labs–are likely to eat too much of them. That's why it's important to use portion control.

Carbohydrates

Carbohydrates are a plant-based source of energy that fuel the Lab to run and retrieve for hours on end. When it needs energy, the body uses carbs first so that protein can be spared for other uses, such as tissue repair and growth. In addition to serving as an energy source, carbohydrates help form the nonessential amino acids produced by the dog's body. When joined with proteins or fats, carbs play a role in the construction of body tissues. Without carbohydrates, the body couldn't synthesize DNA, RNA, or other essential body compounds.

Carbohydrates can take three forms: simple sugars, such as glucose; complex sugars, such as lactose and sucrose; and polysaccharides, such as glycogen and dietary fiber. Sugars provide energy for tissues and are essential to the functioning of the central nervous system. Glycogen, which is stored in muscle and the liver, provides emergency energy for the heart and cells. Fiber helps stimulate bowel movements and speeds waste through the system.

Grains, such as corn, oats, rice, and wheat are the primary sources of carbohydrates in dog foods. They provide the body with complex carbohydrates in the form of starch. Other plant sources, such as beet pulp and rice or wheat bran, provide fiber.

Water

Although we may not think of it as such, water is the most important nutrient in a dog's diet. Water, which comprises almost 60 percent of an adult dog's body and 75 to 80 percent of a puppy's body, plays a vital role in cell and organ function. It helps maintain body temperature, aids in digestion and circulation, transports nutrients, lubricates body tissues, and facilitates elimination of waste. Dogs can go for weeks without food, but without water they can die within days.

A number of factors control water intake: thirst, hunger, metabolic activity (such as growth or pregnancy), and environmental conditions (such as temperature and humidity). The amount of water your Lab drinks and loses each day varies depending on the amount of food he eats. That's why it's important to make sure he has an ample supply of fresh water every day. Dogs that eat canned food, which is about 75 percent water, tend to drink less water than dogs that eat kibble (dry food).

Vitamins and Minerals

In minute amounts, these organic molecules serve a vital function in many of the body's metabolic processes. Vitamins are classified in two groups: fat-soluble and water-soluble. Fat-soluble vitamins–A, D, E, and K–can be stored in the liver, while water-soluble vitamins are excreted in the urine if the body doesn't use them. Among the vitamins you might see listed on a dog-food label are thiamin, riboflavin, niacin, pyridoxine, panthothenic acid, biotin, folic acid, and choline.

With a few exceptions, most vitamins can't be synthesized by the body and must be supplied in a dog's food. Vitamin C is one of those exceptions. Dogs can synthesize the necessary levels of vitamin C, so they don't need it added to their diet.

Because fat-soluble vitamins are stored primarily in the liver, they can quickly reach toxic levels if dogs are supplemented with them too frequently.

Like vitamins, minerals are present in your Lab's body only in tiny amounts, but they too are essential for life. Among other functions, minerals provide skeletal support and play a role in nerve transmission and muscle contractions. Macrominerals, which include calcium, phosphorus, and magnesium, account for most of the body's mineral content. Microminerals, also called trace elements, are present in the body in very small amounts. Microminerals include zinc, manganese, iodine, and selenium.

Proper vitamin and mineral balance is essential, but that doesn't mean you should automatically supplement your Lab's diet. Especially during puppyhood, an overdose of certain vitamins and minerals can cause problems in musculoskeletal development. The level of vitamins and minerals in a dog food should be considered in relation to other components of the diet. The goal is an overall balanced diet.

What Is a Balanced Diet?

For sparkling good health, every Lab needs an appropriate mix of protein, fat, carbohydrates, vitamins, and minerals. A balanced diet contains all the nutrients that dogs are known to need. Nutritional requirements are usually determined as the amount of a given nutrient a dog needs to support growth or to fulfill a needed function.

When dogs don't get enough of a particular essential nutrient, they can develop problems related to that nutrient's functions. For instance, the body uses protein to synthesize new protein, as well as for energy. If the amount of fat and carbohydrate in a diet are not balanced to the amount of protein, then the protein ends up being used for energy instead of for synthesis of new protein. The result is protein malnutrition.

The statement that a diet is complete and balanced has meaning on two levels. Complete means that a food contains all the nutrients that dogs are known to need. Balanced means that a food contains those nutrients in appropriate proportions to one another and also that those nutrients are balanced to the energy level of the diet. For instance, a diet formulated for older dogs is balanced to provide a lower energy level than one formulated for puppies.

Is there a balanced diet that's right for every dog?
No, there is no set balanced diet that's right for every dog. Dogs are individuals, and while a majority of them might do quite well on a given diet, there will always be a few that have special needs. A dog's dietary needs can also be affected by stress, environment, and other factors.

To determine whether a particular food is complete and balanced, look on the label. Manufacturers must state whether their foods meet the nutrient profiles set by a group called the American Association of Feed Control Officials (AAFCO). Growth diets (puppy food) and maintenance diets (adult food) have different nutrient profiles. Some foods are labeled for "all life stages," but for a puppy, a food labeled for growth is a better choice.

Beyond that, look to see whether the food is formulated to meet AAFCO standards or whether the manufacturer conducted feeding trials to see if dogs actually thrive on the diet. Look for a nutritional adequacy statement that says something like "This food is complete and balanced for maintenance [or for growth] based on AAFCO feeding trials." When in doubt, go with a food that's backed by feeding tests.

Choosing Dog Food

When you stroll down the numerous dog food aisles at your pet supply store, you may be overwhelmed by the variety available. You can find foods for puppies, large-breed puppies, old dogs, working dogs, and dogs with allergies. While it's nice to have a selection, it can be difficult to decide which food is right for your dog. Knowing the Lab's special needs will help.

Factors to consider include the dog's energy level and size. Working dogs, or active, high-energy dogs, such as Labs, are probably better off with a diet that's high in caloric density, meaning that it's high in fat and highly digestible. Couch potatoes, on the other hand, who get most of their exercise walking to and from the food bowl, need a much lower calorie diet or they'll become overweight.

With a puppy, you need to be aware of growth rate. Conventional wisdom once said that big dogs with big bones needed lots of calcium and other nutrients during puppyhood. Veterinarians now know that's not true. Because Labs are prone to musculoskeletal disorders, such as hip and elbow dysplasia, it's important that they not grow too quickly.

Large-breed puppies, such as Labs, need less calcium so their bones can develop normally as they're growing. Veterinary nutrition researchers have discovered that by reducing the calcium in diets for large-breed puppies and controlling the calories, the puppies don't grow as quickly and grow up with fewer musculoskeletal problems. Some manufacturers also add nutrients believed to help improve joint cartilage–such as glucosamine and chondroitin–to the foods for large-breed puppies, as well as to diets for large-breed adult dogs.

Keep in mind that a regular puppy food, as opposed to one that's made specifically for large-breed puppies, provides complete and balanced nutrition for any size dog. The difference is that it's not fine-tuned to meet the precise needs of a puppy that will grow up to be a big dog, such as a Labrador. Large-breed dogs are defined as those that will weigh 50 pounds or more in adulthood. Most dogs, such as Labs, that will weigh less than 90 pounds at maturity can be switched to an adult diet at about one year of age. Whatever you choose to feed your puppy, the most important thing is for it to be complete and balanced. As a puppy grows, poor nutrition can lead to all sorts of problems, from poor skeletal development to a compromised immune system.

Canned Food

Canned foods contain either blends of ingredients—muscle meats or poultry, grains, vitamins, and minerals—or one/two types of muscle meats or animal by-products with enough supplemental vitamins and minerals to ensure that the food is nutritionally complete. Depending on the ingredients used, canned foods can vary widely in nutrient content, digestibility, and availability of nutrients. They're prepared by cooking and blending all of the ingredients, canning and cooking the mixture, and pressure-sterilizing the sealed can.

Dogs love canned food. It meets their "smells good, tastes good" criteria. That's because canned food has a high fat content and is calorically dense. Canned food has a long shelf life, although it must be refrigerated after it's opened. It's easier to eat for older dogs that have difficulty chewing. And for you, it's easy enough to open a can and dump the contents into your Lab's dish.

However, canned food does have disadvantages. It's expensive, especially if you're feeding it to a large breed, such as a Lab. Its water content is high—as much as 78 percent—so you're not getting a lot of meat for your money. Canned food sticks to teeth and is a factor in the formation of plaque, which leads to periodontal disease.

Dry Food

This is the most common type of dog food purchased. Kibble contains grains; meat, poultry, or fish; some milk products; and vitamin and mineral supplements. It's made by combining all the ingredients, extruding them into the desired shapes or sizes, and baking. Once the dog food has cooled, the kibble is sprayed with fat or some other substance to make it taste good.

The big advantage to dry food is cost. It's much less expensive than canned food. This is something to consider when you have one or more large dogs to feed. Dry food has a long shelf life and can be left out without risk of going bad.

Dry food has a reputation for helping to prevent the buildup of plaque and tartar on teeth. Dry foods and biscuits can help crack off tartar (the hardened form of plaque), but they don't affect the gumline area. The exception to this is veterinary foods that are designed to have a cross-hatch effect on teeth, scrubbing them all the way to the gumline.

On the downside, kibble generally contains less fat and more carbohydrates than canned food. For this reason, it's often less palatable to dogs than canned food, especially if they're given a choice. A finicky Lab's taste buds can be tempted by mixing a little canned food in with the kibble.

Frozen and Semi-Moist Food

Frozen dog foods are made with fresh meat, vegetables, and fruit, and contain no artificial preservatives. After being mixed and formed into loaves, rolls, or cubes, the food is flash frozen to preserve freshness. Frozen nuggets are as easy to feed as kibble, and loaves or rolls are easy to slice after defrosting. Consider a commercial frozen food if you like the idea of fresh ingredients but don't have time to cook for the dog yourself.

The downside is that frozen dog food is available only in limited distribution. It must be kept frozen until you're ready to use it, and any unused portion must be refrigerated. If you're traveling with a dog, it's difficult to take the food along unless you have some means of refrigeration or of finding it in pet stores along the way.

Some frozen foods also come in freeze-dried form and can be reconstituted with hot water. Some dogs will eat this, while others turn up their noses.

There's no evidence showing that dogs do better on one type of food than another. The choice you make depends on your Lab's dietary needs and preferences, as well as your preferences and budget.

The semi-moist food diet is softer than dry food but not as messy as canned food. The amount of water it contains ranges from 15 to 30 percent. Ingredients include fresh or frozen animal tissues, grains, fats, and sugars.

Other than convenience and palatability, there's not much to be said for semi-moist foods. The level of sugar they contain puts them squarely in the junk food category. In cost, they fall somewhere between canned and dry food, although single-serve packets usually compare in price to canned foods. This type of food is best given in small quantities as a treat.

Understanding the Label

Knowing how to read a dog-food label is a must if you want to choose the best food for your Lab. Important parts of the label that you already know about are the statement of nutritional adequacy—"complete and balanced for growth" or "complete and balanced for all life stages"—and the claim that a food's nutritional value has been proven with AAFCO feeding studies. The next thing to study is the ingredient list.

What's in It?

The label must list ingredients by weight in decreasing order. In other words, the first ingredient—which ideally is some form of animal protein—cannot be exceeded in weight by any of the ingredients that come after it.

Be aware that manufacturers can get around this requirement by a practice called split-ingredient labeling. This involves spreading out, or splitting, ingredients of the same type so they appear farther down the label. For instance, a grain such as corn, rice, or wheat might appear on the label in several different forms, such as flour, flakes, middlings, or bran. A food labeled in this way might end up containing more protein from plant sources than from animal sources.

When you find a food you like, continue to check the label every once in a while to make sure the ingredients remain the same. The best dog food manufacturers use a fixed formula—meaning that the ingredients don't change from batch to batch—but others change ingredients based on availability and market prices. Some dogs with sensitive stomachs can suffer digestive upsets from this kind of unexpected change in ingredients.

You might see certain dog foods described as "premium." These are usually expensive foods that you find only in pet supply stores. The difference between premium and nonpremium foods is density per volume—in other words, a cup of a premium food generally has more usable nutrients than a cup of nonpremium food.

Name Calling

Can you tell anything from a food's name? Surprisingly, yes. There are strict regulations concerning what a food can be called. Let's say that you're looking at a can that reads "Grandma's Chicken for Canines." That food must contain 95 percent chicken, not counting the water used for processing. Once the water is accounted for, the food must still contain at least 70 percent chicken. If the name includes a combination of ingredients—"Grandma's Chicken and Beef for Canines"—chicken and beef must make up 95 percent of the total weight (excluding water), and the food must contain more chicken than beef.

A food name that contains a qualifier such as "dinner," "entrée," "formula," "nuggets," or "platter" must contain at least 25 percent of the named ingredient—lamb, let's say. So "Grandma's Lamb Dinner for Dogs" contains at least 25 percent, but less than 95 percent lamb. What if Grandma makes a lamb-and-beef dinner? The lamb and beef together must make up 25 percent of the product, with at least 3 percent being beef.

Sometimes you'll see a food that highlights a special ingredient, such as bacon or cheese. Manufacturers can list these tasty ingredients if they make up at least 3 percent of the food. If you see Grandma's Beef Dinner for Dogs "with cheese," you know that it contains at least 3 percent cheese. If it says "with cheese and bacon," it must contain at least 3 percent of each ingredient.

Guaranteed Analysis

What else can you learn from the label? Look for the guaranteed analysis. This states the minimum percentages of crude protein and fat and maximum percentages of crude fiber and moisture. Sometimes it includes guarantees for other nutrients, such as calcium, phosphorus, sodium, and linoleic acid.

Because canned food has more moisture than dry food, you'll see differences between the two in the levels of crude protein and most other nutrients. To compare nutrient levels between canned and dry food, multiply the guarantees for the canned food by four. For example, if you're looking at a canned food with a guaranteed analysis of 8 percent protein, and a dry food with a guaranteed analysis of 21 percent protein, you would multiply that 8 percent by four to come up with a dry-matter percentage of 32 percent protein for the canned food.

The label also lists feeding guidelines, which are only a rough estimate. Each Lab is different, so you'll need to experiment to find the right amount of food for your dog. If he starts looking chubby, cut down. If he looks too thin, add more. Remember that a growing Lab or one that works hard in the field all day needs more food than one that lies around the house while you're at work.

Homemade and Raw Diets

The trend toward healthy eating has reached dogdom now, with more pet caregivers showing an interest in preparing a homemade or raw diet for their animals. The attraction of this type of diet is that you can control the quality of the ingredients. A homemade diet can be beneficial if your Lab has food allergies, is sensitive to artificial dyes or preservatives, or has a particular health problem that can be benefited by a special diet.

Proponents of raw diets argue that they are more natural and provide better nutrition. Raw foods retain enzymes and other healthful substances that cooking destroys. People who feed raw diets say their dogs have better health, a beautiful coat, few or no skin problems, and great dental health. Factors to consider before deciding to feed a homemade or raw diet include nutritional completeness, time, and expense.

One of the concerns about homemade diets is that they may lack certain vitamins and minerals, or contain an improper balance of protein, fats, and carbohydrates. Simply feeding human-grade products doesn't make a diet complete and balanced. If ingredients aren't provided in proper proportions, the diet may be inadequate. It's possible to design a nutritionally complete homemade diet for dogs, but it's important to use appropriate recipes from valid sources. Look for a book by a veterinary nutritionist or a layperson trained in nutrition. It's a good idea to rotate the meats, vegetables, and fruits you use so that your Lab receives a variety of nutrients and stays interested in his meals.

Commercial Dog Foods

Commercial dog foods come ready to go in bags or cans. They're easy to measure out and feed. For a homemade diet, ingredients must be purchased, measured, mixed, and cooked (unless you're feeding a raw diet) on a frequent basis. If you enjoy cooking and have plenty of time to spend in the kitchen, this isn't a drawback.

What if you can barely get dinner on the table for your family, let alone for the dog, but you're not satisfied with the diets you find in the grocery store? You may want to consider purchasing a natural or raw diet from a pet supply store or through mail order. Many companies produce so-called natural foods that are preservative-free and contain high-quality organic ingredients. They come in dry, canned, or raw form.

There's no strict definition for what makes a food "natural." Most often, this term is used to refer to commercial diets that are made without preservatives or that use only natural preservatives, such as vitamin E or ascorbic acid. Other foods claim to be natural because they use human-grade ingredients or organic ingredients.

Performance Diets

Working retrievers and show dogs lead stressful lives that call for extra nutrition. They need a diet that's high in caloric density, which means that a food is high in fat to provide energy and highly digestible so the dog's body can make use of it.

This type of food is called a performance diet. It's a good choice for a Lab that competes in field trials, conformation shows, agility, or some other active sport. Labs that get lots of strenuous daily exercise, such as several long walks or hikes, can also benefit from a performance food.

Every Lab is different, so don't be afraid to experiment until you find a food that suits your dog, with just the right mix of nutrients. How can you tell if your Lab's diet is balanced for his individual needs? Simply take a look. A dog eating a well-balanced diet is bright-eyed, muscular, and active, with good breath, a shiny coat, and healthy skin.

Feeding a dog a balanced diet is all about choices. There's nothing wrong with feeding a commercial food if your dog is happy and healthy on it. It's convenient to feed, and it obviously meets your dog's nutritional needs. If your dog has health problems, allergies, or you'd simply like to have more control over what goes into his body, then you may want to consider some form of homemade diet. Whichever type of diet you choose, the most important thing is to make sure that it provides all the nutrients your dog needs.

How and When to Feed

How often should you feed your Lab puppy for optimal growth? That depends on his age. Most puppies start with four meals a day after they're weaned. By the time they're ten to twelve weeks old, they're down to three meals a day. At four months, they can start eating twice a day—a schedule that should be continued for the rest of the dog's life.

How much does a Lab eat?

That depends on the individual dog. Ask the breeder how much he's been feeding at each meal, and go from there. You can also use the recommendation on the food's label as a starting point, but remember that it's only an estimate—it may be too much or too little for your particular Lab.

If you're a working caregiver, though, it's not always convenient to fit in that third or fourth meal. When that's the case, it's perfectly fine to feed puppies only twice a day—morning and evening. It won't make any difference in their activity level or behavior. Just divide the amount of food they need daily into two meals instead of three or four.

As with housetraining, a routine is important. Try to feed your Lab at the same time every day. Feeding meals at set times rather than leaving food out all the time allows you to be aware of how much your dog is eating and whether his appetite is good. And free-feeding (leaving food out all the time) promotes obesity, which can be a problem in this breed.

Supplements

One aspect of feeding a balanced diet is whether to give supplements. If vitamins and minerals are healthful, more of them must be better, right? Not necessarily. Too much of anything can cause problems.

For instance, puppies supplemented with calcium can develop deformed bones or have stunted growth. Too much calcium can also interfere with zinc absorption and cause a zinc deficiency. The result is a dog with skin problems, such as thinning or gray hair, spots where the skin is moist, or increased bacterial infections on the skin.

Too many vitamins can also cause problems. Excessive amounts of vitamin D and C are associated with an increased risk of a certain type of urinary stones. Too much vitamin A can suppress the immune system.

Most veterinary nutritionists agree that supplements aren't necessary if a dog eats a complete and balanced diet. Nonetheless, there are some circumstances in which supplements can be helpful. Dogs with skin problems often benefit from essential fatty acid (EFA) supplements, and older dogs, or dogs with health problems, may need certain supplements because they're less able to absorb nutrients. Of course a dog that's eating a homemade diet needs a multivitamin, which is usually recommended in recipes for homemade dog foods. Ask your veterinarian for advice before supplementing your Lab's diet.

Treat Talk

Like most of us, Labs love treats. Who doesn't enjoy something crunchy, savory, or sweet in addition to the healthy foods that make up our regular meals? Treats are super motivators during training sessions, and it's fun to give them on a dog's birthday, after a great performance at a flyball event, or just for being such a wonderful dog. As with all good things, however, moderation is the watchword.

What kind of treats do Labs like? You name it, they'll eat it. Hard biscuits and carrots satisfy the need for something crunchy, and both are good for the teeth. Frozen baby carrots can help soothe the sore gums of a teething puppy.

Many dogs also enjoy fruits, such as apples, bananas, and strawberries. Rather than giving your Lab sweet, fattening ice cream, choose the more healthful doggie ice cream that's available in the freezer section of grocery stores. Frozen vegetables are also refreshing on a hot summer day. Numerous dog bakeries offer cookies and cakes made just for dogs, with none of the sugar or chocolate that would be harmful to them.

Alert!

Treats shouldn't make up more than 10 percent of your dog's daily food intake. Be aware of how much you're giving, and cut back a little on his food in the evening if you had an extra-long training session or a special event, such as a birthday with doggie cake.

For training treats, use foods that are small, smelly, and quickly eaten. Cut up some hot dogs or cubes of cheese. Cat treats are highly odorous and are just the right size for a training reward. Freeze-dried liver is another favorite, as are tiny bite-size biscuits.

For chewing pleasure, Labs love pig ears and rawhides. There's a risk of choking with these products, especially if your dog tends to gobble them down rather than gnaw on them for hours. Give them only while you're around to supervise.

Nutritional Nightmares

Are there any foods your Lab shouldn't eat? Absolutely! Chocolate, onions, grapes, raisins, and alcoholic beverages are among the items your dog should never ingest.

Chocolate may be the food of love, but it doesn't love dogs. A chemical in chocolate called theobromine is toxic to dogs and can cause vomiting, diarrhea, panting, restlessness, and muscle tremors. Too much chocolate can even kill a dog. Dark chocolate and unsweetened baking chocolate (which doesn't even taste good) contain more theobromine than candy, which is adulterated with sugars and other ingredients. Keep any form of chocolate well out of your Lab's reach.

Raw or cooked onions are off limits, too. A chemical in onions can destroy a dog's red blood cells, causing a serious or even fatal case of anemia.

Lots of dogs love grapes and they seem harmless enough, but grapes and raisins (dried grapes) have been reported to cause acute kidney failure in some dogs. It's not known why the sweet treats cause a problem, but it's best to avoid giving them to dogs. Signs of toxicity from eating grapes or raisins include vomiting within a few hours of eating them, loss of appetite, diarrhea, lethargy, and abdominal pain. These signs can last for days or even weeks. Successful treatment involves activated charcoal to help prevent absorption of toxins and hospitalization with intravenous fluids for at least two days. The veterinarian will monitor blood chemistry for three days to ensure that kidney failure doesn't develop.

You might be able to train your Lab to bring you a beer from the fridge, but don't share it with him. Getting a dog drunk isn't funny, it's dangerous. Alcoholic beverages can be harmful or even fatal to dogs.

Obesity

You might not ever have thought of obesity as a health problem, but it's linked to diabetes and orthopedic problems. Obesity is the most common health problem veterinarians see in dogs, and Labs are no exception. If they eat too much and don't get the exercise they need, they balloon up to resemble sausages on legs.

How Much Weight Is Too Much?

A Lab that's too fat weighs 15 percent or more above the normal weight for the breed (55 to 80 pounds, depending on the dog's gender). Because Labs enjoy their food so much, they're prone to obesity, so it's important to keep their weight normal by feeding measured amounts and providing plenty of exercise.

Most table scraps are high in fat and don't meet a dog's nutritional needs. If it's not good enough for you to eat, don't give it to your dog. Stick to a healthful diet, and give appropriate treats during training sessions or on special occasions.

Putting Your Lab on a Diet

You can tell if your Lab is overweight just by looking at him. As you stand over him looking down, you should see a defined waist. No waist and a rounded or bulging abdomen are signs that your Lab has been tucking into his meals just a little too heartily and lounging around afterward. A hands-on test will confirm your dog's condition. Can you feel his ribs (but not see them) or are they heavily padded with fat?

Your veterinarian can confirm whether your Lab needs to go on a diet and exercise program. The simplest way to start is by reducing the amount of food you give. If you usually measure out a heaping cup of food, level it off. That alone can help.

If reducing the amount of food isn't practical, switch to a brand with fewer calories. There are many such foods in the market. Look for a product that says "lite" or "less active."

Introduce a new food gradually, over seven to ten days, to avoid stomach upset. If you change foods, don't switch to a type that your Lab isn't used to eating. For instance, if you feed him canned food, the new food should be a reduced-calorie canned food, not a dry diet. When that's not possible, mix the canned food with the dry over a period of several weeks so he has time to become accustomed to the change.

If your schedule allows, feed several small meals a day rather than one or two large ones. Eating more frequently helps your Lab feel more full and less deprived. Another way to help him feel full is to add more fiber to his diet. Canned green beans, carrots, and pumpkin (plain, not the sweetened pie filling) are high in fiber but low in calories. Most dogs gobble them down.

Finally, be sure your Lab gets daily exercise. Throw a ball for five or ten minutes, take longer walks, or take him someplace he can swim. If he's seriously overweight, start slowly and work up to longer periods of exercise. As he loses weight, you can increase the intensity and duration of play sessions. Ⓔ

Basic Health Care

PREVENTIVE MEDICINE IS THE BEST WAY to keep your Lab in fetching good health. By taking steps to prevent problems or recognize them before they become serious, you'll save money as well. Preventive health care includes spay/neuter surgery, vaccinations, and regular home health checks.

Spaying and Neutering

Sometimes referred to as "altering," spay or neuter surgery is the removal of a dog's reproductive organs (the uterus and ovaries in a female and the testicles in a male) to prevent it from producing litters of puppies. Spaying (also referred to as an ovariohysterectomy) is the procedure used for female pets, and neutering generally refers to the procedure used for male pets. Both surgeries offer health benefits beyond the prevention of unwanted puppies.

One of the greatest health benefits of spay surgery for females is the reduced risk of breast cancer, especially if the surgery is performed before the first heat cycle. Spayed females also run no risk of developing uterine or ovarian infection or cancer. Neutering of males results in reduced risk of testicular and prostate cancer, less desire to roam, and a reduced incidence of aggressive behavior.

Spaying a female before her first heat can reduce the risk of mammary cancer to as little as 5 percent. The risk increases to 8 percent if she goes through one heat cycle and 26 percent if she goes through two or more heat cycles.

Myths about Spay/Neuter Surgery

Despite these benefits, many myths exist about spay and neuter surgery that may make you reluctant to go ahead with it. Among these myths are "My Lab will get fat," "My Lab's personality will change," "My Lab should have a litter before she's spayed," and "Surgery is dangerous and painful, and I don't want to put my Lab through it unnecessarily." Let's take a look at each myth realistically.

My Lab Will Get Fat

Spay and neuter surgery is usually scheduled when a dog is six to nine months old, just when growth is beginning to slow and hormonal balances change, influencing appetite. Young animals naturally start to put on weight during this time, especially if they're still getting the same amount of food and not enough exercise. It's understandable that people might associate spay/neuter surgery with weight gain, but it's not the surgery that causes the problem. Adjusting a dog's diet and providing plenty of exercise will prevent obesity.

My Lab's Personality Will Change

Yes it will, for the better. Spayed or neutered dogs are more bonded to their owners, less likely to roam, less given to marking territory by lifting a leg and spraying urine around the house, and less likely to develop aggressive behaviors. Spaying and neutering doesn't affect retrieving ability.

My Lab Should Have a Litter Before She's Spayed

Having a litter has no positive effect on a female's emotional state. Dogs don't dream about someday having puppies and don't feel deprived if they don't have them.

Anesthesia Is Dangerous

The risk from anesthesia is much less than it used to be. The drugs used today are very safe, and many veterinarians use high-tech equipment to monitor heart rate and breathing during surgery. If you're concerned, ask if the clinic uses a reversible gas anesthesia, and if the dog is hooked to a heart monitor. These safety features are more expensive but worth the money.

The average cost for neutering a male is $80 to $150. The average cost for spay surgery ranges from $100 to $250, depending on whether it takes place before or after the first estrus cycle. Some veterinarians charge according to the size of the dog, since a larger dog requires more anesthesia than a smaller one.

Surgery Is Dangerous and Painful

Veterinarians use the same high-quality instruments and take the same precautions as medical surgeons. If you're concerned about cleanliness, ask if the instruments are sterilized after every use, if the incision is closed with multiple layers of sutures or staples, and if the veterinarian scrubs between each surgery.

Surgery is performed under full anesthesia, so your dog doesn't feel a thing. Soreness is normal after surgery, but veterinarians today are much more knowledgeable about pain prevention in dogs than they were just five years ago. Medications are also available that can help your dog be more comfortable during the week or so it takes to recover.

When to Spay or Neuter

Most veterinarians recommend that spay or neuter surgery be scheduled at six to nine months of age. In females, it's best if it takes place before the first estrus (heat) cycle. The advantage to surgery at this age is not only because of the decrease in risk of mammary cancer, but also because young dogs are resilient and recover more quickly from surgery. When a male is neutered before puberty, his sexual urges don't develop.

Your veterinarian may recommend running a blood panel before spay/neuter surgery. This is most commonly done if your Lab is middle-aged or older, has a previous history of health problems, or has a current health problem, such as obesity. A blood panel helps ensure that there are no underlying problems that could cause trouble during surgery.

Spay/neuter surgery is generally low risk. Recovery usually takes one week. Keep your Lab quiet during this period. Sedate walks on leash are fine, but hold off on letting the dog chase tennis balls or jump around. If your Lab tries to bite at its stitches, you may need to block the biting with a cone-shaped Elizabethan collar around the neck. When the incision has healed, the veterinarian will remove the sutures unless they are self-dissolving.

Withholding food and water for twelve hours before surgery helps ensure that the dog doesn't vomit and aspirate food into the lungs while under anesthesia.

Vaccinations

Vaccination is the exposure of a dog's immune system to specific heat-killed germs, live germs rendered incapable of causing disease, or toxins and germ products. Once the immune system is exposed to these disease-causing agents, it manufactures antibodies against them. Antibodies are protein substances that neutralize the effects of an antigen, a disease-causing foreign substance in the body.

Today's dogs are fortunate to have vaccinations against a number of killer diseases, including parvovirus (any of several small DNA viruses that cause several diseases in animals) and distemper (highly contagious, catarrhal, often fatal disease of dogs). Before the development of vaccines for dogs, many died every year because their immune systems weren't strong enough to fight off these diseases.

While vaccinations have been a boon to dogs, too much of a good thing can be just as bad as not having it at all. Veterinarians are currently rethinking the requirement that dogs be vaccinated every year. Overvaccination has been associated with autoimmune hemolytic anemia in dogs—a disease that can be fatal.

Many schools of veterinary medicine now recommend a standard three-shot series for puppies to protect against parvovirus, adenovirus 2, parainfluenza, and distemper. The first vaccination is given at six to eight weeks of age, the next three to four weeks later, followed by the final shot in another three to four weeks. A rabies shot is given after sixteen weeks of age. After the initial three-shot series, they recommend that dogs receive booster shots for these diseases at one year of age and every three years after that. Note that some states require annual rabies vaccination instead of every three years.

When dogs are naturally exposed to disease, immunity often lasts a lifetime, but immunity stimulated by vaccination is limited, so booster shots at regular intervals are necessary.

Types of Vaccinations

Three types of vaccines are used in dogs: killed virus, modified live virus (MLV), and recombinant. Killed vaccines cannot cause disease and are stable during storage, but they are often associated with vaccine reactions and require more frequent booster shots. Modified live vaccines are stronger and provide longer-lasting protection against disease. In a dog with a weakened immune system, however, they have the potential to cause disease.

Recombinant vaccines are a new development. They work by splicing gene-sized fragments of DNA from a virus or bacteria and delivering specific antigen material to the dog on a cellular level. This cuts out the risk of vaccination reactions that sometimes occur when vaccinating with the entire disease-causing organism. Recombinant vaccines cannot cause disease. It's not known yet how long the immunity lasts, but there's a good chance they will soon replace MLV and killed virus vaccines. Recombinant vaccines are available for distemper, rabies, and Lyme disease. The future may also bring more nasal vaccines, which may be less likely to cause adverse reactions.

Which Vaccines Are Really Necessary?

Core vaccines—those for distemper, adenovirus 2 (hepatitis), parvovirus, and rabies—are essential for all dogs. These viral diseases are serious (and can be fatal), common, highly contagious, or a threat to humans (rabies). Distemper, hepatitis, and parvovirus can be treated only with supportive therapy, such as intravenous fluids. There's no medication that can cure the diseases, although antibiotics can help ward off secondary bacterial infections. Rabies is fatal once signs develop.

Other vaccines can also be given, based on the amount of risk the dog faces from them. Vaccines for coronavirus, Lyme disease, parainfluenza, leptospirosis, bordetella, and giardia fall into this "noncore" category. For example, Labs that participate in field trials in the northeastern United States (where Lyme disease is common) are much more susceptible to the disease than field trial Labs in Montana or Alaska (where Lyme disease is uncommon or nonexistent). The dogs in the western United States don't need a Lyme disease vaccination because they run little risk from it. For most dogs, tick control is a better preventive for Lyme disease than vaccination.

Some dogs react negatively to vaccines. Reactions range from facial swelling or hives to hair loss at the vaccination site to lethargy or anaphylactic shock. Most reactions occur within twenty minutes after the injection, but it's a good idea to observe your Lab carefully during the twenty-four hours after a vaccination.

Parasite Prevention

Keeping your Lab free of internal and external parasites is one of the guidelines of good health. Worms, fleas, and ticks are not just irritating, they also spread disease among dogs and sometimes to humans. Parasite infestation results in physical problems, such as bloody diarrhea and secondary bacterial infections. Some parasites can even transmit other parasites. The outdoorsy Lab frequently comes in contact with these minuscule pests, so it's important to take precautions against them.

Internal Parasites

One of the more unpleasant aspects of being a dog is the potential for internal parasites. Roundworms, hookworms, tapeworms, and heartworms can all infest your Lab if they're not kept at bay with preventive medicine. Intestinal worms take a toll on dogs by leaching nutrients from the body. They can cause internal bleeding, dull fur, and a potbellied appearance. Heartworms can be fatal if not treated, and some worms can be transmitted to humans. Other potential worm parasites are whipworms, threadworms, and lung flukes.

Here are a few examples of internal worms and methods to prevent and treat them. Please consult with your Lab's veterinarian for more detailed treatment/prevention recommendations.

Parasite	Warning Signs	Prevention/Treatment
Roundworms	Diarrhea; eggs and worms in the feces; respiratory distress; weakness; dull coat; swollen stomach	Routine examination of stool samples; application of deworming medications
Hookworms	Bloody, dark red, or black and tarry diarrhea; weakness; weight loss; pale gums	Routine examination of stool samples; application of deworming medications
Tapeworms	Visible segments in dog's feces (resemble rice grains); dog may rub its anus on the ground because of itching	Routine examination of stool samples; application of deworming medications
Heartworms	Coughing; exercise intolerance; abnormal lung sounds; breathing difficulties; weight loss; enlarged abdomen; congestive heart failure (or no signs may be visible)	Adulticide and filaricide (two-step) therapy; application of vet-recommended medications (heartworm preventives); possible surgery in severe cases
Whipworms	Bloody diarrhea; weakness; weight loss; anemia	Application of deworming medications, or heartworm prevention products (possibly two/three treatments)
Threadworms	Watery or bloody diarrhea	Application of vet-recommended deworming medications

Parasite	Warning Signs	Prevention/Treatment
Lung flukes (flatworms)	Chronic coughing or gagging; loss of body weight; lethargy; weakness	Application of vet-recommended deworming medications
Fleas	Dog scratching and biting its skin	Flea collars, sprays, shampoos, powders; frequent baths and grooming; vet-prescribed monthly pills (such as Program) that inhibit flea eggs from growing and hatching; topical treatment (such as Advantage or Frontline)
Ticks	Visible, spider-like, blood-sucking insects attached to dog's skin	Regular examination of your dog's coat and skin; tick sprays and collars; tick-preventing medications; antibiotics
Mites	Scaly, reddened skin and patchy hair loss; crusty and/or bleeding sores; wounds that dog scratches and bites at	Series of baths with medicated shampoo, topical medication, and antibiotics; possible use of corticosteroids (to reduce itching)

External Parasites

Besides the nasty internal parasites, there are several external parasites that look upon your Lab as a great local restaurant. Fleas, ticks, and mites not only cause your Lab to scratch miserably, they also spread infection and disease. Fortunately, thanks to new pharmaceutical developments, control of external parasites is easier than it has ever been.

With the exception of rabies, no data exists to indicate just how long the immunity provided by vaccination against infectious canine diseases lasts. Rabies vaccine is the only commonly used vaccine that requires studies to determine how long immunity lasts before the vaccine can be licensed in the United States.

On the opposite page are a few examples of internal worms and preventive methods against them. Please consult with your Lab's veterinarian for more detailed treatment/prevention recommendations.

How to Examine Your Lab

You can help prevent problems or catch them before they become serious by giving your Lab a home health check on a regular basis. Doing so helps you get to know your dog and sharpen your observation skills. Even slight changes in behavior or condition can be early warning signs of a health problem. By getting things checked out early, you can protect your pocketbook and your dog. Schedule a weekly health check as part of your Lab's routine, and consider keeping a written "Lab Log" so you'll notice patterns or changes more quickly.

Lab Exam Tips

When your Lab is a puppy, get him used to being touched all over his body. He should let you look at his teeth and inside his ears, handle his paws, lift his tail, and roll him over for a tummy rub and belly check. By accustoming your puppy to being handled, you'll ensure that he's still willing to let you–and the vet–examine him when he's bigger and stronger.

It's not unusual for a dog to skip a meal once in a while, but a steady decrease in appetite—or an unusually ravenous appetite—is cause for concern. Stools should be small and firm. Loose stools or diarrhea may indicate a health problem or the need for an improved diet.

Mouth

"Say aah." Use this phrase (or another of your choosing) to teach your Lab to open his mouth on command. Lift up his lips to check the teeth for tartar (also referred to as calculus) buildup. While you're there, make sure the gums are nice and pink. When you push on the gums, they should regain their color quickly. Pale gums are a sign of many serious problems, including bloat, poisoning, and parasite infestation.

Ears

Lift up the ears and look inside. Do they look clean or dirty? Unhealthy ears may be red or inflamed, indicating an infection, or filled with lots of waxy brown gunk. A small amount of light brown wax is normal, but heavy amounts (or dirt and debris) should be gently cleaned out with cotton balls (not Q-tips) saturated with mineral oil or an ear cleanser, such as Oti-Clens. Never use alcohol, which besides being drying can sting like the dickens. Clean the ears only when they need it; too much cleaning is just as bad as too little.

Give each ear a good sniff. Your Lab's ears should never smell rancid or unpleasant. A bad odor indicates an infection that should be treated by a veterinarian. To finish the ear exam, check for and remove grass seeds or other debris that might have become lodged in or near the ear.

Eyes

Many Labs spend their days crashing through brush or catching tennis balls thrown to them. Both activities can result in eye injury. That doesn't mean you shouldn't let your Lab play, just that you need to pay close attention to his eye condition.

Eyes should be bright and clear, with little or no discharge. Red, swollen, or squinty eyes and heavy discharge are signs that call for a veterinary visit. To tell if an eye is painful, gently press on the surface of a closed eyelid. What seem like minor eye problems can become serious in a heartbeat, so never let an eye injury go without treatment.

Dogs lower their body temperature by panting, which allows water to evaporate from the mouth, tongue, and lungs and exchanges warm air in the body for cooler air from the environment.

Body

Run your hands over your Lab's entire body to check for lumps or bumps, sores, or painful areas. Some dogs are stoic, so a barely distinguishable flinch may be the only response you get if you touch a sore spot. Lift up the paws to check for stickers between the toes or in the pads of the foot. In winter, clean your Lab's feet after he's been outside to remove de-icing chemicals, salt, snow, and ice. Make sure toenails are at a comfortable length. A healthy coat is shiny with no patchy areas or hot spots.

What's Normal?

Heart rate, respiratory rate, temperature, and urination and defecation are all physiologic signs that you can check to make sure your Lab is in peak health. Like people, dogs have ranges for normal temperature, heart and respiratory rates, and elimination, but the following values can help you assess your Lab's condition.

Taking Your Lab's Temperature

The normal temperature range for a dog is 100° to 102.5°F. The average temperature of a dog is 101.3°F. A fever can indicate such conditions as pneumonia, infection, or heatstroke. If your Lab's temperature goes above 103°F, take him to the veterinarian.

To take a dog's temperature, use a rectal thermometer. Bulb and digital thermometers work equally well, but a digital thermometer provides a faster result. Whichever you choose, lubricate the thermometer with petroleum or KY Jelly, and have someone else hold the dog still. Lift his tail and gently insert the thermometer 1 to 3 inches into the anal canal, using a twisting motion. Leave the thermometer in for the amount of time recommended by the manufacturer.

Don't let the dog sit down while you're taking his temperature, or the thermometer may break. If this happens, take the dog to the veterinarian for removal.

Checking the Heart Rate

The normal heart rate for adult dogs at rest ranges from 60 to 160 beats per minute. Heart rate varies depending on such factors as a dog's size and activity level. For instance, toy breeds tend to have higher heart rates than large breeds, and puppy's heart rate is as high as 220 beats per minute. The heart beats faster with exertion, fright, and high temperatures.

You can feel the heartbeat by pressing against the rib cage over the heart (remember, it's on the left side), along the inside of the thigh where the leg joins the body, or just below the left elbow joint. To take a dog's pulse, count the beats per minute. An easy way to do this is to count the beats for fifteen seconds and then multiply that number by four.

The Respiratory Rate

The average respiratory rate—the number of breaths per minute—for a dog at rest is twenty-four breaths per minute. A normal range is ten to thirty breaths per minute. Rapid breathing—as distinguished from panting—or labored breathing can signal serious problems, including fever, pain, anxiety, heatstroke, and heart or lung disease. To estimate respiratory rate, watch your dog's chest rise and fall. Count the breaths for fifteen seconds and multiply by four to get the breaths per minute.

How to Give Your Lab Medication

Even with the best of care, most dogs experience illness at some point in their lives. When that happens, they'll more than likely have to take pills or liquid medications, or be treated with drops or ointments for their eyes or ears. As smart as Labs are, you can't train them to take their medications as needed, so the task of administering them falls on you. Knowing the best way to give a pill, get liquids down the throat, or apply topical medications will help ensure that your Lab gets better faster.

Pills and Liquids

The easiest way to give a pill is to hide it inside something yummy. Cream cheese, peanut butter, canned dog food, soft cheese, and liverwurst are all good candidates for this method.

Most Labs swallow the doctored food so fast that they don't even notice the pill going down. Before you try this method, check with the veterinarian to make sure it's okay to give the pill with food. Some medications work best on an empty stomach.

The most important thing to know about giving medication is that your Lab needs all of it, even if he seems to be better before the medication is used up. To ensure a complete recovery, give all of the medication prescribed instead of saving it "for the next time."

If your Lab refuses the pill or must take his medicine without food, you'll need to make a bit more of an effort. Holding the pill in your dominant hand, gently pry the mouth open by using one thumb to press upward on the roof of the mouth and the other to press down on the lower jaw. Slip the pill in and place it on the back of the tongue. Close the mouth and rub the throat to encourage swallowing. After giving your Lab a pill, see if he licks his nose. If he does, that means he's swallowed the pill.

When your Lab needs liquid medications, a plastic syringe (the kind without a needle) or eyedropper is your best friend. Draw the required amount of medicine into the syringe and place the delivery end into the pouch formed by the cheeks. Hold the lips closed with your fingers and slowly press the plunger to dispense the liquid.

If you aren't able to get the medicine into your Lab this way, ask the veterinarian if you can mix the medicine with the dog's food. This method has drawbacks, however. Many dogs are suspicious of any food that tastes or smells unusual. It's also a less accurate way of giving medication, because you can't be sure the dog has ingested all of it. Using a syringe to give medicine to a squirming dog can be difficult, but a little practice will turn you into a master.

Eye/Ear Drops and Ointments

Eye drops are usually dispensed straight from the bottle. Hold the bottle in one hand, and tilt the dog's muzzle skyward with the other. Squeeze the required number of drops into the eye. Try not to touch the applicator tip to the dog's eye.

To apply ointment to the eyes, hold the head still with one hand, using your thumb to pull the lower eyelid down. With the ointment applicator in your dominant hand, slowly squeeze out a line of ointment. Release the eyelid and close the eye, gently rubbing the surface to distribute the ointment. If possible, ask someone to help you hold the dog still, so you run less risk of poking him in the eye with the applicator.

Ear medications often come in plastic bottles with long applicators to help ensure that the treatment gets deep into the ear. To avoid spreading infection, use separate applicators if you're treating more than one dog. It may cost a little more up front, but you'll save time and money by not having to treat repeated infections.

Pull the ear up over the dog's head with your left hand and hold the head still. (Reverse this if you're left-handed.) Insert the nozzle or medicine dropper into the ear and dispense the appropriate amount. Your Lab will try to shake his head, but don't let him. Massage the cartilage at the base of the ear to make sure the medication is well distributed. Then your dog can shake.

Basic Grooming

BESIDES KEEPING YOUR LAB LOOKING GOOD, grooming serves a number of functions. It's a great way to build a trusting relationship with your dog and to keep tabs on what's going on with his body. Routine grooming allows you to catch problems, such as ear infections, skin disease, parasite infestations, and tumors, before they become serious. Labs that are groomed regularly are more amenable to being handled by veterinarians, groomers, trainers, and dog-show judges. Good grooming serves a psychological function as well. Just as with people, a Lab that's well kept not only looks good but also feels good.

Grooming Supplies

Labs are the original low-maintenance breed. Their short coat is easy to care for—although it sheds heavily. Beyond regular brushing to keep the coat healthy and shiny, all a Lab needs to stay looking handsome is eye and ear cleaning, nail trimming, dental hygiene, and the occasional bath when he's splashed through a swamp or had a run-in with a skunk. A rubber curry brush, a shedding blade, a wire slicker brush, nail trimmers, and a doggie toothpaste and toothbrush are the tools you'll rely on to keep your Lab looking and feeling his best. Other grooming supplies you might want to keep on hand are a shampoo formulated for dogs, a coat-conditioning spray, a flea comb, and a nondrying ear cleanser.

Brushes

Rubber curry brushes are oval-shaped to fit comfortably in the hand. Some come with a strap that fits over the hand. The short, nubby bristles on curry brushes loosen coat hair and dirt, and give the coat a polished look. The massaging action the brush provides just feels good. Variations on the rubber curry include a knobbly glove that fits over the hand (sometimes referred to as a hound mitt) and rectangular brushes with rubber teeth or knobs (such as the Zoom Groom).

Labs have what is known as a double coat: a short hard outer layer offers protection from ground cover and brush, while a soft undercoat provides warmth and helps keep the dog dry.

Hair Removal Tools

The metal shedding blade removes clouds of Lab hair. Use it once or twice a week after first brushing with the curry. Stroke it over the body as if you were peeling a potato. A shedding blade has sharp edges, so don't bear down too hard, and avoid using it on the dog's legs. With the help of the shedding blade, your Lab will leave a lot less hair lying around the house.

A wire slicker brush is rectangular in shape with thin, curved wire bristles on the pad and a handle to make it easy to hold. The slicker brush is useful for removing clumps of dead hair that may build up if a Lab hasn't been brushed for a while. It also stimulates the skin, promoting blood circulation and new hair growth. Use it before a bath if your Lab has clumps of dead hair that need to be removed. You're most likely to find these clumps on the hindquarters, the backs of the thighs, and the chest.

Nail Trimmers

Most Labs' nails wear down quickly, but every once in a while they may need trimming. A dog's thick, tough toenails require a specific type of nail trimmer. Look for pliers-style nail trimmers at the pet supply store. Nail clippers can have two cutting edges or a single blade that works like a guillotine to slice off the nail tip. Most groomers and dog experts like the clippers with the orange handles, which are easy to grasp and have a sharp blade to slice off nail tips.

Toothbrushes and Toothpaste

Toothbrushes and toothpaste made specifically for dogs are available at the pet supply store or your veterinarian's office. For young puppies, use a gentle finger brush (one that fits over your index finger). Once their permanent teeth come in, you can purchase a soft dog toothbrush–it has a large head at one end, and a small head at the other to make it easy to get to all areas of the mouth. Toothpaste for dogs is often chicken or beef flavored to make it more palatable. Avoid using toothpaste made for people, as it can upset a dog's stomach.

When dogs eat, food particles and saliva accumulate on their teeth, forming a soft plaque that hardens into tartar. The bacteria trapped in the plaque contribute to bad breath and gum inflammation (gingivitis). Dogs with gum disease have a brownish buildup on teeth, swollen or bleeding gums, bad breath, or loose or broken teeth.

Shampoo and Conditioner

A dog's skin has a different pH level than that of a human. Shampoos for dogs are formulated not to strip away the beneficial oils that keep the skin and coat healthy. Choose a gentle deodorizing or conditioning shampoo that won't dry out your Lab's coat. Unless your Lab has parasites or other skin problems, he doesn't need a shampoo that contains flea- or tick-fighting insecticides.

Conditioners leave the coat shiny. You can apply one after the dog is shampooed, which is then rinsed out, or use a spray-on conditioner after the dog is dried. Coat conditioners with mink oil make the coat look extra shiny, especially if your Lab has a black coat.

Ear Care

Because Labs are water dogs and have floppy ears that hold in moisture and warmth, they're prone to fungal infections in the ear. To keep the ear environment healthy, wipe it out weekly with a 2-percent solution of acetic and boric acid. You can find appropriate ear cleansers at the pet supply store or from your veterinarian.

Brushing and Combing

Brushing loosens and removes dirt, dead hair, and old skin cells. It also distributes the skin's natural oils through the coat. It's the very foundation of good grooming. Brush your Lab once or twice a week to keep his coat and skin in good condition. While you're brushing, check for signs of potential problems, such as itchiness, hair loss, redness, tenderness, or lumps.

If your Lab's coat tends to be dry, spray him with an antistatic coat conditioner before brushing to prevent a shock from static electricity.

To brush your Lab, use a rubber curry brush or hound mitt. Starting at the dog's neck, go over the body in the direction the hair grows and work your way to his rear. Then switch sides and repeat. Be sure you brush all the way down to the skin. This helps loosen and remove dandruff flakes.

After this first brushing, go over the coat with the shedding blade. Top it off with a spray of coat conditioner to add shine. When you finish, your Lab's coat will be gleaming.

A high-quality steel comb, often referred to as a Greyhound comb, will last for the lifetime of all the Labs you might ever have. Choose one with fine teeth on one half, and wide-spaced teeth on the other. Use the fine-tooth side to search for fleas and the wide-tooth side to remove loose hairs after a bath.

Yes, Labs Shed

Labs shed in small amounts year round. In the spring and fall, their coats undergo a major shed, a process known as "blowing coat." Labs blow coat in the spring to get rid of their heavy winter coat, as well as in the fall to make way for winter hair growth. Lab hairs are like little needles that insinuate themselves into upholstery, carpet, and other fabrics.

The most important thing you can do to keep the level of hair down is to brush your Lab often. A quick brushing every day or a thorough brushing once a week will remove loose hair, placing it onto the brush instead of into your surroundings. To keep hair from flying all over your house, brush outside, in the garage, or over a sheet or towel that you can shake out and throw in the washing machine after the grooming session.

Is the amount your Lab sheds normal?
As long as he doesn't have any bald patches, it probably is. Bald patches may be caused by hypothyroidism or other hormonal diseases. Hair loss caused by stress or illness usually occurs in specific areas, such as the rear or flanks, where hair grows fastest.

Cleaning Ears and Eyes

Clean the ears only when you see an accumulation of wax, dirt, or debris. Cleaning ears too frequently is just as bad as cleaning them too little or not at all. Check them weekly to see if they need cleaning. Don't forget to sniff them to check for a bad odor that might indicate infection.

To clean the ears, moisten a cotton ball, cosmetic pad, or soft cloth with mineral oil or a cleanser recommended by your veterinarian. Gently clean the ears, starting in the deepest part and wiping outward. That way you don't push bacteria and dirt further into the ear canal where they could cause infection or itching. Don't dig any deeper than you can see inside.

Most dogs normally have a small amount of clear discharge in the corners of the eyes. Simply wipe it away with a damp tissue or soft cloth whenever you notice it. Check eyes for redness or other signs of irritation that might call for a veterinary visit. Do this daily.

Dental Hygiene

If you want your Lab to have healthy teeth and fresh breath, you need to brush his teeth frequently. Daily is best, but even two or three times a week is helpful. Periodontal disease caused by tartar buildup is a common problem in dogs, but regular brushing keeps the dentist away.

Get your Lab used to having his teeth brushed while he's still a puppy. Puppy teeth are too sensitive for a toothbrush, but you can gently scrub the teeth with a soft gauze pad that's been moistened with water. When the permanent teeth come in, you can start using a toothbrush and toothpaste made for dogs.

Brush the front teeth first, and then move to the upper and lower teeth in the back. Get down into the crevices where teeth and gums meet, because this is where food is most likely to get stuck, causing bad odor and infection.

If your Lab's teeth develop a heavy buildup of tartar, he may need a veterinary cleaning. He'll be anesthetized with a short-acting anesthetic so the veterinarian can probe the gumline, remove tartar, and polish the teeth.

Hard dog biscuits, dry dog food, and rawhides can help chip off tartar, but brushing is the only way to provide the thorough cleaning your Lab's teeth need.

Bathing

A correct Labrador coat repels dirt, but occasional bathing is still important to keep the dog clean and smelling good. How often you bathe your Lab depends on personal preference and on how dirty he gets. You can bathe him weekly, monthly, two or three times a year, or every time he goes out and rolls in duck poop or other stinky substances.

Since Labs love water, giving them a bath isn't always the same ordeal it is with some other breeds. You can still count on getting pretty wet yourself, though. Gather everything you need beforehand: shampoo, conditioner, towels, and cotton balls to place in the ears to help keep water out. Brush the dog to remove dead hair.

If you're bathing your Lab in a tub or large shower, place a non-skid mat on the floor so he has good footing. Wet him thoroughly with warm water, starting at the head and working your way to the end of the body. Lather with shampoo, then rinse. Be sure you get all the shampoo out of the coat. Shampoo residue can make the dog's coat look dull. A 50/50 mixture of cider vinegar and water is a good final rinse that will help remove shampoo residue.

Towel-dry the dog thoroughly, removing as much water as possible. Your Lab will help you with this process by shaking frequently. Then blow him dry, using the warm setting (not hot). If you brush him while you're drying, you can remove more hair, but you have to dry him completely—not just damp dry—for this to work. If you choose not to blow dry the dog, let him dry naturally inside his crate, which should be in a warm, draft-free place so he doesn't get chilled. Letting him dry in the crate also ensures that he doesn't immediately run outside and roll in the dirt.

If your Lab's fur tends to develop a greasy feel between baths, rub in some dry cornmeal, cornstarch, or oatmeal to absorb the oil. Then brush it out. Double-check with the veterinarian to make sure the greasiness isn't caused by a skin condition.

Dealing with Skunk Odor

Face it—if you live in a rural, or even suburban, area and hunt or hike with your Lab, someday he's going to have a run-in with a skunk—and he's going to come out on the losing side. Before you let him back in the house, you'll want to eradicate that awful, disgusting scent he's sporting. Lots of remedies for removing skunk odor have been suggested, from bathing dogs in tomato juice to dousing them with Massengill douche. The following homemade solution will also work, and you can find the ingredients at most drugstores or grocery stores.

Mix one quart of 3-percent hydrogen peroxide, a quarter-cup of baking soda, and one teaspoon of liquid soap. Wet your Lab down to the skin, then apply the mixture. Work it through his fur and leave it on for several minutes. Rinse thoroughly. Make sure your Lab doesn't drink or lick any of the solution, and throw out any of the mixture you don't use. It's not safe to bottle and store this chemical combination.

Removing Sticky Substances

At some point, your Lab is going to have a sticky encounter with chewing gum, tree sap, tar, or paint. Sometimes the only way to remove these gooey substances is by clipping off the fur where it's stuck, but before you do that, try one of the following techniques.

Rub the area with ice. Chewing gum or sap usually becomes brittle when it gets cold, making it easy to crumble it out of the fur. Work some petroleum jelly, vegetable oil, or oily peanut butter into the sticky substance. They will help soften it so you can work it out of the coat. Wipe with a rag and repeat until all the stickiness is removed.

If these tricks don't work, just clip the offending substance out of the coat. You don't want your Lab chewing on tar, tree sap, paint, or old chewing gum. Never try to remove these substances with turpentine, gasoline, paint thinner, or any similar harsh substance. They can be absorbed through the skin and are toxic to your dog.

Any time your Lab smells bad, check for a reason. It might just be that he found a dead bird and rolled all over it, or he may have an ear infection or skin problem. Whenever you can't identify the source of an odor and a bath doesn't solve the problem, take your Lab to the veterinarian.

Trimming Nails

Most Labs are active enough that they wear down their toenails naturally. You'll know the nails need a trim if you hear them clicking on the floor. Nails that are too long can get caught in carpet and break, which is painful. Also, nails that grow too long curve back into the paw pad, impairing the dog's ability to walk. Don't let your Lab's nails get into this condition.

Get your Lab puppy used to having his nails trimmed by taking just a little bit off the ends every week. Praise him and give him a treat if he holds still. When he's older, he'll be used to having you handle his feet and will be less reluctant to have his nails trimmed, something that most dogs abhor.

When trimming a dog's nails, avoid clipping past the curve of the nail. You don't want to hit the quick, the blood vessel inside the nail. If your Lab has light-colored nails, you can see the quick, which looks like a dark line running through the nail. If you can't see the quick because the nails are too dark, a good rule of paw is to trim the nails parallel to the toe pads. When you're through, smooth rough edges with a metal nail file and give your Lab a treat.

If you accidentally hit the quick, stop the bleeding by applying pressure with a cloth or cotton ball or putting styptic powder on the injured nail.

Anal Sacs

Now we're getting to the end of the grooming process. The anal sacs, or glands, are located on each side of the anus (if your Lab's rear were a clock, you would find the anal glands at the 5:00 and 7:00 positions). The anal glands produce a fluid that's excreted when a dog defecates. Sometimes the glands become clogged. If your Lab is scooting his rear on the ground or frequently biting and licking at it, he may have intestinal parasites or impacted anal glands.

Impacted anal glands require veterinary intervention in the form of emptying, or expressing, the glands. The vet can show you how to do this at home should the situation recur. It can be a stinky job, though, so if you're squeamish you may prefer to just take the dog in whenever the glands need to be expressed.

CHAPTER 

Basic Obedience

MANNERS MAKE THE LAB. Teaching your Lab certain basic behaviors will make him a pleasure to live with. You'll be able to take him anywhere, confident that he'll behave in a way that reflects well on you.

Clicker Training

A clicker is a small plastic box with a metal strip that makes a clicking sound when pushed and released. A clicker or other noisemaker (snapping your fingers or jingling a chain) serves as a bridge between the dog's action and a reward. You may also know clicker training by its scientific term of operant conditioning: the tendency to repeat an action that has a positive result.

Clicker training works by indicating to your Lab what behaviors you like and signals that you will "Pay" for those behaviors with something the dog likes—usually a treat, but also petting or praise. For instance, you might click every time you see your Lab chewing a toy. Then give him a treat. After you've done this a few times, you'll have a dog that grabs a chew toy every time he sees you coming. At this point, you can add a word or a phrase that identifies the action you want, such as "good chew" or "good toy."

Essential

The clicker (a conditioned reinforcer in scientific parlance) is paired with a reward, such as a treat (a primary reinforcer). By clicking when your Lab does something right—not before, not after, but during the action—and following the click with a treat or other reward, you teach him not only what behavior you want, but also that a reward will follow.

In training, timing is everything. The benefit of a clicker is that it gives instant reinforcement of a behavior. Giving a click is much faster than saying "Good dog!" A clicker also allows you to shape precise behaviors that might otherwise be difficult to teach—tilting the head, lifting a paw, or wagging the tail on command, for instance. You won't need those behaviors in obedience trials or other dog sports, but they're great for trick training or getting your Lab to pose pretty for a photo.

▲ **Three female yellow Labs posing for a photo.**

Basic Commands

Here are the five magic words your Lab should know: sit, down, come, stay, and heel. You don't have to wait until puppy kindergarten to start teaching them, either. Your eight-week-old Lab pup is ready, willing, and able to learn—so start practicing these commands at home as soon as you get your puppy, and he'll be the star of the Pre-K class.

Before you get started, make note of a few simple rules:

- Train when you're in a good mood.
- Give commands in a firm tone of voice; praise in a happy tone of voice.
- Stop training if you get frustrated.
- Train in a quiet place with no distractions.
- Train before meals so your Lab will be interested in the treats you're offering.
- Always end training sessions with something your Lab has done successfully.

Be sure everyone practices giving the commands to the dog so that he responds to all family members. This is also a good way to make sure he really understands a command.

"Sit"

"Sit" is a great command. Use it to stop your dog from jumping up on people, to wait politely while you finish a conversation with someone, or to prevent your Lab from mauling you before you set down his dinner dish. "Sit" is also the easiest command to teach, so it's a good one to start with. When you have success with it, you'll be confident enough to move on to other commands.

How to Start

To begin teaching the "Sit" command, stash some training treats (remember, tiny and smelly) in your pockets or nearby where you have easy access to them. Take one treat in your hand and hold it just in front of your Lab's nose. Slowly move your hand upward. As your Lab's nose follows the trajectory of the treat, his rear should start to go down. As soon as he's in a sitting position, give him the treat and say "Good sit!" Always use an enthusiastic tone of voice when you praise your Lab.

Repeat the above scenario three to five times. Any more than that and your Lab may get bored. Wait an hour or so, and have another short training session. You can have lots of five-minute training sessions every day.

Ignoring your dog when he doesn't respond to a command is one way of giving a correction. Another way is to teach your dog a word or sound that means "Wrong, try again." Whatever word you choose, say it in a neutral tone of voice. Avoid using the word "No," which has a negative tone and can discourage your Lab from trying again.

As your Lab begins to get the idea, start giving the verbal command without the hand signal. Give the command only once. If your Lab doesn't respond, walk away. Don't scold him, just leave. Wait a few minutes, and repeat the command. Every time he responds on the first command, give the treat and lots of excited praise.

Teaching "Sit" with a Clicker

Can you teach the "Sit" command using a clicker? Absolutely! Any time you see your Lab sitting, click and treat. Wait to add a verbal command or hand signal (a raised hand) until your dog is sitting every time he realizes you have a treat in your hand. Just before he sits, give the command: "Sit!"

Once your dog understands that the word "Sit" and the action of sitting are linked, begin rewarding only the sits that you ask for.

Again, if he doesn't perform on the first try, don't repeat the command. Walk away.

Practicing the "Sit" Command

When your Lab starts getting good at the "Sit" command, raise the stakes. Reward only the fastest or the straightest sits. Step away from him and expect him to remain in place. Gradually increase the distance you move from him until he remains sitting even if you leave the room.

◀ A 5½-year-old female black Lab awaits the next command.

Practice sits in different parts of the house. You don't want your Lab to associate the command with only one place. It's especially important to teach him to sit at the front door, in the kitchen before giving a meal, and out in public (the checkout line at the pet supply store, for instance). To increase the length of a sit, start to wait a beat before clicking. Gradually increase the amount of time between the sit and the click.

Question?

When should you not teach the "Sit" command?
If you plan to show your Lab in conformation, some people recommend against teaching the "Sit" command. Dogs aren't supposed to sit in the show ring, and some dogs make that very mistake because they're used to sitting when their people are otherwise occupied.

"Down"

This command is a little more difficult to teach than sit. It puts the dog in a submissive position, which many dogs prefer to avoid. Nonetheless, down has the same benefits as sit, and it's a must if you plan to compete in obedience.

Ways to Teach "Down"

The classic way to teach the "Down" command is by placing a treat in front of the dog's nose and then moving it down between the legs and forward. (It can help to sit on the floor when you do this.) The theory is that the dog will automatically go into the down position in an attempt to follow the treat. If he does, say "Good down!" and give the treat. Follow with the same techniques you used to teach the "Sit" command.

If this approach doesn't work, move on to the clicker method, which usually works very quickly. Click and treat every time you see your Lab in a down position. Follow with the same techniques you used to teach the "Sit" command. Add a downward sweep of the hand at the same time you say "Down!" Soon you'll be able to give the command using only the hand signal.

Perfecting the "Down" Command

Once your Lab knows the command, gradually increase the length of the down, just as you did for the sit. Any time he breaks

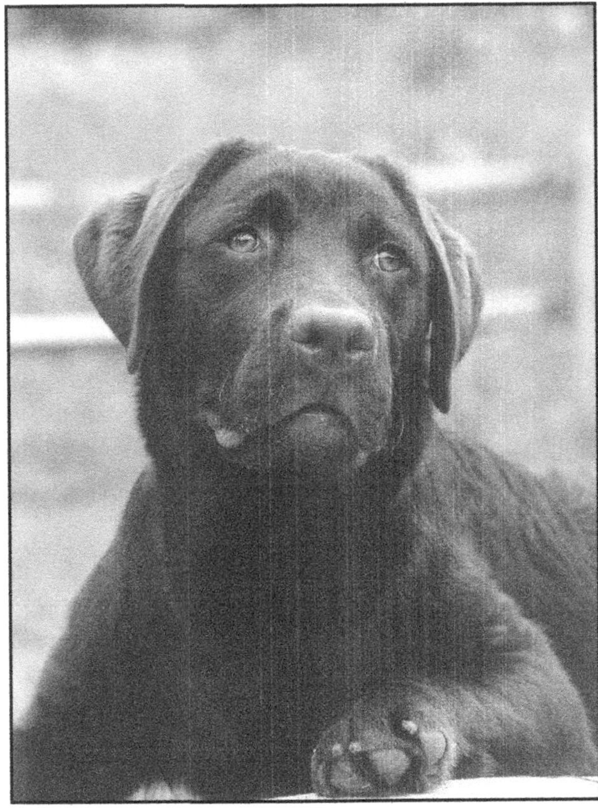

◀ A five-month old chocolate female Lab in the "down" position.

the down and comes toward you, put him back in the same place and start over. Practice doing the down in different areas of the house, in public, and on different surfaces: the floor, grass, asphalt. Use it when you're on the phone, working at the computer, or having dinner with the family.

"Stay"

When your puppy has mastered the "Sit" and "Down" commands, you can start working on the "Stay" command. Put your Lab in a sit or down position. Standing next to or in front of him, place your hand in front of his face, palm up. Say "Stay" (in a firm, less high-pitched tone of voice than the one you use for other commands) and back up just a few inches. Wait a couple of seconds and say "Good stay!" and give him a treat. Then give a release word, such as "Okay," meaning that it's all right for him to move. If he moves before you release him, simply put him back in place and start over.

Practice Daily

Schedule a training session for the "Stay" command a few times each day. It's a good idea to practice this command when your puppy is already tired or calm. Try it after a meal, walk, or playtime.

Gradually increase the length of time you ask your dog to stay by just a few seconds–work up to ten seconds, fifteen seconds, thirty seconds, and so on. Start increasing the distance you move away from him as well. Remember, if he breaks the stay, put him back where he was and start over. It's not necessary to scold him.

Ignoring a dog's incorrect response is a form of negative reinforcement. Dogs like attention, so taking it away is a pain-free method of correction. It's much more effective than repeating a command five or six times in an increasingly louder tone of voice.

Add Distractions

When your Lab has established a good understanding of stay, start adding some distractions to test his mastery of the command. Drop your keys, clap your hands, ask someone else to walk by him. Praise him ("Good stay!") and give a treat whenever he ignores the distractions and stays in position. If he breaks the stay, put him back in place and start over.

Gradually increase the level of distractions by dropping a treat or tennis ball near him, having someone ring the doorbell, or having someone walk another dog beside him. Practice indoors and outdoors so he'll encounter different types of distractions that aren't set up by you (cars driving by, kids playing next door).

Eventually your dog should remain in position until you release him—whether that's ten minutes or an hour later.

He should also stay even if you're not in the room. When you're sure that his knowledge of the "Stay" command is solid, start leaving the room after giving the command. It's best if you have someone else in the room who can put the dog back in place if he breaks his stay to follow you. Wait thirty seconds, and then go back and praise him for staying. Gradually increase the length of time you're out of the room before returning, then have your assistant introduce distractions while you're out of the room.

Whatever command you're working on, pay attention to how your dog is progressing. If he doesn't respond or frequently breaks the command, don't hesitate to go back a few steps in training to a point where he was being successful. Work from there to improve his mastery of the command.

"Come"

Besides being generally useful, the "Come" command is one that can save your Lab's life if he's ever in danger. Use it to call him for dinner, to get him ready to go somewhere, or to get him out of the path of a speeding car. The "Come" command is easy to teach; the trick is making sure your Lab responds to it instantly, every time. This takes time, consistency, and plenty of praise and other rewards.

A Fun Command to Teach

Start teaching the "Come" command as soon as you bring your puppy or dog home. Puppies, especially, will follow you instinctively. Use this behavior to your advantage by saying "Come!" every time your pup is headed toward you anyway. Use your most excited tone of voice, and reinforce the verbal command with body language by squatting down and holding your arms open. When the pup reaches you, give him lots of praise and petting. This is one command your dog just can't get wrong.

Gradually start calling your dog from a greater distance. Vary the rewards he gets for coming so that he'll always want to see what's going to happen when he reaches you. In addition to praise and hugs, good rewards might be an extra-special treat or a game of fetch with a tennis ball. Practice this command several times a day, every day.

Labs need only light correction when they make a mistake. If your Lab ignores a command, a sharp word or the withholding of praise and reward is punishment enough.

Testing the "Come" Command

When you are sure your Lab understands the "Come" command, start testing him in controlled situations. Practice in a confined area or make sure he's wearing a long line (such as fifteen- to thirty-foot clothesline) so you can enforce the command if he doesn't respond. Let him wander off. When he's no longer paying attention to you, give the "Come" command, using your happy voice. He should respond right away. If you call him and he doesn't come, wiggle the line to encourage him to come toward you (don't drag or jerk him) and give lots of praise when he comes.

If he's not wearing a leash, go get him and walk him to the place where you gave the command, saying "Come" as you go. When you reach the spot, say "Good come!" Practice until he comes reliably no matter how far away he is from you or how interesting his other activity is. As his recalls improve, add on a request that he sit in front of you or at your side when he reaches you. When he's mastered that, reward him only for straight sits or only for very fast responses to the "Come" command.

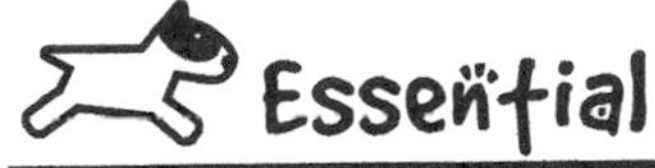

Never call your dog to you and then scold him because he was doing something wrong (like chewing on your shoes). Praise your dog every time he comes at your call. And avoid calling him for something he dislikes, such as taking medication or getting his nails trimmed.

To teach the "Come" command using a clicker, click every time your dog walks toward you, saying "Come!" as he heads in your direction. Click the instant your dog moves toward you and reward him when he gets to you. Start with very short distances of 2 or 3 feet, and gradually increase the distance from which you call him.

"Walk Nicely on a Leash"

Dogs love to explore on walks. Their noses are always alerting them to interesting things to smell. And, of course, there are other dogs to meet and ducks to chase. All of that can make for a difficult walk if your Lab is constantly pulling on his leash in search of the next best thing.

You can, however, teach your Lab to walk nicely without pulling. He doesn't have to walk sedately at your side in a formal heel position, but not pulling is a must. There should always be some slack in the leash.

"Let's Go for a Walk"

To begin, attach the leash to your Lab's collar. Hold it in your left hand with your Lab standing by your left side. Encourage him to walk forward by saying, "Let's go!" (or whatever phrase you choose). Praise him or click and treat (or praise, then click and treat) when he starts to walk with you. He'll probably stop to eat the treat. When he's finished, begin again, this time clicking for more steps forward. Click only when the dog is moving.

Alert!

Don't reward your dog for pulling. This can be done inadvertently when he pulls you toward another person and is then allowed to greet them or pulls you to the park and is then let off leash to play. Require him to walk nicely before he's allowed to do any of those things.

As you walk, reward (praise or click and treat) your Lab any time he is paying attention to you and not pulling. Gradually increase the length of time he walks before you give a reward. Vary the rate at which you give rewards so that your Lab is motivated to walk nicely all the time.

One way to keep your dog's attention on you is to hold a lure, such as a favorite (small) stuffed animal or toy. Some dogs are crazy about feathers and will focus on those. Your Lab will learn quickly that watching you is a good thing.

Any time your Lab starts pulling, stop walking. When he looks at you and there's slack in the leash, you can start up again, reminding your dog to focus on you ("Watch me!") and rewarding him periodically as long as he's walking nicely without pulling. Stop and start again as necessary. If your Lab is very strong and these techniques aren't working, you may want to try using a head halter. (See the section on head halters in Chapter 16.)

Mastering the Walk

Practice walking nicely inside your home, in the yard, and around your neighborhood. Introduce distractions so your Lab learns to stay focused on you. Distractions could be the approach of a child or another dog or walking by a pond or lake where birds gather. Schedule walks after a play session so that your Lab has already worked off some of his energy. Here's one trainer's test for mastery of the art of walking nicely: when you can walk your dog while holding an open cup of liquid without spilling it.

CHAPTER 12

Teaching Manners

IN ADDITION TO KNOWING BASIC COMMANDS, your Lab needs to have boundaries that he can recognize. By establishing yourself as his leader, you can teach him the household rules he needs to know, such as staying off the furniture, dropping items when told, and refraining from chewing on forbidden objects.

Setting Rules

Wild and domestic dogs are guided by a leader and live by the rules the leader sets. Because your Lab is living in a human household, you need to be his leader and lay down the rules for him to live by. Dogs like knowing who's in charge and what the rules are, so don't let your Lab down. Unless you set boundaries for him, he can't help but get in trouble.

Displaying Leadership

You set rules by showing your Lab what he can and can't do. You express your leadership by expecting your Lab to behave toward you in certain ways. Leaders don't get jumped on or knocked out of the way, and their commands are obeyed as soon as they're given. Leaders are in charge of food, playtime, and everything else in the dog's life. Here are some kind, but effective ways you can show your Lab that you are top dog.

Working for a Living

Children learn to say the magic words "Please" and "Thank you" when they ask for and receive something. Your Lab can learn to do the same thing by performing a command first. When he wants to play fetch or tug, ask him to sit first. Then release him ("Okay!") for the game. When you feed him a meal, require him to sit or down before you give him the food. Again, he's not allowed to eat until you give the okay. Interactions like these are a daily reminder that you're in charge.

Showing Respect for You

Other ways your Lab can show you respect are by moving out of your way or waiting for you to go first out the door. If he's standing where you want to walk, ask him to move. If he doesn't obey, put a leash on him and move him where you want him to be. Then require him to sit or down until you release him.

Fact

"Down" is an especially good command to work on. It's a naturally submissive position that can help your Lab learn to accept your leadership and respond better to all your commands. Use this command as often as possible throughout the day.

Teach your Lab to wait before you go out the door, until you start walking, or until you tell him it's okay to jump in the car. Practice waiting at curbs before you cross the street. "Wait" is a variation on the "Stay" command and is taught in much the same way (see page 160). You're simply using it in specific circumstances and giving it a different name.

Regular training sessions also help your Lab understand his place in the family pack. They don't have to take long. Spending five minutes in the morning and five minutes in the evening working on obedience commands will do wonders for your Lab's attitude. Don't forget to praise him for a good performance. Being a leader means letting your dog know when he's done a good job, as well as when he's made a mistake.

Give your Lab attention on your schedule, not his. If he's constantly demanding attention, petting, or playtime from you by jumping up, nudging you with his nose, or pawing at you, teach him that you are the one who initiates these things. Either ignore his requests or—if you're inclined to grant them—require him to perform a command first. Crate him for an hour or two if you need to get things done around the house. Being in the crate gives him a chance to relax in his own space and keeps him out of trouble.

The "Off" Command

It's cute when a Lab puppy jumps up for attention, but a few months later when he's a much bigger dog, it's not so much fun. Labs are big dogs, and they can easily knock people over with an exuberant leap. If nothing else, their paws can get dirt on a freshly cleaned outfit or snag a pair of stockings. Use the "Off" command when your Lab is jumping up on people or to get him off the furniture.

Don't use the "Off" command interchangeably with the "Down" command. The two words mean different things, and you want to avoid confusing your dog.

Teaching "Off"

To teach the "Off" command to prevent jumping up, you've got to move fast. When you see that your Lab is about to jump on you, say "Off," turn aside, and walk away so he misses his target. Then tell him to sit, and praise or pet him for doing so. Show your Lab that he gets attention when he sits, not when he jumps up.

Another way to respond to jumping up is to ignore the dog (fold your arms, turn your head away from him, and stand like a tree) until he sits back down on his own. The second he does, click and treat the desired behavior, saying "Good off!" This method is best used with a puppy rather than a full-grown Lab. Whichever method you use, your Lab needs to learn that "Off" means four feet on the floor.

Counter Jumping Up

Lots of dogs like to jump on guests as they come through the front door. To put a stop to this behavior, practice sits and downs with your Lab at the door. Then ask family members or neighbors to get in on the act. Have them come to the door and knock or ring the doorbell. Put the dog in a sit/stay or down/stay and open the door. Praise or click and treat if your Lab remains in place. If he jumps up, use your "try again" word and start over. Don't let visitors pet or talk to him until he performs correctly.

Be sure that everyone in the family knows how to respond to jumping up. Training must be consistent, or your Lab won't understand what you're trying to teach. Avoid using unnecessary and painful physical corrections, such as kneeing the dog in the chest.

Don't let strangers undermine your training by saying "Oh, it's okay" when your Lab jumps on them. Explain that you're training him not to behave that way, and ask for their cooperation.

Some people enjoy having their dogs jump on them. They just want to be able to control when the dog jumps. When your Lab fully understands the "Off" command, you can teach him to jump up on invitation. Pat your chest and say "Up!" When he responds, say "Good up!" Then give the "Off" command. Practice until your Lab understands that it's okay to jump up only when you invite him.

"Off the Furniture"

Once your Lab understands that "Off" means all feet on the floor, you can also use the command to tell him to get off the furniture. Firmly say "Off" and point to the floor. If he complies, praise him ("Good off!") or click and treat the behavior. Also say "Off" any time you see him getting off anything so that he learns to make the connection between his action and the command.

If he doesn't make the connection, help him off the furniture by luring him with a treat or toy, or gently guiding him with your hands or the leash, saying "Off" as you do so. Then praise him or click and treat once he's on the floor. Use the treat lure only two or three times in the beginning, or your Lab will start to demand a treat in exchange for getting off the sofa or bed. In this case, the treat's only purpose is as a lure to get the training process started.

To practice some more, encourage your dog back on the forbidden furniture by patting it and saying "Up!" This serves two purposes: It allows you to repeat the "Off" command sequence, and it starts the process of teaching your Lab that it's only okay to get on the furniture when you invite him. As he improves, you can pair the verbal command with a hand signal, such as a sweeping motion of your forearm.

You can teach your Lab that he's allowed on the furniture only when you invite him up. And before you invite him up, require him to perform a "Sit" or "Down" on command. Any other time you spot him on the sofa or bed, use the "Off" command. You can also designate certain pieces of furniture as "his."

"Go to Your Bed/Place"

The "Go to your bed/Place" command is easy to teach. It comes in handy when you need to put your Lab in his safe place before you go out somewhere or at bed time. Use this command any time you want your Lab in his crate, on his bed, or in his safe room.

Teaching "Place"

Every time you put your Lab in his crate, say "Crate" or "Bed" in a happy tone of voice and give him a treat. It doesn't have to be a large biscuit; a training-size treat will do just fine. You can also click and treat, and say "Crate" every time you see him go into his crate on his own. Your Lab will quickly learn that the word "Crate" means good things. If he's very food-oriented, it won't take long before all you have to do is say the magic word to see him go running for the crate.

To transfer this command to a dog bed or safe room, use the same technique. Say "Bed!" or "Place!" every time you see him there, and praise him ("Good bed!") or click and treat him for being there. Then practice giving the command, rewarding him when he responds correctly, taking him to the designated area, and repeating the command if he doesn't.

Using "Place" in a Boat

"Place" is also a useful command if you and your Lab enjoy boating. Teach him that a particular area of the boat is his "place," using the techniques described above. This is especially important in small boats, where you risk the boat overturning if your Lab doesn't stay in place. If you and your Lab will be in a small boat, such as a rowboat or canoe, start training with the boat on land.

Encourage him to get into the boat, and show him where his place is. Say "Place," followed by "Stay." If your Lab is accustomed to his "place" being a crate or folded blanket, you can help transfer the idea by putting the crate bottom or blanket in the boat where you want him to be. This technique works for any size boat. When he understands what "place" means in the boat, you can remove the cue object and start practicing near the water's edge or in shallow water near the bank.

On land or in shallow water, practice having your Lab jump into the boat, go to his place, and then come out of the boat on command. When he gets good at this, you can add retrieving from the boat and returning to his place. Soon the two of you will be able to go out on the water with confidence. Working from a boat is your Lab's heritage, after all.

Use your dog's name as part of the command any time you want him to move; for instance, with "Come" or "Let's go." Any time he needs to stay in place ("Sit," "Down," or "Stay"), use only the command word, without his name.

"Leave It/Drop It"

Dogs, especially retrievers such as Labs, are highly oral, meaning they like to pick things up in their mouths. While this can be a good thing when you're teaching your Lab to retrieve, it's not so good when he starts to pick up things that could be harmful or that you simply don't want in his mouth—decaying animal carcasses, for instance, old bones that he's found on the ground, or your favorite pair of shoes. To ensure that your Lab doesn't eat or chew on anything he shouldn't, teach the "Leave it" and "Drop it" commands.

Practicing "Leave It"

Practice the "Leave it" command on walks. Any time your Lab shows interest in something you don't want him to have, say "Leave it" in a happy tone of voice. If he turns to look at you, click and treat him for paying attention to you and walk away from the object. If necessary, you can mine the sidewalk with items you want your Lab to ignore, such as food, socks, or shoes.

Another way to teach "Leave it" is to have some extra-special treats on hand as you walk. When your Lab stops to investigate something, show him the treat and then move it in the direction you want to go. When he follows the treat, say "Leave it" as you walk away. Give the treat when you're several feet away from the item he was interested in. Your Lab will learn that "leave it" means to move away from something.

With all commands, teach your dog that he's to remain in the requested position until you give a release command, such as "Okay."

Testing the Command

When your Lab starts making the connection between "Leave it" and moving on, practice the command without the treat. Test your dog's willingness to obey by mining the walkway with enticing items. Give lots of praise every time he responds correctly to the words "Leave it."

If you want to practice "Leave it" another way, hold a good-smelling treat in a closed hand. Hold the hand out so your Lab knows you have a treat. If he starts to sniff, paw at your hand, or nudge you in an attempt to get the treat, say "Leave it." Don't repeat the command, and don't open your hand. As soon as he stops trying to get the treat, say "Good leave it!" and give him the treat. Practice until your dog ignores the hand with the treat as soon as you say "Leave it."

Other Ways to Teach "Leave It"

You can also teach "Leave it" using the tree method. Set up distractions with items your Lab will want to get, such as treats, bones, an empty food carton, or fast-food wrapper. Stand just out of range of the object and let your dog make all the attempts he wants to get it. During this time, simply stand silently—like a tree. The second he stops trying to reach the item, and either sits or looks toward you, click and treat, saying "Good leave it" as you do so.

Continue this scenario until your Lab learns that staying with you is rewarded, while going for the gusto isn't. Up the ante by requiring him to walk by the item before you click and treat. Any time he tries to go for the item, ignore him until he returns his attention to you. It can be useful to have a helper who can whisk the item out of the dog's reach (so that you don't have to be the bad guy) and pull the dog away from it.

In advanced "Leave it" training, walk the dog closer to the object, add objects that are even more desirable, or have a helper offer the dog some type of food. This is necessary to ensure that your Lab will leave anything you tell him to. Eventually, you can reward him for paying attention to you in the face of something he really enjoys.

The "Drop It" Command

To teach the "Drop it" command, give your Lab something he likes, such as a favorite toy. Avoid giving him anything he shouldn't be chewing on in the first place. When he has the item in his mouth, take it in your hand and say "Drop it." If he lets go, give him lots of praise, then return the item to him. Let him have it again for a minute, then repeat the command. Practice with different types of items so he learns to drop anything you tell him to.

If he doesn't drop the item, gently remove the item from his mouth, saying "Drop it" as you do so. When it's out of his mouth, say "Good drop it!" Then return it to him and start over again.

The other way to approach a refusal is with an offer of a trade. If your Lab doesn't want to release a treasured item from his mouth, show him a treat or toy that he especially likes. If he drops the item in his mouth to get the new object, say "Drop it" as he does so, then praise him and give him the treat. Then give back the original item. From this exchange, your Lab learns that he gets rewarded for obeying "Drop it," both by a treat and by getting the first item back.

Practice the "Drop it" command frequently until you're sure your Lab associates the action of dropping something with the words "Drop it." Then you can start using it as a command. Gradually reduce the number of times you reward him for responding until finally you're giving only praise.

"Wait"

Start teaching this command at doorways, either in your home or outside at the car. Take your Lab to the door, and tell him to sit. Palm up in front of his face, say "Wait." Then start to open the door. If he moves, close the door and start over. Repeat until he remains in the sit position as you open the door. Click and treat every time he waits without moving. When you're ready, say "Okay" and let him follow you out the door or get into the car. Practice this command every day until your Lab stays steady as a rock, and until you give the okay to move out.

Socialization

THE KIND OF DOG YOUR LAB BECOMES depends in large part on how well you socialize him. Socialization is the act of introducing your Lab to the people, places, and things in the world around him. The experiences a puppy encounters in its new environment are key factors in shaping its personality and temperament as an adult. Dogs are social animals, and Labs are naturally friendly, but they still need to learn about the different types of people, sounds, and activities that they are likely to encounter during life. Ways to socialize your Lab include experiences in the home, daily walks, "field trips" to places such as the veterinary office or a dog-friendly business nearby, training class, and play dates with other dogs. No matter what the situation, you can't overdo socialization.

In the Home

Your Lab begins learning about his environment the minute he walks into your house. Some of the things he will learn about (if he hasn't already encountered them at the breeder's home) are vacuum cleaners, blenders, doorbells, fireworks, and thunderstorms. Be careful how you react the first time your Lab pup encounters these things. He'll take his cue for future behavior from your response.

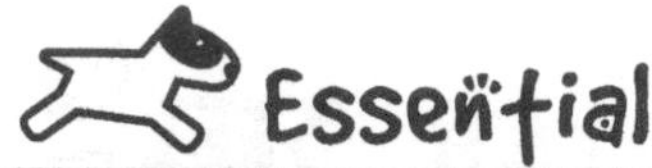

Whether your puppy reacts to different noises with surprise, fear, or curiosity, be matter of fact: "That's just the dishwasher/vacuum cleaner/blender." Don't comfort him if he seems frightened by the noise. Your reassurance will only create a dog that's afraid of loud noises.

Start your Lab's socialization process by providing him with plenty of attention and affection from everyone in the family. Introduce him to the neighbors and to delivery people who regularly visit your home. Invite neighborhood kids to come play with him, and show them how to hold and pet him. Also, let your Lab meet other dogs, as long as you know they are vaccinated.

Out and About

You know that walking your Lab is important for his physical health and provides emotional release, but it's also a great way to introduce him to the things he'll encounter in your neighborhood: other animals, birdlife at a nearby lake or park, children on bicycles or skateboards, and more. A walk is also a good opportunity to practice the many obedience commands you've been teaching your Lab, such as not pulling on the leash, sitting, and waiting at curbs before crossing the street.

Meeting People and Dogs

As you meet people along the way, give your Lab an opportunity to greet them. He needs to learn how to walk up to people appropriately and greet them politely by sitting instead of jumping. If the person you encounter has a dog as well, that's another opportunity for socialization. Keep leashes slack so the two dogs can sniff each other without feeling tension at the end of the lead. You want your Lab to look forward to meeting other people and dogs.

Your Lab should meet people of different ethnicities. Expose him to people doing different activities, such as walking, running, riding a bicycle or skateboard, hopping, crawling, or swimming in a pool. He should see people using walkers, wheelchairs, or crutches, and people carrying packages or pulling suitcases or wagons. Take him to outdoor shopping centers, pet supply stores, parks, and beaches.

As you socialize your Lab, be patient and persistent, and give lots of praise when he greets people happily, shows curiosity at something different, or remains calm in a new or noisy situation. And don't expose him to a bunch of different things all at once. Take things one day at a time.

City Sights and Sounds

Urban Labs will encounter traffic noise and large crowds of people on a daily basis. Accustom them to these sounds early on. A dog that's startled by sudden noises or the approach of a stranger can bolt and be lost or hit by a car. As soon as your veterinarian says it's okay for your pup to go out in public, start taking him on walks that will expose him to the sights and sounds of the city. You can do this as early as eight to ten weeks of age, as long as he doesn't come in contact with other dogs and his paws don't touch the ground—carry him or put him in a crate and pull him in a child's wagon.

Is Your Lab Antisocial?

It's unusual for a Lab not to love people, but it can happen on occasion—especially if a pup isn't well socialized by the breeder. If your Lab is shy around other people or dogs, you can help him develop more confidence and trust. Gradually introduce him to strangers and other dogs in carefully controlled situations.

Working with a Shy Lab

Before you introduce your shy Lab to someone new, lay down some guidelines. Ask the person to remain still and quiet, refraining from petting the dog or making eye contact. Let the pup approach on his own terms, even if it takes a few minutes. Give him plenty of time to sniff and circle the person. When the puppy seems comfortable, the new person can slowly crouch down—so he or she will be at dog level. Let him or her offer the puppy a treat.

If your Lab seems more confident after this introductory period, the new person can slowly reach out to scratch the dog beneath the chin. Don't let him or her try to pat the dog on the head, as many dogs view this as an aggressive move. Have the person continue giving small treats, so your dog learns that meeting people is fun and rewarding. Repeat this pattern every time your Lab meets someone new.

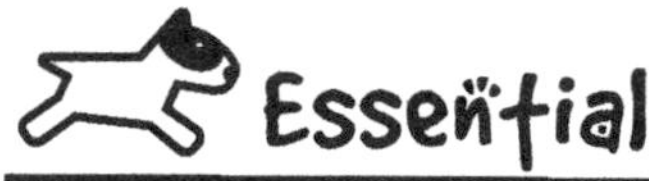

Never force your dog to go up to someone he's afraid of. Fearful dogs that feel trapped may bite. At the very least, your dog will lose trust in you as the person who protects him from frightening things.

Praise Improvements, Ignore Fear

Praise the puppy for any willingness to approach the person, be petted, or take the treat. Ignore any fearful behavior. Whatever you do, resist reassuring the puppy with soothing words when he shows fear. This only encourages him in the belief that there's something to be afraid of.

If your Lab is anxious around other dogs, start by introducing him—one at a time—to dogs that you know are very friendly and easygoing. It's best if the other dog is smaller than your dog, so he'll feel less threatened. As his confidence grows, gradually introduce him to bigger, rowdier dogs, and dogs of different breeds.

Puppy kindergarten and obedience class are great places for your Lab to interact with other dogs, under the supervision of an experienced trainer.

Play Dates

Even if your Lab is well socialized, regular play dates with other dogs are highly beneficial. This is especially true if your Lab is an only dog. Playing with other dogs helps burn off all that Lab energy, and it's a great way for your Lab to learn proper dog etiquette from older, more experienced dogs. A play group is also a good place for you to meet and talk to other dog owners and share information about behavior, health, and nutrition. It's nice to have a support group you can count on when you have questions about or problems with your dog.

▲ **Three black Lab puppies playing keep away.**

Starting a Play Group

To find or set up a Lab play group, talk to people in your neighborhood or training class who might be interested in getting together on a weekly or monthly basis. You can also find like-minded Lab owners in your area by posting a suggestion for a dog play group on a Lab e-mail list, or asking your local Labrador Retriever Club to print your request in its newsletter or on the Web site. Pick a date, time, and place that's convenient for most of the people interested, and send out an e-mail reminder a week beforehand.

Some play groups arrange an occasional speaker, such as a veterinarian, to discuss various dog-related topics. Play groups can also form spontaneously at dog parks or when a couple of Lab lovers decide to get together on the spur of the moment with their dogs.

Dog Park Etiquette

Rules and manners make life better for everyone, dogs and humans. Here are some guidelines to keeping things civil and healthy on play dates or at dog parks:

- Dogs should be friendly and well trained.
- Keep your dog on leash until you're sure of his behavior.
- Pick up your dog's waste and dispose of it appropriately.
- Don't let rough play get out of hand.
- Make your apologies and take your dog home if he behaves aggressively or starts a fight.
- If your female Lab isn't spayed, leave her at home when she's in heat.
- Bring water for your dog.
- Be sure your Lab is fully vaccinated before taking him to a dog park.

Visits to the Veterinarian

A visit to the vet is a great way to socialize your Lab. He'll encounter new people, strange smells, yowling cats, and barking dogs. Strangers will handle him, which can be stressful for some dogs. There are plenty of ways you can help prepare your Lab for this new experience so that it's a happy one for him.

First, stay calm yourself. If your Lab senses that you're nervous about the visit, he'll pick up on your anxiety and reflect it himself. Project a calm, happy demeanor. If you've been examining your Lab at home by looking in his ears, examining his teeth and eyes, playing with his paws, and touching his tail and other parts of his body, he'll be more prepared for a veterinary exam. Have other members of the family examine him too, so that he's used to being touched by different people. Your veterinarian will be grateful that your dog is so easy to handle.

A well-socialized Lab walks into the veterinary office with a smile on his face and a wagging tail. To help ensure that your Lab enjoys visiting the vet, take him there early and often. Schedule a first visit just on a "getting-to-know-you" basis. The vet can examine your dog, but schedule shots for another time, so there's no painful association with that first office visit. Let staff members give your Lab a treat or two to seal the new friendship.

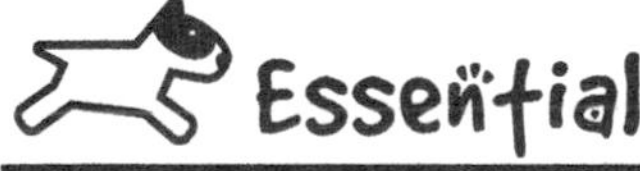

Even if your Lab doesn't need to visit the vet for a health problem, you can drop by occasionally to have him weighed. In most offices, this doesn't cost a thing and takes only a few minutes of your time.

Becoming Accustomed to New Situations

Dogs are pretty adaptable creatures—and they've had to be, to live successfully with us for so many millennia. Nonetheless, it helps for them to have some guidance when they encounter new situations. Welcoming a new baby into the home and moving to a new house are two examples of changing circumstances that call for your guidance in helping your Lab adapt.

A Baby in the House

Dogs in the wild live in packs like families, and every pack member helps to care for pups. Like their wild cousins, Labs love the family "pups," and they can accept babies willingly, if they're prepared for the new arrival. Begin introducing your Lab to the idea of a baby months before your baby arrives.

Learning about Babies

Most dogs are curious about babies, which sound, smell, and look different from older humans. If possible, arrange for your Lab to meet other babies so he can become accustomed to their scent, sound, and appearance. This helps him learn to recognize them as humans, not prey.

With the consent of the parent, let the dog sniff the baby, so he can add "infant smell" to the all the other scents stored in his brain.

Don't hold the baby out to the dog, or he may mistake it for prey or a toy and try to grab at it. Sit, cuddling the baby in your arms, and have the dog sit in front of you as he sniffs. This is best done only with a Lab that is well trained.

Training Is a Must

If you haven't obedience-trained your Lab, do it before the baby arrives. A dog can accidentally injure mother or baby by jumping up on or running into Mom while she's carrying the child. Teach your Lab to respond faithfully to the commands "Sit," "Down," "Off," "Stay," and "Come."

Practice these commands while holding a doll or walking back and forth with it. Wrap the doll in a baby blanket and let the dog sniff it. Praise or reward your Lab with treats for behaving calmly toward the "baby." Record the sounds of a baby crying or making other noises and play them frequently so your Lab learns to recognize and accept them.

Scent of a Baby

When the baby arrives, send a blanket impregnated with the baby's scent home with the new father. Let your Lab sniff it to his heart's content so he'll recognize the baby's scent when it comes home. When mother and baby arrive from the hospital, let your Lab greet Mom first, without the baby. Introduce the baby and dog later, after your Lab has had some time to assimilate the presence of the new family member.

Making Introductions

To make the dog-baby introductions, attach your Lab's leash and tell him to sit or down and stay. Keep the introductions gradual and controlled. If you're concerned that the dog might try to lunge at the baby, put a halter or muzzle on him first. (Practice having him wear it before the baby comes home so he's used to it.)

From a distance of 10 or 15 feet, show your Lab the baby. If he remains calm, the person handling him can gradually walk him closer to the baby to get within sniffing distance. Again, don't hold the baby out to the dog, but cuddle it close.

Keep your Lab on leash for his first few interactions with the baby. Reward him for behaving nicely and calmly around the baby. You want him to associate the baby with good things. Once you're satisfied with his behavior in the baby's presence, you can let him in the room off leash. Put him in a sit/stay or down/stay so he doesn't get underfoot.

Continue giving your dog attention after the baby arrives. Your Lab is used to being an important member of the family, so don't shunt him off to the garage or backyard because you don't have time for him. Involve him in the baby's daily routine by taking the two of them for walks or letting him stay in the room in a down/stay or sit/stay while you perform baby-care chores. With your help, your Lab should adjust well to the baby's presence.

It's unusual for Labs to be aggressive toward people or protective of objects, but if such is the case with your dog, take extra precautions when the baby is around. Never leave a baby unattended with the dog. In fact, never leave any baby (or toddler) unsupervised with any dog, no matter how sweet and loving the dog is.

Moving to a New Home

"Whither thou goest, I go" may well be the canine motto. Dogs are territorial animals, to be sure, but they associate home with their people, not with a specific place. As long as you're there, your Lab will be satisfied with any place you choose to live. Nonetheless, there are steps you can take to help him become comfortable in a new home.

Consult with the Veterinarian

Relocating to a different city or state? Visit the veterinarian to make sure your Lab is up to date on vaccinations and in good physical health. If he's prone to carsickness, stock up on his prescription medication so he'll have a comfortable car ride or flight to the new location. Ask your veterinarian if he or she can refer you to a vet in your new area.

Make Your Lab Feel Comfortable

If the previous homeowners had a dog, your Lab may want to mark his new territory. Before you move in, have the carpets cleaned to eliminate or reduce the scent of the other dog. This can also help get rid of any fleas that might be lurking, just waiting to pounce on your Lab.

If possible, move your furniture in before you bring your Lab to the new house. He'll recognize the smell of your furnishings and feel more comfortable in the new place. When you bring him into the new house, take him first to his food and water dishes, and show him his bed or doghouse. Then let him explore his new yard. Maintain his old routine as much as possible during the move and the subsequent unpacking.

Take your Lab on a walk around the new neighborhood, so that he can investigate the territory to find out where other dogs lift their legs and what paths the local cats take. You might not be able to tell any of these things, but your Lab's nose smells all.

Boundary Training

Many new home developments do not permit fences. If this is the case where you live, you can teach your Lab the boundaries of his territory so he doesn't stray. To be successful, be patient and spend plenty of time training to keep your Lab safely in his yard.

Take your Lab out on leash every time you go into the yard. Walk him around the edges of the yard. If he tries to go outside the yard, say "Aaaght" and bring him back inside the boundary. Do this several times a day for three or four weeks. Avoid letting him roam the yard off leash.

When you think he understands the concept of not leaving the yard, put him to the test. (This is called "proofing" in dog training parlance.) Attach a long line to his collar (a clothesline is a good choice) and toss a tennis ball outside the yard. If the yard faces a street, post another family member outside the yard to make sure no cars are coming and to stop the dog from running into the street.

If your Lab tries to leave the yard to chase the ball, step on or grab the line to keep him from crossing the perimeter, and say "Aaaght." Keep up with your training and try again later. If he doesn't go after the ball, shower him with praise and treats. Practice occasionally so he doesn't forget that he's not to leave the yard. Boundary-training isn't as good as a real fence–a taunting squirrel can test the most well-trained dog–but for the most part it should keep your Lab safe at home.

Travel

LABS MAKE WONDERFUL TRAVEL COMPANIONS. They're agreeable—never arguing about where or when to stop for a break—and so friendly that you're sure to make new acquaintances along the way because people won't be able to resist your Lab's wagging tail. With your Lab along, you'll notice things you might otherwise have missed, such as wildlife or a beautiful park. And having a dog along adds a touch of home to an otherwise sterile hotel room. Whether you're taking your Lab to a new home, a dog show, or a vacation spot, here's what you'll need to know about car, air, and boat travel; finding accommodations; traveling abroad; and—when he can't go along—choosing a boarding kennel or pet sitter.

Car Travel

Going for a ride is a favorite canine activity. But teach your Lab car manners so trips will be fun and safe. Car manners include waiting to get in the car until you give the okay, sitting politely in the seat, restrained by a doggie seatbelt; riding in a crate without complaint; and not hanging his head out the window and barking at other dogs.

A dog seatbelt keeps your Lab from roaming the car, or jumping on you while you're driving. It can also save his life by preventing him from being thrown from the car in the event of an accident. And depending on where you live, state law may require that your dog be secured in the car. Look for a dog seatbelt that has padding to prevent chafing, adjustable straps for a snug fit, and that allows the dog to sit, stand, or lie down. It should attach to your car's seatbelt, which locks into place when you stop suddenly, ensuring that the dog stays on the seat. If possible, the dog should ride in the back seat, so he's not injured by an inflating airbag. Some cars have a switch to turn off the passenger-side airbag, which should be done if your dog is riding in the front seat.

When going on a road trip with your Lab, simply pack his duffle bag, cover your backseat with a blanket or beach towel to catch dog hair, load a crate into the back of your car, and you're good to go. Well, there's a little more to it than that, but not much.

Finding Accommodations

It's unusual these days not to be able to find a hotel or motel that accepts dogs. Some limit the size or number of dogs, but in most cases well-behaved dogs are welcome everywhere—from Motel 6 to the most upscale luxury palaces.

Start your search at Web sites that list pet-friendly hotels (see Appendix A). You can also check a specific hotel's Web site, or look in one of the many books written for people who travel with pets (see Appendix A). Be aware that listings, especially in books, are often out of date. Call to confirm a hotel or motel's pet policy before trying to make a reservation. When you find the right place and make a reservation, request a room on the first floor or a low floor so that potty trips don't involve a long wait for the elevator.

Help your Lab be a good hotel guest. Don't let him on the bed, or cover the bed with a blanket so he doesn't get hair on it. Crate him when you're not there to supervise so he doesn't destroy anything. If he's prone to lifting his leg, put a belly band on him, and if he barks, take him with you so he doesn't disturb other guests.

Belly bands work by wrapping around the midsection of a male dog, across the end of the penis, serving as a gentle reminder not to lift his leg indoors. They're also useful for older male dogs that are incontinent. Some belly bands have an absorbent center to help contain any accidents, or a sanitary napkin can be enclosed to soak up urine.

What to Pack

Choose a duffle or tote bag that will hold grooming tools, plastic bags for poop pickup, food and water dishes, a measuring cup for scooping out kibble, a bag of treats, a couple of toys, and an extra leash. Stash a copy of your Lab's vaccination records in a side pocket in case you need to board him somewhere for the day or are asked to show them at a border crossing. If you're planning to do some day hikes, bring along a daypack that will hold a couple of water bottles and your Lab's folding nylon water dish (a great travel accessory). Don't forget a blanket or fleece mat for lining the crate or laying on a hotel room floor.

You'll also need a supply of dog food. Dry food is the most convenient form for traveling, and if you feed a national brand, you probably won't have any trouble finding supplies of it on the road. If you feed a more obscure brand, go to the company's Web site to see if it lists stores that carry it where you'll be traveling. Get directions to the stores, or map them from your computer before you leave.

On the Road

After checking to make sure you have everything, load your Lab into the car. Depending on the length of the trip, plan rest stops every two or three hours so your Lab can work the kinks out of his legs, go potty, and enjoy a few minutes sniffing around a new area. The break will be good for you, too.

To accustom your Lab to riding in the car, take him on brief errands. Picking up the dry cleaning, going to the drive-through bank teller, or stopping off at Taco Bell are all great practice rides for your dog.

Car Rules

Make it a rule that your dog must always be restrained in some manner. No wandering loose in the car where he can distract you while you're driving or be thrown through the windshield in the event of a sudden stop or accident. You can get him a doggie seatbelt or confine him to his crate.

Teach your dog to wait at the car door until you give him the signal to jump in. This gives you time to get his crate arranged or set up his seatbelt if necessary. Use the "Wait" command that you learned in Chapter 12. Have a leash available when you arrive at your destination. Tell your Lab to wait, and snap on the leash before you let him out of the car.

Dealing with Carsickness

Sometimes dogs get motion sickness, just like people do. Signs of carsickness are yawning, whining, drooling, and vomiting. To help your dog recover from a bout of carsickness, roll the window down to let in some fresh air. It can also help if the dog is able to see out the window. If your Lab gets carsick in the crate, try restraining him with a doggie seatbelt so he can sit up and see the view.

With behavioral modification, you can help your Lab overcome carsickness and learn to love car rides. This can take several weeks and—like all dog training—requires patience and practice. Start by just sitting in the car with your dog. If he doesn't show any signs of carsickness just sitting in the car, praise him and give him a treat. Do this for several days.

After your dog has gone for at least three days without being carsick in a motionless car, get in the car with him and start the engine. Don't go anywhere, just sit in the driveway for a few minutes. Again, praise and treat your dog if he's able to sit in the car without getting sick. Practice this for several days.

If he's doing well with the practice sessions, start the car and back down the driveway. Then drive back in. Continue praising and treating your dog for riding calmly without getting sick. Gradually increase the length of the rides until your Lab no longer gets sick in the car.

If your Lab gets carsick, ask your veterinarian for medication. Whether your veterinarian recommends a natural concoction, such as Rescue Remedy, tabacum (a homeopathic medication), or a pharmaceutical product, test its effectiveness a few days before you leave to make sure that it works. Give the drug an hour to an hour and a half before the trip begins.

Air Travel

Among the reasons your Lab might need to board an airplane are moving to a new home or going to a dog show. Ideally, your Lab would travel in the cabin with you, but most airlines don't permit that unless your Lab is a pup still small enough to ride in a carrier that fits beneath the seat. (Exceptions are made for guide and assistance dogs.)

For travel in the cargo hold, your Lab will need to ride in a molded plastic crate rather than a wire crate. The crate should be large enough for him to comfortably sit, stand, and turn around inside it. Line the crate with a towel or shredded paper in case he potties in it during the flight. Put water in his dish and freeze it before the flight. That way it won't spill as the crate is loaded onto the plane and will thaw during the flight.

The following list, based on suggestions from the American Society for the Prevention of Cruelty to Animals (ASPCA), will help you ensure that air travel is safe, comfortable, and hassle-free for you and your Lab.

- Take your dog in for a veterinary exam ten days before departure to make sure he's healthy and his vaccinations are up to date.
- At that time, obtain a health certificate from the veterinarian, even if the airline, hotel, state, or country you're traveling to doesn't require it.
- If your Lab isn't already microchipped, have it done at this veterinary visit.
- Make sure your Lab's identification tag carries an up-to-date phone number or a cell phone number that will reach you anywhere.
- Book a direct flight whenever possible to decrease the likelihood of your dog being left on the ground during extreme weather conditions or mishandling by baggage personnel.
- If the crate isn't already labeled, write the words "Live Animal" in letters at least 1 inch tall on the top and sides of the crate and use arrows to show the crate's upright position.
- Firmly attach a label to the crate noting the name, address, and telephone number of your Lab's destination, whether you are traveling on the same flight, or the name of the person who will pick up the dog.
- Attach a small pouch of dry food to the top of the crate so airline personnel can feed your Lab in case of delay.
- Latch the crate door, but don't put a lock on it; airline personnel may need to open it in case of emergency.
- Carry a photograph of your dog with you for identification purposes in case he escapes from the crate.

Don't hesitate to let airline personnel, such as desk agents and flight attendants, know you're traveling with your dog. The more people who know, the better, and they'll be more likely to pay close attention to your Lab's welfare if you've alerted them that he's on board. Give his name to the person who takes him at check-in so that he's personalized. Ask if you can watch him being loaded. If that's not possible, ask the gate agent before you board the plane if he or she can track your dog's location so you can make sure he's safely on board. Any time the plane is delayed or you have any concerns about your Lab's welfare, ask airline personnel to check on him. Your active involvement will help make the trip more safe for him.

Should you tranquilize your Lab before the flight?
In most instances, that's not a good idea. Drugs can have different effects at 8,000 feet above sea level, which is the approximate pressurization in the cabin and cargo area during flight. Sedation can also lower blood pressure, which can leave your Lab more prone to hypothermia.

Boat Travel

Labs are the quintessential boat dogs. They love being in and on the water, so there is no one better to have as your first mate, whether you're planning a short jaunt around the harbor or around-the-world cruise on your own vessel. Taking a dog on board with you is rewarding in many ways, but only if you're properly prepared.

Before you set sail for more than a day or two, make sure your Lab is amenable to life in confined quarters and a relative lack of physical activity. Unless you're hugging the shore or making brief hops from island to island, it's not as if you'll be able to pull over to a rest stop and let him run every few hours, or even every day. You can help make things more interesting by teaching your Lab to perform chores on the boat, such as bringing you things.

Take Precautions

Even the most water-loving dogs can fall overboard. They may even jump overboard if fish or dolphins attract their attention. Until your Lab gets his sea legs (and even afterward), protect him with a pet life preserver. Choose a bright yellow or orange vest with a loop or handle. Let your Lab get in the water while wearing the vest so you can see how it works. Practice grabbing the loop or handle with a boat hook, or teach your Lab to swim to a ring thrown in the water so he can be pulled in.

Another safety measure is to have your Lab wear a harness attached to a safety line. Run a jack line along the port and starboard (left and right) sides of your boat, connected by a ring to safety lines attached to your Lab's harness. He can move freely about the boat, dragging the line behind him. For added safety, put up netting between the stanchions all the way around the boat, and make a point of knowing where your Lab is at all times. He doesn't know to bark if he falls off, and you might not hear a splash.

Health Tips

Seasickness, sunburn, and skin problems can all affect the seagoing dog. Fortunately, seasickness seems to be rare, but if your Lab does start looking a little green, a dose of Dramamine will usually take care of it. Ask your veterinarian what the proper dosage should be.

Just like people, dogs can become sunburned, especially if they have light-colored fur. The nose and ears are especially at risk. Monitor your dog's sun exposure, and make sure he has a shady place to retreat to. (This is one of those instances when the "Down" and "Stay" commands come in handy.) Apply sunscreen to the nose and ears for extra protection. Salt water can dry out your dog's fur and cause skin problems, so provide a freshwater rinse after any planned or unplanned dunkings.

Essential

If you're planning to visit any Mexican ports, be sure your dog has a current health certificate from your veterinarian. The incidence of rabies is higher in Mexico than in the United States, so a current vaccination is a must if your dog will be going ashore.

Most of the same injuries that happen to people on boats can happen to dogs, so the supplies in the first-aid kit you carry can be used for your Lab as well. See Chapter 19 for advice on stocking a first-aid kit.

Physical Needs

The two primary physical needs your dog will face on board are eating and elimination. For the first, carry a good supply of your pet's regular food, especially if you're planning to visit foreign ports where it might not be available. If you start running out and won't have access to more for a while, begin mixing the dog's regular food with whatever you plan to feed so the digestive system will have time to adjust. The last thing you want on a boat is a dog with diarrhea.

Stainless steel food and water dishes are the popular choice to use, since they're easy to clean and won't break. Some dishes are weighted at the bottom or angled outward so they won't slide around. If water sloshing out of the dish is a concern, you can buy a specially made bowl with a lid on top and a hole in the middle for the dog to drink out of.

For potty breaks, choose a spot that's easy to hose down, and teach your Lab to go there. To give him the idea, capture some of his urine in a sponge or container and use it to scent a small mat on the boat, so the dog recognizes that it's an acceptable place to eliminate. Commercially available scented pads can also indicate to your dog where to go.

Behavior

Most marinas and yacht clubs welcome pets as long as they are well behaved. No matter where you're docked, the same rules of good pet ownership apply. Keep your Lab leashed so he doesn't chase people or other pets, and pick up waste. Boaters tend to be early to bed, early to rise, so don't permit barking after 9 P.M.

Be sure your Lab always wears a collar and tag with your name, the name of your boat, and your slip number.

It's likely that your Lab will be so fascinated by watching you, the birds, and the fish that he won't have time to get bored or destructive, but take a favorite toy or two along just in case. The occasional trip to shore will allow your dog to stretch his legs and sniff some exciting new scents. When you're in port, take him for long walks every day. Having your Lab on board is a sure way to make friends in any port, and he's one friend that won't contradict you when you're telling that big-fish-that-got-away story.

Boat Life Tips

Let your Lab become accustomed to the boat before you go out on the water. Spend time just hanging out on the boat so your dog can familiarize himself with it. This is a good time to practice getting on and off the boat. Some dogs find it unnerving to walk a gangplank or jump onto a surface that rocks when their paws hit it. Take things slowly, and give lots of praise when your Lab successfully makes it on board.

Keep your first trip short, no more than a couple of hours. This will give your Lab a chance to get his sea legs, and you can find out if he's prone to seasickness. Ladders can be slippery, and dogs aren't really built for climbing them anyway. Make it easier for your Lab to negotiate a ladder by applying nonskid adhesive strips to the steps. If you're taking your Lab on a powerboat, consider getting him a pair of doggie goggles to protect his eyes from dryness and windblown debris.

▲ These two six-year-old female black Field Labs love to swim.

Traveling Abroad

You might not want to take your Lab for a one- or two-week vacation abroad—that's an awfully long time for him to spend in cargo each way—but if you're moving overseas or planning a stay of a month or more, you will surely want to have your best friend along. Dogs are welcome in most European countries, and there are no lengthy quarantines or difficult requirements to meet before your Lab can enter the country.

France, Germany, Switzerland, and the Netherlands are especially dog-friendly. Your well-behaved Lab will be welcome in hotels, many shops, on public transportation, and even in restaurants (especially in France and Germany). Plan for travel to these countries just as you would for any other trip, as far as packing for your Lab and finding accommodations.

The United Kingdom, Sweden, and Russia are another matter, however. Dogs that do not meet strict entry requirements face long quarantines of thirty to sixty days (Russia), four months (Sweden), or six months (United Kingdom). Australia has a four-month quarantine. You'll need to plan well in advance to take your Lab to one of these places.

In the United States, only Hawaii has a quarantine period, which has recently been reduced to five days or fewer, as long as the dog meets the entry requirements of two rabies vaccinations, a microchip, and blood serum test results.

Boarding Kennels

It's not always possible or desirable for your Lab to travel with you. Business trips, cruises, and honeymoons to Hawaii are just a few examples of trips on which your Lab is best left at home. For those times, you'll want to have the phone number of a good boarding kennel in your address book. By finding a boarding kennel in advance and preparing your Lab for being boarded, you can jet off knowing that your pal is in in good hands.

Boarding kennels have several advantages. Your dog will receive daily attention from people who love animals, and he'll be in a secure place—so you don't have to worry that he's destroying or escaping from your home or yard. Finally, many boarding kennels have staff, or even a veterinarian, who are trained to spot health problems.

Finding a Boarding Kennel

Word of mouth is the best way to start your search for a boarding kennel. Ask your veterinarian, trainer, and dog-owning neighbors or coworkers for recommendations. You can also check the Yellow Pages, under "Kennels." Once you have some names, set up interviews so you can make sure the kennel you choose is a place you'd feel comfortable leaving your Lab.

Evaluating the Kennel

Start by taking a tour of the facility. It should look and smell clean. Check to see that kennels have sufficient ventilation and light and are maintained at a comfortable temperature. Most kennels have indoor/outdoor runs for dogs, so they can enjoy pleasant weather and escape from inclement weather. If no outdoor run is available, ask how often the dogs are taken out for exercise. Kennels that house dogs outdoors should offer protection from wind, rain, and snow. Ask whether bedding is provided, what kind it is, or whether you must provide your own bedding.

Mealtime is another issue to consider when placing your Lab in a boarding kennel. Ask how often dogs are fed. If your Lab is on a special diet, find out if you can provide your own food. Some kennels charge extra for feeding a special diet.

Expect the kennel to require a copy of your Lab's vaccination records. Dogs being boarded must be current on their vaccinations, including the bordetella (kennel cough) vaccine, for their protection and the protection of other dogs. If you have your Lab on an alternative vaccination schedule, ask if the kennel will accept a letter from your veterinarian stating that the dog is protected from disease.

Find out if the kennel belongs to the American Boarding Kennels Association (ABKA). The ABKA promotes professional standards of pet care and requires members to follow a code of ethics. ABKA inspects kennels on a voluntary basis–meaning the kennel must request the inspection–and offers accreditation to kennels that meet its standards of professionalism, safety, and quality of care.

Other questions to ask include whether there is a veterinarian on staff or on call; whether other services, such as grooming, training, and day care, are available; and how rates are calculated.

As you conduct your interview and tour the kennel, make note of staff attitudes. Do the staff members seem caring and knowledgeable? Can they meet any special needs your Lab may have, such as giving medication or insulin injections on a regular basis?

Preparing Your Lab for Boarding

Basic socialization is the easiest way to ensure that your Lab will breeze through a stay at a boarding kennel. If he's used to meeting new people and dogs, and going to new places, staying at a kennel will be fun for him, especially if there are daily activities to keep him occupied. Nonetheless, it's a good idea to work him up to a long stay by starting with a short stay of a day or a weekend. This will give you an idea of how he reacts to being boarded. Many dogs enjoy boarding, just as kids enjoy a stay at summer camp.

Before you leave for the kennel, make sure you have everything you need:

- Vaccination records
- Food, if you're providing a special diet
- Medication, if needed
- Favorite toy or bedding
- Itinerary, noting where you can be reached in case of emergency
- Phone numbers for your veterinarian and a local contact in case you're unavailable

Find out if your state requires boarding kennel inspections. If it does, ask to see the license or certificate of the kennel you're considering. Make sure the dates are current. You can also check with your local Better Business Bureau to see if the kennel has any complaints against it.

Take your Lab in, get him checked in with the staff, and say a quick goodbye. Just as you do at home, make your departure unemotional. If you sneak a peek as you go out the door, you'll probably see your dog happily going off to his kennel, without a care in the world. Enjoy your trip, secure in the knowledge that your Lab is well cared for.

Pet Sitters

You may prefer to leave your Lab in the comfort and security of his own home when you travel. This is especially nice for older dogs, who are less amenable to change and more likely to suffer stress when being boarded. Finding a reliable pet sitter who will either visit your dog once or twice a day, or even stay in your home allows you peace of mind when you must travel and leave your Lab at home.

There's more to pet sitting than providing basic care. Besides feeding, walking, and playing with your Lab, a good pet sitter will keep a watchful eye on his health and emotional state. While asking a neighbor to take care of your Lab when you travel is convenient, your neighbor isn't necessarily qualified to give your Lab the supervision he needs (unless she's also a Lab owner or experienced with dogs in general). Hiring a professional pet sitter ensures that an experienced person will show up every day to give your Lab the attention and exercise he needs while you're gone. Most pet sitters also perform such daily tasks as bringing in mail and newspapers, watering plants, and turning lights on and off—giving your home a lived-in look.

To find a pet sitter, start with that favorite method, word of mouth. Ask friends, neighbors, coworkers, your trainer, or your veterinarian for recommendations. Many veterinary technicians do pet sitting on the side. A vet tech is a great choice if your Lab has special health needs, such as requiring regular medication or insulin injections. You can also find pet sitters listed in the Yellow Pages, under "Pet Sitting Services."

Ask how your Lab will be cared for in case something happens to the pet sitter. Ideally, the pet sitter will have a partner or some kind of contingency plan in the event of a personal emergency.

Look for someone who has professional experience, has completed pet-care study courses, is bonded and carries commercial liability insurance, and belongs to a professional organization. A pet sitter should have a brochure or other written material that details prices and services. He or she may ask you to sign a contract that spells out exactly what will be done. This protects both of you from misunderstandings.

Two organizations offer accreditation to pet sitters who meet their standards. For more information, contact the National Association of Professional Pet Sitters or Pet Sitters International (see Appendix A). Both organizations can provide referrals to members in your area.

Behavior Problems

LABS ARE GOOD-NATURED DOGS OVERALL and learn quickly, but even they can develop behavior problems at some point. Usually behavior problems occur during adolescence, at six months to eighteen months of age. Depending on the circumstances, however, problems can develop at any age. Fortunately, knowledge of canine behavior has advanced greatly in just the last ten years, and there are many positive, successful techniques you can use to solve behavior problems.

Potential Behavior Problems

Unwanted behaviors you may encounter in your Lab include excessive barking, begging, chewing, digging, mouthing and nipping, scavenging, and whining. Aggression is rare in Labs, but you should be able to recognize it and know how to handle it if it occurs. Other potential problems include fearful behaviors, such as noise shyness and separation anxiety.

If your Lab develops a behavior problem, the most important thing you can do is to remain patient. Continue to show him what you want, and provide firm, fair discipline when he breaks the rules. Help him with behavior modification if necessary. Below, you'll see ways to manage or retrain your Lab if he develops one of these common behavior problems.

Many of the behavior problems will never develop—or can be easily solved—if your Lab learns early in life that you are his leader and that following you and doing what you ask will always lead to good things.

Aggression

Aggression is defined as a forceful action with the intention of dominating another. In dogs, this would include biting, growling, curling the lip, and other threatening behaviors. Labs in general don't have aggressive tendencies, but any dog can become aggressive given the right circumstances or poor temperament inherited from parents. Aggression is a normal behavior for dogs–one of the many ways they communicate–but that doesn't mean it's okay for your Lab to ever behave aggressively. Because he lives in a human family, he needs to learn to temper his behavior to human standards.

Understanding Aggression

Dogs can show aggression toward their owners, strangers, or other animals. Although it doesn't seem that way to us, most forms of aggression are motivated by fear. Some fears that can cause aggression in dogs include an invasion of territory by a stranger, another dog, or a new baby in the home; the fear of a mother dog that her pups will be harmed by an approaching stranger; or the fear of being hurt physically in some way. What are some of the types of aggression?

- Conflict (dominance) aggression usually occurs when a dog doesn't understand his place in the family pack or fears that his position is threatened. They guard food and toys, refuse to move off the furniture when asked, or display aggressive body language.

- Fear aggression is associated with a frightening experience, which could be anything from a bad visit to the vet to associating the owner with something the dog is afraid of, such as fireworks. These dogs bite when they feel trapped.
- Territorial, protective, and possessive aggression occur in defense of what the dog considers his property: home, yard, owner, toys, or food.
- Maternal aggression occurs when strangers—or even family—approach a mother dog's pups.

Dealing with Aggression

Fear and possessive aggression can often be prevented through plenty of socialization to people, places, movement (a hand throwing a ball or a toddler's awkward petting), and activities in early puppyhood. Practice taking away your Lab's food dish or toys and giving them back. One way you might do this is by adding a treat to your dog's bowl, removing the bowl, adding another treat, and returning the bowl. Smart dogs learn quickly that letting you take the food bowl away is a good thing.

If you're not sure whether your Lab is smiling or snarling, study his body language. A lip curled upward, in combination with a body that's stiff and quivering, is a sign of aggression. Lips pulled to the side and a wagging tail indicate a friendly dog.

Puppy kindergarten, obedience class, and play dates at parks with other dogs and people are good ways to deter territorial aggression. These situations teach your Lab that he must share neutral territory (the park or the class area) with others. Training helps your Lab learn to defer to you as the family leader and protector of territory. Neutering at adolescence can also help reduce the incidence of territorial aggression.

How should you deal with aggression? If your Lab is behaving aggressively for no apparent reason, take him to the veterinarian to rule out a physical problem that could be causing pain. If that's not the issue, seek the help of a qualified behaviorist. Serious forms of fear or conflict aggression often require behavior modification, sometimes in conjunction with drug therapy.

Barking and Whining

Dogs can't talk, but they do verbalize by barking and whining. Each of these vocalizations can have a variety of meanings, depending on the situation. Dogs bark in greeting, to warn intruders off their territory, in excitement, or out of stress or boredom. They may whine for attention or because they're in pain.

It's okay for your Lab to bark or whine, but only in appropriate circumstances, which might include welcoming you home from work, alerting you to the presence of someone approaching the house, or in warning because of a fire or other danger. With training, your Lab can learn when it's okay to bark and when silence is golden.

Teaching Appropriate Barking

Start training the first day he comes home with you. If he barks when someone comes to the door (either before or after they knock or ring the doorbell), praise him for his alertness. If he doesn't bark, help him get into the spirit of things by saying "Who's there? Who is it?" Do the same for any other situations in which you want your Lab to bark.

To help your Lab understand that he must obey the rules of the house, be consistent with corrections. Look him in the eye and say "Aaaght" or "No" to deter an undesirable activity.

When your Lab has learned to alert you to people approaching the house, teach him how to be quiet. Let him bark once or twice, then say, "Enough" or "Quiet." Your voice should distract him enough that he stops barking. If he does, say "Good quiet," and give him a treat. Gradually extend the length of time between his silence and giving him the treat. Use the same technique to stop whining.

How to Correct Barking

If your Lab won't stop barking, should you wrap your hand around his muzzle to stop him? That's a technique recommended by some trainers, but if you're not careful your dog could accidentally bite you. Instead, try calling the dog or giving him a down command. Either action can distract him from barking. When he's quiet, praise him and give a treat.

You may have to employ a more negative correction if your Lab still won't stop barking. Solutions to try include a squirt from a spray bottle or tossing a small throw pillow toward the dog (don't hit him with it). Try to avoid loud verbal corrections for this behavior. Your Lab may decide you are joining in the barking and will bark even more loudly.

What if your Lab barks too much for no reason? The first thing to understand is that there's always a reason. It's your job to discover why he's barking excessively. Is he bored because he's alone all day? Are the squirrels in the yard taunting him? Is he running off all the delivery people that come down the street during the day?

Alert!

Never reward your dog for barking unless it's a situation in which you want him to bark. Don't accidentally reward him for barking by letting him out of his crate, tossing his ball, or giving him his food immediately after he's been barking at you. Wait for him to be quiet for at least thirty seconds before you give him what he wants.

If your Lab is barking because he's bored, punishment is not the way to go. The easiest solution to this type of barking is to bring the dog inside the house. He should certainly be there at night, so he doesn't keep the neighbors awake. If your Lab barks during the day because he's bored while you're gone, rotate his toys so he always has something new. Prepare a goodie bag full of treats that he has to work at to get into. Use a paper bag, fill it with toys and treats, and tape it closed. Give it to your dog before you leave for work. He'll be so busy getting into it that he won't have time to bark.

Dealing with a Whining Lab

Dogs whine when they want something, when they're frustrated or excited, or when they're in pain. Make sure to know the reason for your Lab's whining. If he is whining out of frustration or for attention, don't offer a verbal correction. Instead, ignore the behavior and distract him with some other activity, such as practicing commands. If you know your Lab is in pain, comfort him and give him much affection and attention. Contact a veterinarian if you suspect there's something seriously wrong with him.

As with barking, never reward whining by giving the dog what he wants. If he's whining to get out of his crate or because he wants some of the chicken you're cutting up for dinner, turn your back on him. He doesn't get anything until he's quiet.

Begging and Scavenging

The easiest way to deal with begging is not to let it start in the first place. Never feed your Lab from the table or offer him scraps while you're cooking. It's a sure route to a Lab that will be constantly underfoot, hoping for a tidbit. That's not only annoying, it's dangerous. You could trip over the dog while you're moving around in the kitchen, injuring one or both of you.

Feed your Lab his meal before the family eats. His hunger will be assuaged, and he'll be less likely to bother you at the dinner table. If he's allowed in the room while the family is eating, put him in a down/stay. Do the same thing if he likes to hang out in the kitchen while you're cooking. Choose a corner away from where you're working, and require him to stay there.

Besides begging for food at the dinner table, all dogs love to raid the trash. Often, the best way to deal with your scavenging Lab is deterrence. Place contact paper (sticky side up) over the top of the trash, keep the trash behind closed doors (store it beneath the kitchen sink and put child locks on the cabinet doors) or use a can with a tightly fitting lid that your Lab can't remove. Problem solved.

If you can't resist giving your dog a treat while you're preparing a meal, make him sit or do a down first. Then send him back to his place. Only give him treats when you've called him to come and then required a sit or down.

If that doesn't work for you, make getting into the trash counterproductive. If your Lab enjoys playing with empty paper towel rolls—which can make great dog toys—and pulls one out of the trash, take it away. Later, you can give him a different roll to play with. Eventually he'll learn that paper towel rolls that come from you are fair game; those raided from the trash get taken away.

Catch your Lab with his head in the trash? Lob a shake can at the side of the trash can. The noise will startle your dog into pulling his head out. This works best with metal trash cans; plastic ones won't produce as much noise. Still, the thud should startle your dog. Then you can praise him for not being in the trash—"Good no trash"—and put the can away.

Chewing

Because of their heritage as retrievers, Labs are very oral dogs. This means they like to chew. Young Labs have a physiological need to chew; it's simply part of their development. Older Labs may continue the chewing habit simply because it's enjoyable. Chewing is a way to pass the time when there's nothing else to do. Since you know your Lab is likely to chew no matter what, it's your job to provide him with a variety of acceptable chew toys, as well as to teach him what not to chew.

Make a shake can by putting a few pennies or stones in a clean, empty soda or beer can and taping the top closed. You can use this noisemaker to distract your dog from any forbidden activity. Toss it in the dog's direction, but don't hit him with it. The noise will startle him into stopping whatever he's doing: digging, chewing, barking, and so on.

Teach Appropriate Chewing

To teach good chewing habits, praise your Lab every time you see him gnawing on a toy. Help make toys even more appealing by handling them frequently so they bear your scent. Your Lab wants to be close to you, even when you're not home, so chewing on something that smells like you is the next best thing. That's often why dogs chew up their owners' favorite shoes or other items of clothing. It's not spite; it's admiration.

You can also make some chew toys more attractive by mining them with treats. A Kong toy or hollow rubber bone is great for this purpose. Fill it with peanut butter and stud the peanut butter with small biscuits or baby carrots. Your Lab will spend hours trying to get at all the sticky, crunchy goodness.

Prevent Inappropriate Chewing

The two best ways to prevent inappropriate chewing are to put your things out of reach and to leave your Lab in his crate or safe room when you can't be there to supervise. That way, your possessions don't get destroyed, and your dog doesn't get scolded for misbehaving. It's a win-win situation, but make sure he has something nice to chew on when he's confined.

When you catch your Lab chewing something he shouldn't, give an immediate verbal correction: "Aaaght" or "No!" If he's chewing on something life-threatening, such as an electrical cord, instantly follow the verbal correction with a squirt from a spray bottle or the toss of a throw pillow. Your Lab needs to learn that there are serious consequences to chewing on cords–before he gets electrocuted.

If he's chewing on something not so dangerous–but still forbidden–give the same verbal correction. That should be enough to distract him. When he stops chewing to look at you, give him a toy to chew on instead. Don't forget to praise him every time you see him chewing on something appropriate.

Preventing inappropriate chewing can save your dog's life. Chewing on the wrong things can lead to electrocution (electrical cords) or intestinal blockages (chewing and swallowing socks or dish towels). Protect your furniture and your clothing, as well as your dog's life.

Digging

Digging is a normal behavior for dogs. In the wild, dogs dig to make a bed, find prey, or hide a cache of food. Domesticated dogs dig primarily for entertainment, although an ancestral impulse may be at work as well. The point is that your Lab isn't digging to annoy you; he's just occupying himself while you're gone. Fortunately, there are ways you can redirect or prevent digging.

Digging Deterrents

One way to prevent digging is to provide your Lab with more exercise and playtime. You want to make him too tired to dig.

When that's not possible, make sure he has plenty of interesting toys that are more fun than digging. Look for a Giggle Ball or Buster Cube. Giggle Balls make—naturally—a giggling sound when they're pushed, and Buster Cubes can be filled with treats, which the dog can only access by manipulating the cube. Stuff a large Kong with treats, and leave out a soccer ball or a supply of tennis balls.

Redirecting digging is another option. Give your Lab his own sandbox or dirt pile where he can dig to his heart's content. Define it with a border of railroad ties and stud it with toys or rawhides that he can dig up and enjoy. Whenever you see your Lab digging in a forbidden area, distract him by saying "Aaaght" or "Leave it," and then show him his digging spot. When he digs there, give lots of praise: "Good dig!" Reward him every time you see him digging in the right spot.

Never use cruel and ineffective methods to prevent digging, such as filling a hole with water and forcing the dog's head into it. Instead, try filling holes with rocks, gravel, or pine cones, so that it's no longer comfortable for the dog to dig there.

If your Lab likes to dig in your garden, put a picket fence or chicken wire around it to deny him access. You may also want to consider surrounding the garden (or other favored digging spot) with a new type of electronic fence. The dog must wear a special collar that activates whenever he crosses the boundary, giving off a burst of citronella spray. Dogs don't like the smell of citronella, so this type of fence offers a self-correcting method of preventing digging in specific areas.

Try a Change of Scenery

Is your dog digging to find a cool place to lie when it's hot outside? Consider moving his doghouse to a more shaded area. In warm weather, provide a plastic wading pool for your Lab to splash in. If all else fails and your yard is starting to look like a minefield, keep your Lab indoors when you can't be there to supervise. Another option is to build a dog run in the yard where he can be confined when you're not home. Give the run a concrete base to prevent him from digging beneath the fencing.

Mouthing and Nipping

Dogs use their mouths as surrogate hands. Mouths are great for picking up, carrying, and tasting things. Labs, especially, are famous for their soft mouths—the ability to carry an object without marking it. Dogs also use their mouths to defend themselves or objects they perceive as theirs. While this is all perfectly natural and understandable, your Lab must learn that he can never use his teeth on people. In some places, a single dog bite is enough to require a dog to be euthanized, so teaching your Lab not to mouth or bite people is a must.

A Lab puppy's lessons in how to use his mouth and teeth begin with his littermates and mother. They yelp loudly or cuff him with their paws if he bites too hard. You can continue that lesson by screeching loudly and then walking away any time your pup bites down too hard on your hand. Remember, dogs hate being ignored.

Help your Lab develop a soft mouth by offering tiny treats held in your fingers. Again, if you feel his teeth bite down, yell "Ouch" and walk away with the treat. Try again in a couple of minutes and repeat until he learns how to take food gently. This technique also works during games of fetch or tug.

Noise Shyness

Loud noises are startling to most of us, but we usually jump a little and then go about our business. Some dogs, however, develop a debilitating fear of thunder, fireworks, gunshots, and other loud noises. A noise-shyness in dogs is distressing because it often leads to destructive behavior or a dog that runs away and gets lost or hurt. You can, however, take steps to help your Lab overcome his fear of loud sounds.

Training classes won't magically solve all your Lab's behavior problems, but they can increase the bond between the two of you, as well as increase your dog's confidence, making him more willing to work with you and less likely to behave fearfully.

What to Do

First and most important, don't cuddle or talk soothingly to your Lab while he's displaying fearful behavior. By doing that, you reinforce the idea that there's something to be afraid of. Behave normally and ignore the dog's behavior. On the flip side, don't force your dog to be around the noise or punish him for behaving fearfully; both actions can make the problem worse.

Note whether your dog heads for a perceived safe place whenever loud noises occur. Determine what that place is and make sure he has easy access to it if a storm is brewing or dusk is falling on the Fourth of July. Don't lock him up in the safe place, whether it's a crate or a room. He should be free to leave it if he wants to.

Distraction is another technique that can work well. Try using it when there are signs of a thunderstorm, but your Lab hasn't yet started to display fearful behavior, such as hiding or whimpering. Play a game of tug or fetch–inside–or practice some obedience commands. Give lots of praise and rewards for participating in the play or training session. The activity may help delay the onset of fearful behavior. Stop the game or training if your Lab starts acting afraid, and let him go to his safe place if he chooses.

Behavior Modification

Counterconditioning and desensitization are behavior modification techniques that can help dogs overcome fears. They involve gradually accustoming the dog to the sounds (or other stimuli) that cause fear and replacing the fearful response with one that's more acceptable. Like most behavior modification, these techniques require time and patience.

Get a recording of thunderstorm noises or make a recording of firecracker sounds or whatever noise frightens your Lab. Play the recording at a very low volume, so that it's almost inaudible. While the recording is playing, do something your Lab enjoys. Play fetch, give treats, or feed a meal.

Do the same thing each time you play the recording. Over a period of days, weeks, or months, very gradually increase the volume. If you notice your Lab starting to display fearful behavior, stop the recording. Try again later with it set at a lower level. Eventually, your Lab should start to associate the frightening sound with good times.

Talk to your veterinarian about getting a short-term prescription of an anti-anxiety drug for your dog. Medication alone won't solve the problem, but it can help the behavior modification process. It can also be a good idea to get the help of a behaviorist if your Lab's noise phobia is severe.

Never give your Lab a dose of your own Paxil, Valium, or other drug. Just because a certain medication helps you doesn't mean your dog will respond to it in the same way. And an amount that's safe for you could be fatal to your Lab.

Separation Anxiety

Separation anxiety is a panic response that occurs in a dog when his caregiver leaves home. Dogs with separation anxiety become highly distressed, usually within an hour of the person's departure. They may respond to being alone by digging, chewing, or scratching at doors or windows in an attempt to get out and find their caregivers; howling, barking, or whining; or losing control of their bowels or bladder.

Gradually accustom your Lab to being left alone. Start by teaching your Lab to remain calm during brief absences. Practice by doing all the things you would normally do before leaving: get your purse or wallet, pick up your keys, and put on your coat. Don't leave. Repeat this several times over several days until your dog stops showing interest in your preparations.

Gradually add more elements of departure: stepping outside, closing the door, and coming right back in; leaving, closing the door, waiting a few seconds, and coming back in; and so on. Eventually, you can practice leaving for short periods. Say "I'll be back" or some other phrase to indicate that you're leaving. Step outside the door, close it, and wait one minute. Then re-enter in an unconcerned manner. You can greet your dog quietly or just ignore him.

Behaviorists aren't sure why some dogs develop separation anxiety while others don't, but it sometimes develops when the dog is unused to being left alone; after the dog has been boarded at a kennel; or after a change in the family routine, such as moving to a new home, the addition of a baby or new pet, or the departure of a teenager for college.

Practice leaving and returning at different times of the day. Your Lab needs to learn that it doesn't matter what time you leave; you'll always come back. Once he's comfortable with your absence for periods of thirty to ninety minutes, you can jump up to longer intervals, such as half a day. Ⓔ

Choosing a Trainer

ONE OF THE UNEXPECTED PLEASURES you'll encounter with your Lab is the great feeling of accomplishment you receive from training your otter-tailed bundle of fun. A good dog trainer is one of the best partners you can have in raising your Lab. Especially if you are new to dogs in general, a trainer can help you understand what's normal and what's not, what behavior to expect at different stages of your Lab's life, and how to teach your Lab manners, tricks, and various dog sports.

Why Hire a Trainer?

With a quick trip to the nearest bookstore or library, you'll see that there are scores of books on how to train dogs. Why spend money on a trainer when you could do it yourself at home? Labs are easy to train, that's true, but with proper guidance you can help your Lab learn more things more quickly.

Experience Counts

The main advantage of working with a trainer is that he or she has experience with large numbers of dogs. Although each breed has a characteristic temperament, all dogs are individuals and learn differently. What works with one Lab may have no effect at all with another. A trainer who has worked with many retrievers can call upon a variety of stratagems to see what works best with your dog.

Opportunity for Socialization

Another advantage of attending training class is the socialization aspect. Puppy kindergarten and, later, basic obedience class are great places for your Lab to meet and learn to get along with other dogs and people. Just as important, he'll learn to pay attention to you even with their distracting presence.

You'll want to find a trainer who can help you bring out the best in your Lab, using positive training techniques that make learning fun. Effective dog trainers use humane training techniques, such as clickers, praise, treats, and head halters.

Finding the Right Trainer

Anyone can claim to be a dog trainer since no special instruction or certification is required to set up business in this field. Some trainers, however, do have credentials—such as a diploma from a dog-training school or a degree from a university—in behavioral psychology or ethology (animal behavior). Whatever the educational background, the most important characteristics of a good dog trainer are excellent communication skills and a thorough understanding of learning theory, training techniques, breed characteristics, general dog behavior and physiology, and human nature. After all, the trainer's job isn't to teach your dog: it's to teach *you* how to teach your dog. Here is a checklist for finding a good trainer for your Lab:

- Contact professional dog-training organizations for member referrals.

- Ask if your local Labrador Retriever Club offers training classes.
- Attend a class before signing up to evaluate the training style.
- Interview the trainer about his or her experience and education.
- Protect your Lab from harsh training methods.

Where to Look

Start your search for a trainer with one of the professional dog-training organizations, such as the American Pet Dog Trainers, International Association of Canine Professionals, and National Association of Dog Obedience Instructors. (See Appendix A for contact information.) Membership in this type of organization indicates a trainer's interest in continuing education, staying informed about advances in behavioral knowledge, and learning from others in the field.

Evaluating the Trainer

When you've found several trainers in your area, make an appointment to visit their classes as an observer. You'll want to make sure you're comfortable with the trainer's teaching style. Look for the following signs of an experienced trainer:

- Explains and demonstrates each behavior clearly before teaching it
- Explains and demonstrates how to teach the behavior, providing written instruction if pertinent
- Allows time during class to practice the behavior
- Spends time individually with students to work on problem areas
- Treats people and dogs courteously

As well as learning, dogs and people should be having fun in the class. Unless you enjoy being yelled at, avoid trainers with a drill sergeant mentality. Training techniques have evolved over the years, and it's no longer considered constructive to jerk dogs with choke chains, or yell at them when they don't perform correctly.

If you believe a trainer is mistreating your dog, don't be afraid to put a stop to it. Hitting, hanging, kicking, or shocking are all unacceptable. No training method should ever be harmful to the dog.

Ask participants whether they're satisfied with the progress they've made with their dogs. Are their training needs and goals being met? A six-week class should give you basic skills to work competently with your dog at home. Interview the trainer about his or her experience. Here are some questions to ask:

- How long have you been training dogs?
- How did you acquire your knowledge of dog training?
- What's your experience with Labrador Retrievers?
- What training techniques do you find work best with Labs?
- Do you belong to any professional organizations?
- What will my Lab and I learn in this class?

Whether you are successful in training your Lab depends on several factors. Your trainer's ability plays a role, of course, but so do your dog's temperament and your level of commitment and experience. You will only get out of training as much time and effort as you put into it.

Training Classes

Training your Lab can be a lifelong endeavor, not because Labs aren't smart–they are–but because there's so much they can learn. From puppy kindergarten to dog sports to therapy work, there's a class for just about anything you might want to teach your Lab.

Puppy Kindergarten

We used to think that dog training should begin at six months of age, but puppies are capable of learning good manners at a much earlier age. The earlier you begin to train your Lab, the more quickly you will develop a deep and powerful bond with him that will last throughout your life. Puppy kindergarten is the perfect place to learn how to be your Lab's leader and friend, using only positive reinforcement techniques–no choke chains or physical manipulation, such as jerking or pulling.

What Your Lab Will Learn

A good puppy kindergarten class provides opportunities for puppies to develop social skills with dogs and people. You'll learn how to communicate effectively with your Lab and cope with typical puppy behaviors, such as barking, play biting, chewing, digging, stealing food or trash, and jumping up on people. Pups learn basic commands ("Sit," "Stay," "Come," "Down," and "Off"), and walking nicely on a leash without pulling is also part of the curriculum. Trainers may also cover such issues as spaying, neutering, grooming, health care, safety, and tattooing or microchipping for identification.

Some trainers offer regular "puppy parties" for socialization purposes. These informal get-togethers are a great opportunity for puppies to let off some steam, especially if they don't have another dog at home to play with or are alone during the day. Puppy parties have the same vaccination requirements as puppy kindergarten classes.

Class Size and Makeup

Look for a class with a manageable number of puppies, so the trainer is able to give individual attention to everyone. It's also a good sign if puppies are divided by size during playtime. Dogs play rough, and it's all too easy for a big dog to accidentally injure a small one. Local breed clubs often offer training classes, and this can be ideal for you and your Lab, allowing the two of you to meet other Labs and Lab owners.

Puppy kindergarten is aimed at puppies ten weeks and older. Be sure the class you attend requires dogs to be vaccinated and flea-free before attending class. Expect all puppies older than eight weeks to have written proof of distemper and parvo vaccination; puppies older than twelve weeks to have written proof of their second distemper and parvo vaccination. Run the vaccination requirements by your veterinarian to make sure he or she is comfortable with your puppy attending the class. Some vets prefer not to expose puppies to strange dogs until the vaccination series is complete at four months of age.

Well-behaved children of appropriate age (six years or older) should be welcome at dog training class. They need to learn how to work with the dog just as much as you do. A reputable trainer encourages participation of the entire family.

Obedience Training

Basic obedience classes build on the lessons learned in puppy kindergarten or introduce them if the dog didn't attend puppy kindergarten. In this class, your Lab will hone the skills learned in puppy kindergarten. The class may emphasize some especially important behaviors, such as stay, heel, and come. Again, the trainer will stress the use of positive reinforcement methods, but you'll learn how to reduce or phase out the amount of treats you give. The goal is for your Lab to learn to respond to your verbal commands and hand signals.

Once your Lab has the basics down, he can advance to more difficult lessons. These can include walking off leash, retrieving on command, jumping, scent discrimination games, and staying in position even though you've moved out of sight. Learning hand signals is another aspect of advanced training.

These are skills you can use at home with your Lab to help keep his mind sharp and his body active. Some trainers also offer classes designed for people who plan to compete in obedience with their dogs. In these classes, you'll be able to practice your skills in simulated conditions before facing a real judge in the ring.

Training for Sports

Among the many dog sports you and your Lab can participate in are agility, flyball, and freestyle. It's not difficult to find classes for each of these activities. Ask your trainer if he or she offers such classes, contact your local Labrador Retriever Club, check the offerings at your local community college, or search the Internet. Agility, flyball, and freestyle all have national organizations (as listed in Appendix A) that can direct you to people in your area who participate in a given sport.

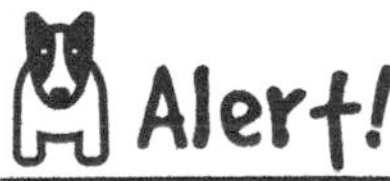

Your Lab shouldn't train over any but the lowest jumps until he's at least eighteen months old. At this age, his growth plates will have fused and won't be damaged by repetitive motions that can lead to orthopedic problems.

Before you sign up for a class in a particular dog sport, be sure your Lab is ready for competition—he should know and respond to basic obedience commands. If you have to call him several times before he comes or if he won't sit or lie down the first time you tell him to, do a little remedial work at home or in a class before trying a dog sport.

Training for Therapy Work

Visits from pets to people in hospitals and nursing homes have proven healing benefits, from lowering blood pressure to raising spirits. If you and your Lab would like to do this special work, you'll need to become certified as a therapy team. Organizations such as the Delta Society, Therapy Dogs International, and Love on a Leash offer certification programs. You may also be able to find one through your trainer.

Training Tips and Techniques

Do you remember your parents swatting the family dog with a newspaper for some misdeed, or rubbing his nose in the mess when he had an accident in the house? These harsh methods used to be how many people "broke" their dogs to house rules, but training techniques have come a long way since those days. Gentle guidance, prevention, and positive reinforcement are the rules of the day, and dogs are better off for it.

The techniques trainers find most effective now are praise, rewards, use of a clicker to signal correct behavior, and use of gentle training devices, such as head halters. These can all be used to motivate desired behaviors. The focus is on communicating with the dog rather than forcing him to obey.

Praise

You probably know from your own life experience that you respond better to praise than criticism. Your Lab is no exception. Saying "Good dog!" in a happy, excited tone of voice lets your Lab know that he's pleased you.

You don't have to reserve praise for formal training situations. Use it any time you see your Lab doing something you like. Is he lying quietly while you read or watch television? Say "Good relax!"

(or "Settle" or whatever term you want to use). Is he in a down position on his own? Tell him, "Good down!" Take every opportunity you can to reinforce good behaviors with praise.

Hand signals aren't just for use in the obedience ring. You can use them at home as well. If your Lab is jumping up on you while you're talking on the phone, simply give him the hand signal for sit (hand moving up in the air above his head) or down (hand moving downward toward the ground) and follow it with the hand signal for stay (palm up in front of his face).

Rewards

As with praise, people and dogs work better when they're rewarded for their efforts. A reward can be anything your Lab likes, from a treat to a special toy to a favorite game. You can give a reward immediately for a job well done, or delay it until after the training session. For instance, you might offer a treat when your Lab puppy sits (instant gratification) or pull out a favorite tug toy after he completes a great agility run (delayed gratification). Both types of rewards are beneficial.

When you give treats as training rewards, choose something that your Lab doesn't get every day. Training treats should be small (easily swallowed) and aromatic. Cut-up hot dogs, small cubes of cheese, dried liver, and cat treats, such as Pounce, are all good choices.

Using a Clicker

To use a clicker effectively, you must first teach your Lab that "treat" follows "click." Click, then give a treat. Repeat this twenty or thirty times, and it won't take your Lab long to make the association. Then start clicking and treating every time your Lab does something you like—sits, lies down, comes toward you, potties outside—even if it's something he's done on his own. Carry a clicker and treats around with you so you can always reinforce the behaviors you want.

Once your dog understands a behavior and starts offering it on his own, you can give the action a name: sit, down, fetch. Start clicking for the action if the dog performs it during or after the time you give the cue word. The same holds true if you're teaching a hand signal rather than a verbal cue. As your Lab's skills improve, increase your standards: Require a straighter sit, a longer down, a come from farther away before you click. In this way, you shape the behavior to what you ultimately want the dog to do. With a clicker and the help of a trainer or a good book on clicker training (see Appendix A), you can teach your Lab all kinds of things.

The clicker is strictly a bridge to a reward. Don't use it to get your dog's attention or as a signal to perform a certain command. Doing so diminishes its value as a training aid.

Head Halters

Head halters have been around for more than a decade, but their use still isn't well known. A head halter works in much the same way as a horse halter, allowing you to control the dog's head. One strap fastens around the neck behind the ears and the other wraps around the muzzle. When the dog pulls, the halter puts gentle pressure on nose and neck.

The pressure exerted by the head halter evokes the same kind of neurochemical response that makes a puppy relax when its mother picks it up by the scruff of the neck or takes its muzzle into her mouth as a disciplinary measure. In the case of the head halter, the dog relaxes and stops pulling, essentially correcting his own behavior. (Then you can click and treat him for walking nicely.) A head halter doesn't cause any pain, and a dog wearing one can still eat, drink, pant, bark, and even bite—although the latter isn't desirable, of course. Brand names for head halters include Gentle Leader, Promise Collar, and Halti.

For a head halter to be effective, it must fit well. Read the directions carefully or work with your trainer to achieve a proper fit. The neck strap should rest just behind the ears, with enough give that you can fit one finger between the strap and your dog's neck. Adjust the nosepiece so that it sits below your dog's eyes. It should be loose enough that it can slide down to the top of the nose, but not so loose that it slips off the nose. The metal ring to which the leash attaches goes beneath the chin.

Alert!

Be careful not to jerk your Lab while he's wearing a head halter, or you could hurt him. Use it with a regular leash, not a retractable lead, or he could jerk himself if he abruptly comes to the end of the line, so to speak. Take the head halter off when you're not walking your dog.

When you first put the head halter on, your Lab may paw at it or rub his nose on the ground in an attempt to get it off. Ignore his behavior and encourage him to walk with you by using praise and treats. When he learns that the halter means he's going for a walk, he'll come to accept it happily.

Never forget that your Lab needs positive motivational training if you want him to learn well. A treat or a quick game of fetch is always a welcome reward for this breed. A Lab that's forced or bullied into something will quickly become stubborn. Show your Lab what you want and give him the opportunity to learn, and he will bend over backward to please you.

Advanced Training

ITS VERSATILITY IS ONE OF THE MANY reasons the Labrador Retriever is such a popular breed. The Lab is an all-around athlete, capable of excelling not only in the conformation ring but also in the field and in competitive dog sports. There aren't many breeds that can lay claim to so many areas of expertise. In this chapter, you'll learn about conformation showing, field trials, hunt tests, agility, flyball, freestyle, and tracking.

Conformation

A dog show is an event where dogs are judged on how well they measure up to the breed standard and to the other dogs in the ring on that day. It's much more than a beauty pageant, though. The conformation show brings together breeders and their dogs in a hunt for those Labs that are most suited for breeding. Each Lab's structure (conformation), movement, and attitude is judged against the breed standard. The dogs that most closely meet the standard earn championships and are considered good breeding prospects.

Dogs earn points toward championships at all-breed dog shows. Each win brings one to five points, depending on the number of dogs defeated. A three-, four-, or five-point win is called a major. Dogs must receive fifteen points under three different judges to earn a championship. Two of the wins must be majors, each won under a different judge.

Because Labs are such a popular breed, show-ring competition is stiff. Statistically, only 2 percent of the Labs that are registered with the American Kennel Club (AKC) finish their championships.

Besides proper conformation, a good show dog has character, expression, attitude, and showmanship. He's well muscled and not overly fat. He moves effortlessly, looking as if he could go all day in the field—as indeed he should be able to do. His eyes should have a kind, soft, intelligent expression since lack of expression is considered a weakness.

The best show dogs have a style and quality that draws all eyes to them. Some Labs just seem to "ask" for the win, and they often get it, even if they might not be the best in the ring that day.

Grooming for Conformation

Lots of breeds must be endlessly curled, combed, and styled before they enter the show ring—not the Lab. This is a wash-and-go dog. Nonetheless, a few grooming tips can help your Lab look his best on the big day:

- Bathe him two or three days before the show, not the day before. His coat should have a hard but not harsh texture to it rather than being soft and fluffy.
- If you like, you can trim the whiskers for a neater, cleaner look. Your Lab won't lose any points with or without whiskers, however.
- With some training from an experienced Lab exhibitor, you can use thinning shears to clean up the dog's lines and subtly shape and round the tail.

Specialty Shows

Specialty shows are limited to dogs of a single breed—in this case, Labradors. They are usually judged by breeders who are experts in all aspects of the Lab, and it's at a specialty where you'll see many of the finest Labs in the country.

Specialty shows can be local, regional, or national. The annual national specialty celebrates the Lab's versatility, and draws more than 1,500 entries. Besides conformation, it includes agility, hunt tests, obedience, and tracking events.

Are there any Labs that can't participate in conformation?
A Lab that's shorter or taller than the breed standard calls for will be disqualified. Blind or deaf dogs cannot participate, nor can spayed or neutered dogs. Dogs with missing teeth may also be penalized.

Some of the classes at specialties that aren't normally found at the average dog show are the veteran, brood bitch, and stud dog classes. The veteran classes showcase dogs that are still sound, even at ten or more years of age. They represent the lines that smart breeders want to breed into. Brood bitch and stud dog classes showcase the offspring of the dogs entered.

Another class unique to a specialty show is the sweepstakes. The puppy sweepstakes put on display the up-and-coming generation of Labs. These young dogs will carry on the versatile heritage of their breed. The climax of a national specialty is the best of breed competition, where the best Labrador in the country is chosen.

Conformation Training and Handling Tips

You can start teaching your Lab to stand as early as eight weeks of age. Keep things fun, and don't ask him to hold his position for more than a couple of seconds. When he's about twelve weeks old, start moving him on a lead and let him stand on his own. Again, keep practice sessions short—only a minute or two each time. Remember to keep things fun.

For more formal preparation for the show ring, consider attending a handling class at your local dog club. You can sign up for this when your Lab is about three months old. (He can't enter a show until he's six months old.) It's a great way to pick up tips, especially if you plan to show your Lab yourself. You'll learn how to display your dog's outline in the show ring (called stacking), gait (move) him properly, and groom him appropriately.

The Labrador Retriever Club offers a noncompetitive Conformation Certificate open to all Labrador Retrievers (more than one year old), including spayed and neutered dogs. The evaluation scores a dog in eight conformation and temperament categories and should demonstrate that the dog possesses the basic attributes of a Labrador Retriever.

At home, practice in front of a mirror. Stack your dog in different ways to see what looks best. This can help you enhance your Lab's appearance and bring out his best points. Some Labs set themselves up squarely with no assistance from their handler, called free-stacking. If your Lab looks good standing on his own, go with it, but consider who the judge is as well. Sometimes, breeder judges prefer the natural free stack, while some all-breed judges like to have dogs presented to them in a stacked position.

As far as gait goes, show your Lab on a loose lead, moving at a slow trot or brisk walk. One of the most common complaints judges have is that dogs are moved too quickly around the ring. If your Lab is put together properly, he'll move correctly at a brisk walk, and you won't have to gait him quickly to hide movement faults.

Make showing fun for your Lab. He should be happy in the ring, not on edge—because he feels your tension traveling down the lead—or bored because he'd rather be doing something else. Use liver or a favorite toy as bait to keep his attention and put a sparkle in his eyes. Your own style is important, too. Dress appropriately and professionally, and look like you want to win. In the words of the late Lina Basquette, a grande dame of the show ring, "Always dress like you're going to win something big." Don't be afraid to ask for help. Watch and talk to and learn from other handlers, both amateur and professional.

Professional Handlers

A good Lab should be able to finish with his owner showing him. Handling your Lab to his championship is a great achievement that you can always cherish. Nonetheless, some people choose to hire a professional handler, for perfectly valid reasons. They may not enjoy being in the spotlight, even though the dog is the one being judged; they may be poor handlers—not everyone has the skill and coordination to handle a dog well; or they may simply not have enough time.

Professional handlers show ten to twenty dogs a show at 120 shows a year. Not surprisingly, they understand the physical and mental conditioning show dogs need. Not just any handler will do, however. You want someone who knows the breed: how to care for it, how to condition it, and how to motivate it. Some handlers specialize in sporting breeds and have a deep understanding of the particular issues involved in showing a Lab.

The handler should have a rate card or rate sheet that explains exactly what expenses you're paying for (travel, food, advertising, and so on). A contract should spell out the yearly budget, travel plans, who gets the trophies, and so on. It's important that you and the handler are honest with each other from the beginning.

The health and welfare of your Lab is the most important thing. If your Lab will be living with the handler in another city or state, find out how he will be cared for, where he'll be housed, whether the kennel has heat and air-conditioning, what he'll be fed, how he'll travel to shows, and so on. Tour the handler's facility yourself to make sure you're satisfied with how and where your Lab will be living.

Next, understand where your Lab falls on the handler's list of priorities. If you simply want your Lab to earn a championship, he may be handled by an assistant if the handler has a more important dog to show. Many top handlers end up with as many as four or five dogs in one string in the best-in-show ring, and they can't handle all of them at once. Be clear on how the system works and accept that your Lab isn't always going to be top dog.

Field Trials and Hunt Tests

Labs are the ultimate field dogs. They are the winningest breed in field trials, and they earn more hunt test titles than all other retriever breeds combined. Approximately 20 to 25 percent of the Labs in this country are used for hunting or participate in competitive and noncompetitive events, such as field trials and hunt tests. Individual dog clubs sponsor field trials and hunt tests, which are held under AKC rules and regulations.

Field trials and hunt tests are performance events that evaluate a Lab's ability to retrieve game, the function for which he was originally bred. A good retriever is able to follow the trajectory of a shot bird and find where it landed. He isn't afraid to go after a bird, no matter where it is, and he retrieves with style. He pays attention to his handler, has a good sense of smell, and doesn't shy away from the sound of gunfire. Retrievers should perform equally well on land and in water. Just as important, a good retriever has a soft mouth, meaning he doesn't damage the bird during the retrieve. Retrievers are judged on their ability to mark, or remember, the location of downed birds, retrieve them quickly, and then deliver them gently to their handlers.

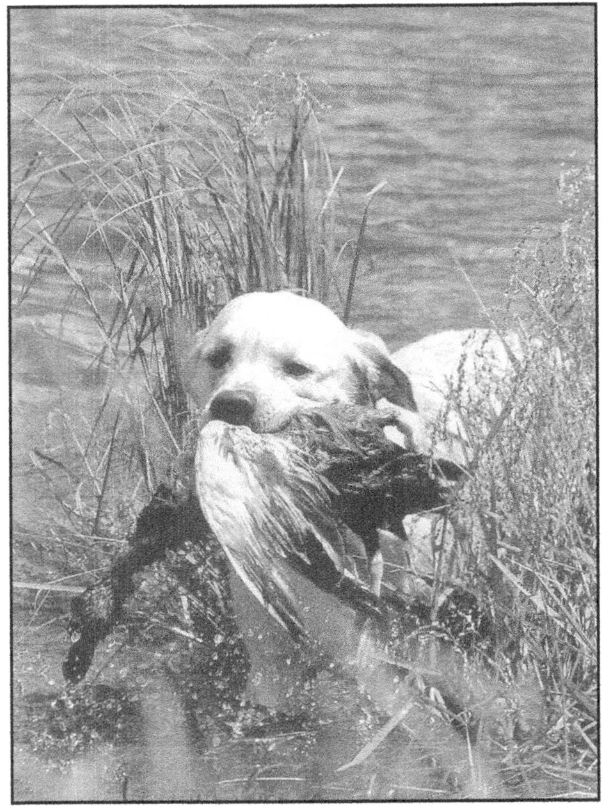

◀ Labs were bred to retrieve game birds while hunting, just like this male yellow Lab is doing.

Field Trials

A field trial is a competitive event, meaning that dogs compete against each other for placements and points toward a field championship. Titles that can be earned are field champion (FC) and amateur field champion (AFC). Once earned, these titles become part of the dog's name. For instance, a dog with a field championship would have a registered name that looks like this: FC King Buck.

Like a conformation show, the purpose of a field trial is to determine the best breeding stock, so spayed and neutered Labs may not compete. To participate, dogs must be at least six months old and registered with the AKC. Field trial classes, known as stakes, test dogs of varying ages and levels of experience. Stakes also separate amateur and professional handlers. Retriever field trials have four stakes, two major and two minor.

The major stakes are classified as open all-age and amateur all-age; the minor stakes are classified as qualifying and derby. Championship points are earned in the two major stakes, with at least two judges officiating.

Some Labs do more than retrieve. They point as well, making them the perfect hunting partner in the eyes of some hunters. Fewer than 5 percent of Labs are born with this ability, but the International Pointing Labrador Association and the American Pointing Labrador Association have been formed to identify and perpetuate these dogs.

Judges determine the tests that will be given and try to test each dog equally. They call back the best dogs and continue testing them until they decide their placements. Dogs are judged on natural abilities–memory, intelligence, attention, nose, courage, perseverance, and style–and on trained abilities, such as steadiness, control, response to direction, and delivery. As retriever trials increase in difficulty, the dogs must mark (find) multiple birds or find unmarked birds, a skill called a blind retrieve.

Field Trial Championships

Championship points are awarded based on the dog's placement in open all-age and amateur all-age stakes, with five points for first-place wins, three points for second-place wins, two points for third-place wins, and a half point for fourth-place wins. The field champion or amateur field champion titles require the dog to earn ten points in the open all-age stake, of which five points must be for a first-place win. To earn an amateur field champion title in amateur all-age stakes, the dog must earn fifteen points, of which five must be for a first place. Open all-age points can be combined with amateur all-age points for an AFC title.

Retrievers can be eliminated from trials for such behaviors as failure to enter rough cover, water, ice, mud, or any other unpleasant or difficult situation; returning to the handler before finding a bird in a marked retrieve; stopping the hunt; repeated evidence of poor scenting ability; or failing to pick a bird up after finding it.

Training for Field Trials

Lab puppies show retrieving instinct early and can be introduced to birds as early as eight to nine weeks of age. Labs that are going to participate in field trials also need basic socialization and training. They should be comfortable around other dogs and with having strangers touch them. And of course they need to become accustomed to the sound of a gun.

Commands that form the foundation for hunting training include "Sit," "Down," "Stay," "Come," "Fetch," and "Give." A retriever in a field trial should come at heel, sit promptly where the handler indicates, and stay quietly until given further instructions. Barking or whining is penalized and can even cause a dog to be eliminated from the stake.

The only dog ever to appear on a federal duck stamp (issued by the U.S. Fish and Wildlife Service) was the black Labrador Retriever Nilo's King Buck, who earned back-to-back field trial championships in 1952 and 1953.

Other preparation involves conditioning, making sure the dog is in good shape for the amount of work he'll be doing. Work him gradually until he's able to walk or run for several miles a day. He also needs to be familiar with environments similar to those at a trial. Take him for walks in woods, fields, and parks so he becomes accustomed to different types of foliage, the sounds of snapping twigs and crunching leaves, and the presence of many different smells.

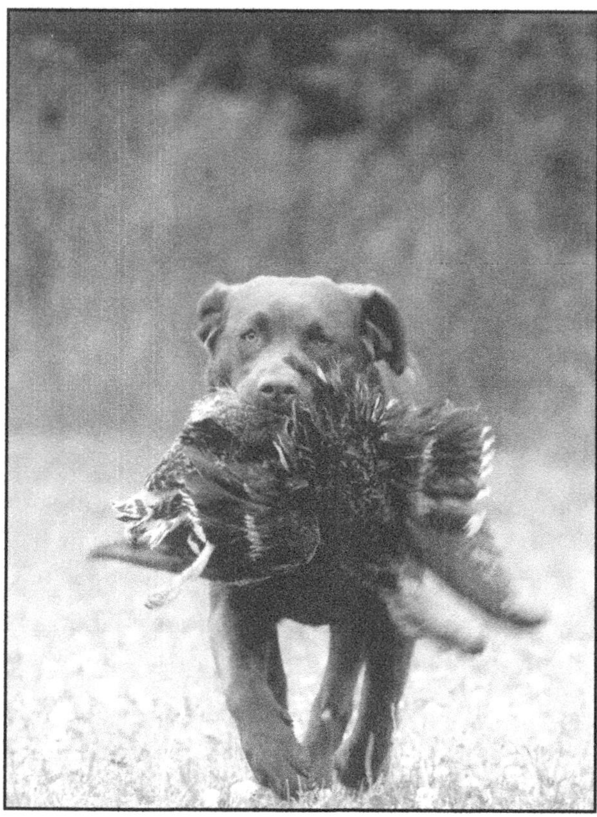

◀ **Labs make great hunting dogs, including this 2½-year-old female chocolate.**

Hunt Tests

Hunting tests are a means of judging the dog's ability to perform against a standard of perfection established by the AKC regulations. Unlike field trials, they are noncompetitive, meaning the dogs must simply meet a standard of performance, rather than beat other dogs. Labs receiving qualifying scores at a given number of tests can earn the titles junior hunter (JH), senior hunter (SH), and master hunter (MH). Each successive title requires more skill, and dogs are judged more strictly as they advance. Once a dog has qualified at a higher level, it cannot move back to a lower level.

Beginners start with marked birds, meaning they can see the bird or bumper fly and fall. They must then stay until the handler gives the command to retrieve the bird. As the dog advances, hunt tests become more difficult, but at all levels the dog is usually not required to retrieve from a distance greater than 100 yards.

Dogs with an indefinite listing privilege (ILP) number—meaning they are recognized as a given purebred, although they have no registration papers—are eligible only for hunt tests. Owners may handle their own dogs or hire a professional handler.

To get started in hunt tests, find a local retriever club and join it. Joining a club gives you other people to train with and other resources. By training with a group, you can benefit from the experiences of other people and see a variety of training techniques. Choose the ones that work best for you and your Lab.

The National Retriever Championship Stake

The National Retriever Championship Stake is the retriever Olympics. All retrievers are eligible to compete, not just Labs. To qualify for the National, a Lab must be the previous year's champion or amateur champion, the winner of the previous year's Canadian National, or the winner of a first-place, with five championship points in open, limited, or special all-age stakes in trials held within the past year.

The National Retriever Championship Stake includes at least ten tests, or "series," equally divided between those on land and those on water. The judges place only the winner, and that dog is entitled to bear the official designation "National Retriever Field Trial

Champion" for that year. Since the National began in 1941, all but four of the championships have been won by a Lab.

Organizations that sponsor agility competitions are the American Kennel Club, the United States Dog Agility Association, the North American Dog Agility Council, and the United Kennel Club. Titles vary from organization to organization.

Agility

This fun, fast-paced sport requires the dog—directed by his handler—to navigate a series of obstacles, such as A-frames, balance beams, tunnels, and weave poles, as well as different types of jumps: through tires, hoops, or over single or double bars, for instance. The dog is judged on speed and accuracy. Labs love the rowdy nature of agility competition, which appeals to their mischievous side.

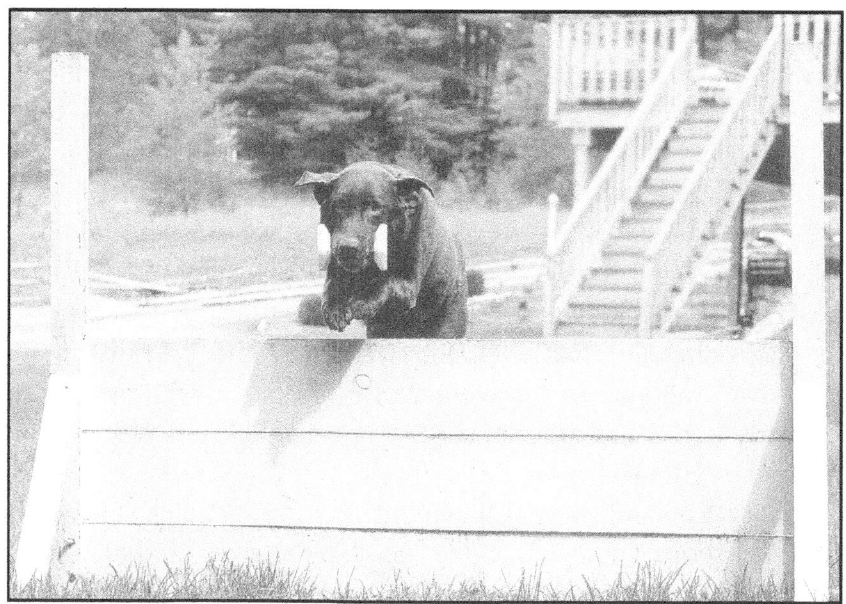

▲ **This ten-year-old chocolate Lab performs a retrieve over the panel jump.**

A Lab's athleticism, learning ability, and willingness to please all make him a good agility prospect. He's independent enough to think for himself but takes direction well—a plus in this sport. He might not have the speed of top agility breeds, such as the Border collie, but he's capable of a solid, consistent performance. And here's a plus: He doesn't mind working in the rain! Drawbacks are the breed's sense of smell and love of birds, both of which can cause him to become distracted while running the course.

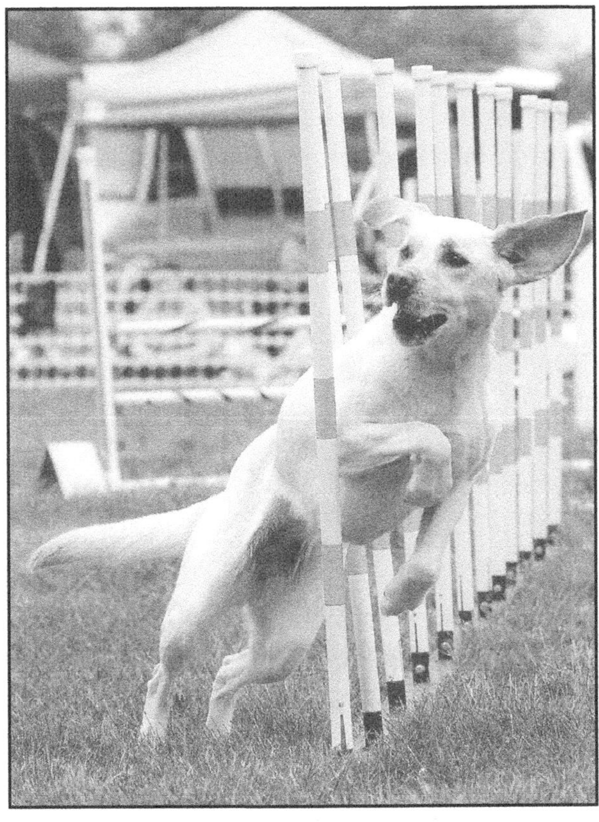

◀ A 3½-year-old female yellow Lab blasts out of the weave poles during agility training.

Before starting agility training, your Lab should know and respond to the commands "Sit," "Down," "Stay," and "Come." Young puppies can start learning elements of agility, such as going through tunnels, balancing on the teeter-totter, weaving through poles, and going over the A-frame, but avoid jumping them higher than elbow height (theirs, not yours) until they reach physical maturity at eighteen months of age. Remember to keep things fun.

As with any sport, a Lab that competes in agility must be in excellent physical condition. Take your Lab in for a veterinary exam before beginning training. Health conditions that would preclude participation in agility are hip dysplasia or other musculoskeletal problems, decreased vision, heart problems, and obesity.

Flyball

A Lab's strong desire to retrieve and obsession with tennis balls make this relay race the perfect sport for the breed. The object is for each of four dogs on a flyball team to go over four hurdles to reach the flyball box. There, they step on a lever that triggers the release of a tennis ball. Ball in mouth, the dog returns over the hurdles, and the next dog takes his turn. The first team to run without errors–skipping one or more hurdles, for instance–wins the heat.

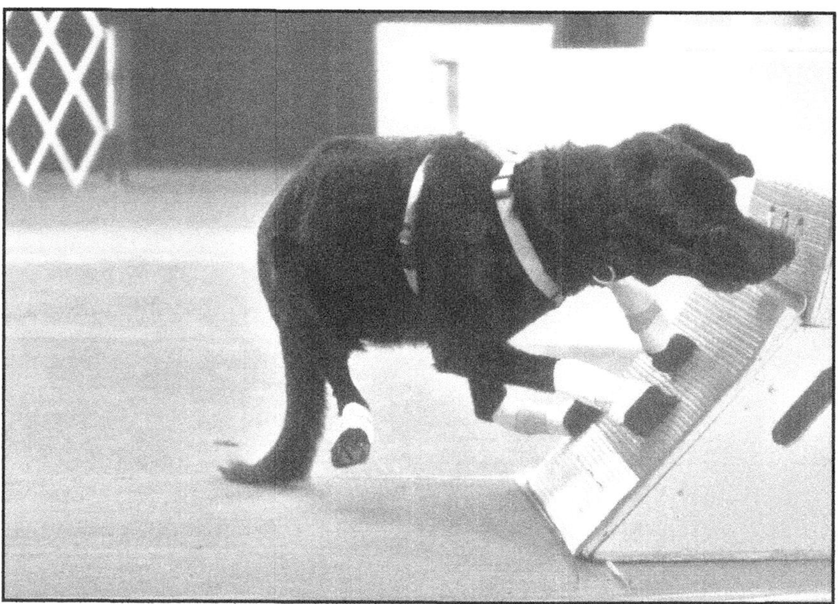

▲ This two-year-old male black Lab pounces on the Flyball box during a Flyball tournament.

The ideal Lab for flyball is lean and well muscled, with good endurance. You can start teaching your young Lab the basics of flyball by having him run down a line of jumps toward a target, with boards on the ground replacing the jumps. Puppies can also learn swimmer's turns, used to turn away from the box.

Flyball is hard on the body, and joints such as hocks, elbows, knees, and shoulders take a beating. Before getting started, take your Lab to the veterinarian to be x-rayed for hip and elbow problems. Many serious competitors also x-ray shoulders, knees, and backs, just to be on the safe side. It's also a good idea to have your veterinarian check for eye problems.

Avoid repetitive boxwork and jumping—except over low jumps—until your Lab's growth plates have closed. And don't let flyball be your dog's only exercise. It's important to build muscle and endurance in an athletic Lab daily with varying activities such as swimming, off-leash play, walks up and down hills, and retrieving games.

Freestyle

Nicknamed the tail-wagging sport, freestyle involves developing a routine set to music that shows dog and handler working together, expressing their creativity through movement and costume. Routines can be based on obedience exercises, tricks, or any other behaviors the dog knows and enjoys. It's perfect for athletic, attentive, and trainable Labs.

There are two types of freestyle: heelwork to music (which involves heeling on all sides of the handler, with the dog no farther away than 4 feet), and musical freestyle (an anything-goes routine that often encompasses jumping and fancy tricks). Handlers choose the beat that goes with the dog and choreograph moves based on their dogs' abilities. Labs can start training for freestyle at any age, and even dogs with health issues can participate. Simply adapt your choreography and music to the dog's speed and ability level.

Tracking

Labs aren't scenthounds, but they do have a superb sense of smell. Teach your Lab to track and you'll have a dog with a useful skill, as well as a new way to enjoy the outdoors with him. Your Lab can earn an AKC tracking title by completing a single successful track.

Titles that can be earned by following a human scent trail are tracking dog (TD), tracking dog excellent (TDX), and variable surface tracking (VST). For the TD test, the track is 440 to 500 yards long, with a minimum of two right-angle turns, and must be half an hour to two hours. The person laying the track must be unfamiliar to the dog. At the end of the track, the person laying the track drops a scent article, which the dog must locate. The TDX track is longer, older (three to five hours), more complicated, and takes in varied terrain, such as ditches, streambeds, and tall grass. Its length is 800 to 1,000 yards, and it has several turns and two cross tracks. Along the way are dummy scent articles meant to lure your dog off the trail.

Whatever sport you try, always keep things fun. Use toys and treats to help motivate your Lab and keep him focused.

TD and TDX tests usually take place in rural areas, but the VST tests a dog's tracking ability in more developed locales, such as suburban neighborhoods or city streets. The length of a VST track is 600 to 800 yards, and it goes over at least three types of surfaces, such as asphalt, concrete, grass, gravel, or sand. To add to the difficulty, a portion of the track must lack vegetation, which helps hold scent. The track must be three to five hours old with four to eight turns. A dog that passes all three tests earns the title champion tracker (CT).

Common Illnesses and Injuries

LABS ARE BIG, ACTIVE DOGS, but sometimes an injury or illness can lay them low. Most dogs at some point will itch and scratch from allergies, hot spots, or flea bites, suffer the unpleasantness of diarrhea or vomiting, or develop lumps or bumps that should be checked out. Being the outdoor athletes that they are, Labs are also prone to such injuries as broken toenails, cuts and scrapes, or ruptured cruciate ligaments. Knowing what to expect and what to do about these potential problems will help you recognize and deal with them when they occur.

When Do You Need to Visit the Vet?

Every dog should be examined annually by a veterinarian. Even if you choose not to vaccinate your Lab every year, he still needs a physical exam to make sure his overall health is good. During this physical exam, the vet will listen to the dog's heart and lungs; take his temperature, pulse, and breathing rate; weigh him; check the eyes, ears, and skin for infection or parasites; look inside the mouth to make sure there's no tartar buildup on teeth or other dental problems; test his range of motion to make sure his movement is smooth (not stiff); and palpate (feel) his body to make sure the organs don't seem enlarged and that there are no suspicious lumps or bumps that could indicate infections or tumors.

Besides this annual exam, your Lab should go to the veterinarian any time he has a serious injury or illness. A small cut or scrape can usually be treated at home, and minor bouts of vomiting or diarrhea usually aren't a problem. A visit to the veterinarian is warranted if vomiting or diarrhea is frequent or lasts for more than forty-eight hours, if the dog's behavior is unusual—say, lack of appetite for more than a day—or if the dog suffers an injury that causes lameness or that you can't treat with your canine first-aid kit. Following are some examples of the common illnesses or injuries that your Lab might encounter and what to do about them.

The annual exam is also a good time to take in a fecal sample to make sure your Lab doesn't have any intestinal parasites.

Allergies

An allergy is a reaction of the immune system. It's caused by exposure to an allergen, which is any substance—medications, insect bites or stings, grasses, pollens, molds, and foods—capable of causing an allergic reaction. Dogs can inherit allergic tendencies or acquire allergies, and it's estimated that one in seven dogs suffers from some type of allergy.

Allergic Skin Disease

Labs are among the breeds that are prone to allergic skin disease. It usually appears when a dog is young—one to three years old. Atopy, which is usually an inherited tendency, is characterized by an itch-scratch cycle that's usually triggered by pollens. Eventually, the dog may begin reacting to all kinds of allergens, from dust and feathers to molds and wool.

Dogs with atopy itch and scratch constantly, resulting in hair loss and scabbing. The skin becomes thick and flaky. It's also not unusual for dogs with atopy to develop other infections that develop as a result of the wounds caused by scratching.

It takes lots of testing to determine whether a dog is suffering from allergic skin disease or some other type of allergy. The veterinarian may order skin scrapings, bacterial and fungal cultures, intradermal skin testing (which involves injecting tiny amounts of known allergens and observing the skin reaction), and even a trial period on a special diet. A good flea-control plan is also important, because FAD can resemble atopy.

Once atopy is diagnosed, there are several ways to manage it. The first is to change the dog's environment—as much as possible—by limiting exposure to known allergens. Antihistamines, essential fatty acid (EFA) supplements, and medicated shampoos can help control itching and scratching. A Lab that suffers severe itching may need intermittent low doses of corticosteroids to relieve itching. When all else fails, allergy shots (hyposensitization) can be given. This involves skin testing (to identify specific allergens) and then desensitizing the dog to these irritants through a series of injections.

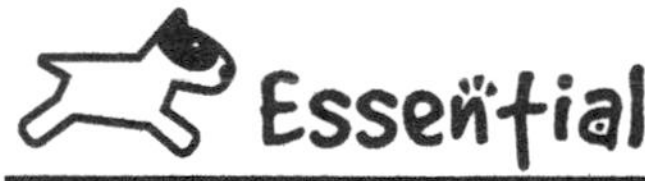

Atopy usually starts out as a seasonal condition but can become a year-round problem if the dog develops multiple allergies to common household or environmental substances, such as wool or house dust.

Flea Allergy Dermatitis (FAD)

A single bite from a single flea can trigger flea-allergy dermatitis, which is the most common allergy seen in dogs. The allergy occurs because many dogs are sensitive to a particular substance in flea saliva. Dogs with FAD itch like crazy, and their skin is inflamed, red, and bumpy. Depending on where you live, FAD can be seasonal or year-round.

The best treatment for FAD is a good flea-control program, so talk to your veterinarian about appropriate products to use. Until fleas are under control, itching can be controlled with antihistamines and—if necessary—short term doses of corticosteroids. Some dogs develop skin infections from chewing at the itchy spots. These can be cleared up with topical (on the skin) and oral (taken by mouth) antibiotics.

Food Allergies

Signs of food allergies are severe itching and red, bumpy, or raised patches of skin. This rash is usually seen on the ears, feet, stomach, and back of the legs. Wheat and corn are common food allergens.

Feeding your Lab a hypoallergenic food won't prevent allergies from developing. These foods contain unusual proteins that most dogs haven't been exposed to, which makes it easier to figure out which ingredients are causing the problem.

When a food allergy is suspected, the veterinarian will recommend putting the dog on a hypoallergenic diet for a certain period of time—usually six to ten weeks. A hypoallergenic diet contains unusual ingredients—catfish and potatoes, for instance—that the dog has likely not encountered before. It's also free of artificial colors, flavors, and preservatives. If the food allergy goes away while the dog is on a hypoallergenic diet, it's necessary to add ingredients back to the diet until the allergenic culprit is identified. Then a homemade or commercial diet can be chosen that doesn't contain the allergy-causing ingredient(s).

Contact Allergies

This type of allergy occurs when a dog comes in contact with a substance that irritates the skin. Common items that contain such irritating substances are soaps and shampoos, plastic or rubber dishes, flea collars, wool or synthetic fibers, and topical medications containing neomycin. If your Lab develops skin irritation on the nose or lips (plastic or rubber dish allergy), irritation or hair loss around the neck (flea collar), or irritation on the feet, legs, and stomach, suspect a contact allergy. Try to identify and remove the offending substance. In the meantime, your veterinarian can prescribe medication to help relieve the itching.

What Are Hot Spots?

These warm, painful, swollen patches of skin usually develop in response to flea bites, allergies, other skin diseases, or lack of grooming (when dead hair gets trapped against the skin). If your Lab gets a hot spot, clip away the hair and clean the skin with chlorhexidine. Severe or numerous hot spots may require a trip to the veterinarian so the dog can be sedated or anesthetized during this procedure. Your veterinarian can also prescribe medication to relieve the itching until the hot spot clears up. Your Lab may need to wear a cone-shaped Elizabethan collar to prevent him from biting or scratching at the area.

Cuts, Scrapes, and Foxtails

There are all kinds of ways that active Labs can acquire cuts, scrapes, or foxtails. For cuts and scrapes, simply clean it with chlorhexidine (Nolvasan), available from your drugstore—unless the wound is deep and requires stitches. (Hydrogen peroxide is out of favor as a wound cleanser because it can cause cellular damage.) Then apply an antibiotic ointment (also available from the drugstore) to help prevent infection. Check the injured area regularly to make sure it's healing nicely and doesn't need veterinary attention. Signs of infection are redness, tenderness, and swelling.

A foxtail is a type of grass with spikes that resembles brushes. Dogs that spend time outdoors—the average Lab, for instance—will most likely encounter foxtails at some point. The grassy heads start to dry in the spring and are most likely to cause problems in summer and early fall. With their sharp ends and microscopic barbs along the sides, foxtails can become embedded in your Lab's eyes, ears, nose, paws, and fur. They can work themselves into the body, causing infection and even death if they migrate to the brain, heart, lungs, or spinal cord.

If you live in an area where foxtails are common, check your Lab for them after every excursion outdoors. Remove any that are clinging to the surface of your Lab's coat or that are outside the ear canal. It may help to soften the foxtail first with mineral oil, vegetable oil, or baby oil. Suspect a foxtail in the ear, eye, nose, or paw if your Lab is shaking his head or pawing at his ears; if he's squinting or his eye appears "glued" shut; if he begins sneezing repetitively or sneezes blood; or if he constantly licks his paw or it appears swollen.

Trying to remove a foxtail from the ear can push it in further, and foxtails can't be flushed from the eye with water or saline solution. Take your Lab to the vet to have these removed.

Diarrhea, Vomiting, and Lack of Appetite

If your Lab's stools appear loose or liquid instead of firm and compact, he has diarrhea. Diarrhea has many causes, ranging from eating something that doesn't agree with the dog's digestive system to intestinal parasites to excitement or anxiety. Some infectious or chronic diseases may also cause diarrhea. Depending on the signs, diarrhea may or may not require a veterinary visit.

If you suspect that your Lab's diarrhea results from anxiety or excitement, or because he stole some spicy or fatty food and is suffering the consequences, withhold food for twenty-four hours, but make sure he has plenty of water to drink—diarrhea can cause dehydration. For the next couple of days, you can feed him a bland diet of skinless boiled chicken with white rice, or cottage cheese. Other easily digestible foods you can give are boiled hamburger meat, cooked macaroni, and soft-boiled eggs. Gradually replace the bland diet with his regular food. If diarrhea continues for more than twenty-four hours, take the dog to the veterinarian. Diarrhea that's bloody, black, or tarry looking or that's accompanied by vomiting, weakness, or fever calls for an immediate veterinary visit.

It's not unusual for Labs to eat gravel or even rocks. If your Lab starts throwing up gravel or has intermittent vomiting and diarrhea, an intestinal obstruction may be the problem. Surgery may be necessary for large objects such as rocks, but if your dog eats gravel your veterinarian may suggest dosing him with mineral oil for a week to clear out the tiny stones.

Like diarrhea, vomiting can be caused by any number of problems, including anxiety or excitement, eating too quickly, or eating something that doesn't agree with the digestive system. Vomiting is also a sign of some infectious or chronic diseases. If your Lab is healthy and you suspect the vomiting is related to eating something that didn't agree with him, withhold food and water for twelve hours, then feed a bland meal, such as boiled chicken and rice. Give only one or two tablespoons at first to make sure your dog can keep the food down. If he can, gradually return him to his regular diet. Take your Lab to the vet if he has projectile (violent) vomiting, if the vomit smells like feces, if the vomiting is accompanied by diarrhea, if the vomiting continues even though the dog hasn't had any food, or if the vomit contains blood or worms.

Labs love to eat, so a consistent lack of appetite is cause for concern. Not wanting to eat can have any number of causes, from poor dental health (when it hurts to chew) to viral diseases, such as distemper or infectious canine hepatitis. Any time your Lab loses interest in food—especially if appetite loss is accompanied by lethargy or other signs of problems—take him to the veterinarian.

Lumps and Bumps

Dogs can develop all kinds of lumps and bumps on or beneath the skin. Some are harmless while others require veterinary intervention. Look (and feel) for lumps and bumps whenever you groom your Lab.

Abscesses, Hematomas, and Adenomas

A soft, painful lump may be an abscess or hematoma. An abscess is an infected area caused by a bite or puncture wound, whereas a hematoma is a blood clot beneath the skin. Ear hematomas are common in dogs. Abscesses must be drained by the veterinarian and treated with antibiotics, whereas some hematomas disappear on their own—if they don't they must also be drained by the veterinarian.

Some lumps look like small, smooth, pink warts and appear on the eyelids or legs. These benign (harmless) tumors are sebaceous adenomas and are commonly seen in older dogs. Tumors on the eyelids should be removed to prevent damage to the cornea.

Ceruminous (wax-producing) gland adenomas can develop in the ear canal. They're a pinkish-white color and dome-shaped. Sometimes they become ulcerated or infected. Small tumors of this type are usually harmless, but large ones can become invasive and must be treated with surgery and radiation therapy.

Warts and Cysts

Papillomas (warts) are caused by a virus and can grow on the skin or inside the mouth. They are usually harmless and don't need to be removed unless they're causing a problem because of their location on the body.

Cysts are firm lumps beneath the skin. They form when hair follicles become blocked with hair and a cheesy material called sebum. Cysts are generally harmless, but they can become infected and may need to be drained surgically or removed.

Skin melanomas are usually harmless, but melanomas in the mouth and nail bed are usually malignant. They should be removed surgically, but they often recur. Dogs with melanomas in the mouth don't have a good prognosis.

Skin Cancer

Dogs can develop several different types of skin cancer: basal cell tumors, mast cell tumors, melanomas, and squamous cell carcinomas. Fortunately, none of these conditions are especially common in Labrador Retrievers.

Basal cell tumors are common, usually occurring on the head and neck. They feel firm and have distinct borders. Surgical removal is the best treatment. Mast cell tumors make up 10 to 20 percent of the skin tumors seen in dogs. They have many nodules and usually look red, hairless, and ulcerated. Mast cell tumors can be either benign (harmless) or malignant (harmful) and should be removed surgically. Dogs with malignant mast cell tumors may also need radiation or chemotherapy.

Melanomas develop from cells in the skin that produce melanin, which is what gives your Lab the dark pigment on his nose and skin. Melanomas look like brown or black nodules and can occur on the eyelids, lips, in the mouth, on the nail beds, and elsewhere on the body.

Squamous cell carcinomas are caused by exposure to the ultraviolet radiation in sunlight. They're usually found on lightly pigmented areas of the body. Appearance ranges from a firm red patch to a cauliflowerlike growth to a hard, flat, grayish-looking ulcer that doesn't heal. They can be removed surgically or treated with radiation therapy if surgery isn't possible.

Tumors

Other lumps that you might find on your Lab are perianal gland tumors or venereal tumors. Perianal gland tumors are solitary or multinodular growths around the anal area and occur in older males that haven't been neutered. The tumors are removed surgically, and the dog is neutered. Radiation and chemotherapy may be necessary for malignant tumors.

Venereal tumors, which can resemble cauliflower or single nodules on a stalk, are unusual. They're spread sexually or by licking, biting, or scratching. Chemotherapy is the usual treatment, and spaying or neutering is recommended as well.

Orthopedic Problems

Musculoskeletal problems, which affect the bones, joints, and muscles, are common in dogs, and Labs are no exception. As a breed, they are prone to hip and elbow dysplasia and osteochondritis dissecans. Other problems that can occur include ruptured cruciated ligament and toe injuries.

If your veterinarian determines that your puppy has unusually loose hip joints, you may want to look into a surgical technique to close the area between the two halves of the pelvis. The surgery must be performed before five months of age, so the pup must be evaluated early.

Hip Dysplasia

Hip dysplasia occurs when the head of the thigh bone (femur) doesn't fit properly into the hip socket, causing joint laxity (looseness), inflammation, pain, and lameness. Signs of hip dysplasia include limping and a lack of enthusiasm for exercise—very unusual in an active Lab puppy! An x-ray of the hips and pelvis can confirm whether there's a problem. In mild cases, nutraceuticals, such as glucosamine and chondroitin, and pain-relieving medications, can help a Lab get along. When hip dysplasia is severe, though, total hip replacement is the best treatment.

Elbow Dysplasia

Elbow dysplasia is caused by the failure of the elbow bones of one or both forelegs to unite and move properly, or by bone fragments within the joint. Lameness is the primary sign of elbow dysplasia, and the problem can be confirmed with x-rays. Like hip dysplasia, it can often be managed with nutraceuticals and anti-inflammatory medications. Exercise, such as swimming and walks on leash, can help maintain the range of joint motion and strengthen the surrounding muscles, improving joint stability and the health of the joint fluid. Severe elbow dysplasia may require surgery to fuse the joint and relieve the pain.

Osteochondritis Dissecans (OCD)

Osteochondritis dissecans (OCD) is a problem of cartilage development that usually affects shoulder joints but can also affect the elbow, hocks, and stifles (knees). Labs with OCD may gradually become lame or show pain when the affected joint is flexed or extended. X-rays provide a definitive diagnosis. The recommended treatment for OCD is rest and joint-protective nutraceuticals to help prevent pain, inflammation, and further degeneration. If the elbow or shoulder joints are affected, your veterinarian may advise surgery to scrape away defective cartilage or remove cartilage flaps loose in the joint.

Ruptured Cruciate Ligament

Also known as an anterior cruciate ligament (ACL) tear, this is a common injury in retrievers. It usually occurs when the knee twists suddenly or hyperextends. ACL tears are one of the major causes of arthritis in the canine knee joint. If your Lab suffers an ACL tear, you'll know. He'll hold up the injured leg or cry out. The knee joint will be swollen and painful. A surgical procedure called tibial plateau leveling osteotomy (TPLO) is the best treatment.

If an ACL tear occurs in one knee, the ligament in the other knee is likely to tear at some time in the future.

Toe Injuries

Active dogs are likely to suffer toe injuries at some point. These can range from a broken toenail to a dislocated or sprained toe. Toes can become broken, dislocated (rupture of ligaments), or sprained (rupture of tendons) if the dog bangs the toe hard against something, steps in a hole, or lands wrong from a jump. A toe injury might be the problem if your Lab is limping.

Sometimes toes heal on their own, but surgery may be necessary to repair the structure. Run any toe injuries by your veterinarian to make sure they're not serious. An x-ray can find slight fractures that might otherwise be missed.

When nails are kept short, broken toenails are unlikely. If your Lab does break a toenail while running or by snagging it on carpet fibers, the injury is likely to bleed profusely. It looks scary, but you can stop the bleeding by putting pressure on the wound with a cloth or towel until the bleeding stops. If the toenail doesn't break off cleanly, it's a good idea to take the dog to the veterinarian to have it removed. Removal can be painful and may require anesthesia. Usually, the toenail will grow back.

Eye Diseases

Common eye diseases in Labs are retinal dysplasia, cataracts, and progressive retinal atrophy. These hereditary problems can be screened for before dogs are bred. Ask the breeder for documentation from the Canine Eye Registry Foundation (CERF) that your pup's parents are free of these conditions.

The term retinal dysplasia applies to a number of conditions in which the retina doesn't develop properly. Some are acquired, while others are hereditary, and Labs are among the breeds in which inherited retinal dysplasias are found. It's sometimes the case that Labs with skeletal abnormalities also have retinal dysplasia, and it may be that the same gene causes both problems. Signs of retinal dysplasia range from lines or curves on the back part of the eye—known as retinal folds—to generalized retinal detachment. Some dogs with retinal dysplasia have little visual loss, but blindness results if the retina detaches.

Researchers at the University of California at Davis Institute of Genetic Disease Control have established a registry for Labradors diagnosed with tricuspid valve dysplasia (TVD), so they can track the disease's prevalence and mode of inheritance in the breed. Ask the breeder if your pup's parents have been screened by echocardiogram to be free of TVD.

A cataract is an opaque spot on the eye's lens, which is normally clear. Cataracts can be acquired as a consequence of aging or are inherited, and can eventually lead to vision loss. Labs are one of the breeds in which congenital, or juvenile, cataracts have been documented. With their great sense of smell, Labs can get around just fine without their eyesight, but if necessary, cataracts can be removed surgically.

Progressive retinal atrophy (PRA) is an inherited degeneration of the retina that results in lowered vision or blindness. Signs of PRA are fear of the dark and obvious night blindness. This eye disease has no treatment or cure, although genetic research is promising. The best way to prevent PRA is to breed only Labs that are certified free of PRA.

Tricuspid Valve Dysplasia (TVD)

This congenital (meaning it's present from birth) heart disorder is increasingly common in Labrador Retrievers, and it is believed to be inherited. A deformity of the heart's tricuspid valve causes abnormal blood flow and increases the workload of the right side of the heart. Eventually, the dog suffers congestive heart failure. Signs of TVD include a heart murmur or lack of energy. An echocardiogram (ultrasound) is the best way to diagnose TVD, but electrocardiography (EKG) or x-rays may also be used.

Unfortunately, there's no treatment or cure for TVD. Drugs can be given to control fluid retention and help regulate the heart, but the life expectancy for a dog with TVD is only one to three years. Sometimes dogs don't show signs until congestive heart failure occurs.

Epilepsy

Epilepsy is a brain disorder that causes recurrent seizures—convulsions that are set off by abnormal bursts of electrical activity in the brain. It's one of the most common neurologic diseases in dogs, and some forms are heritable. Inherited epilepsy is referred to as idiopathic, meaning the cause is unknown. Labs are one of the breeds prone to idiopathic epilepsy.

The length of epileptic seizures can range from a few seconds to a few minutes. In rare cases, they can continue for an hour or more. Mild forms of epilepsy can be treated with medication to control the seizures. There's no screening test for epilepsy, and it often doesn't appear until a dog is older. The incidence of epilepsy can be reduced through selective breeding, however. The breeder should be able to tell you the frequency of epilepsy in his or her dogs.

Emergencies

THE INJURIES AND ILLNESSES DESCRIBED in the previous chapter can be serious, but they're not emergencies. An emergency is a life-threatening situation. It's to be hoped that your Lab will never suffer an injury or illness that's an emergency, but it never hurts to be prepared. Knowing what to do for fractures, bites, choking, and other dangerous health circumstances will help you stay calm and give your Lab a better chance at survival.

First-Aid Kit

A first-aid kit for dogs is much like one for humans. You can probably use the same one you keep on hand for your family, or you can put together a separate one for your Lab.

Keep the first-aid kit in your bathroom or on top of your dog's crate, so it's easily accessible when you need it. Make sure everyone in the family knows where the first-aid kit is in case you may need to send one of them to find it some day. The following items, available from drugstores, should be part of any well-stocked first-aid kit:

- Ace bandage
- Adhesive tape
- Antibiotic ointment
- Blunt scissors
- Gauze pads and rolls
- Muzzle
- Needle-nose pliers

- Compressed activated charcoal
- Cotton balls
- Cotton-tip applicators
- Disinfectant, such as chlorhexidine (Nolvasan) or povidone iodine (Betadine)
- Eye dropper
- Petroleum jelly
- Rectal thermometer (bulb or digital)
- Rubbing alcohol
- Sterile saline eye wash
- Surgical gloves
- Tweezers

Other useful items to have on hand are a blanket to keep the dog warm in case of shock, and clean towels or cloths for putting pressure on wounds that are bleeding. A penlight is helpful for examining eyes, mouth, and ears. Keep the phone numbers for your veterinarian's office, your veterinarian's on-call pager, the nearest animal emergency hospital, and a local or national poison-control center by your telephone or in the first-aid kit.

How to Muzzle Your Lab

When a dog is hurt and scared, he's liable to bite at anyone who tries to handle him, no matter how friendly he is normally or how much he loves the person trying to help him. A muzzle can keep your Lab from accidentally biting you, making it easier to care for him as needed. Before you try to examine him, put a muzzle on him, as a precaution for both of you.

Whatever muzzle you choose should be designed to allow the dog to breathe easily. It should be open at the end in case the dog throws up. Look for one with an adjustable-length strap and easy snap-in or Velcro fastener.

Muzzles can be made of cloth, nylon, or leather, and come in several different styles. Basket-style muzzles have a leather, wire, or plastic front that looks like a woven basket. A strap fastens the muzzle behind the dog's head. Some muzzles are made of fabric and are placed over the dog's nose and mouth, with a strap that goes around the head to hold it in place. Others fit around the nose and mouth with a strap that fastens behind the head. A soft cloth muzzle that fastens in the back with Velcro is probably easiest to use.

To put the muzzle on, kneel or stand at the dog's side rather than coming at it with the muzzle from the front. Slide the muzzle over the dog's nose and mouth and fasten it behind the head. If possible, have someone else hold the dog while you put the muzzle on. Speak soothingly during the process. It's a good idea to try the muzzle on your Lab before you need it so that it will already be properly adjusted for size if you need to put it on in a hurry.

Are there any times you shouldn't muzzle an injured dog? Yes. Never muzzle a dog that's unconscious or one that's coughing, vomiting, has a mouth injury, or is having difficulty breathing. And trying to put a muzzle on a dog that's actively resisting it by biting or snarling is not worth the risk of being bitten.

Does Your Lab Need CPR?

Cardiopulmonary resuscitation, or CPR, combines artificial respiration and heart massage. Artificial respiration is the act of breathing into a dog's nose to get the lungs going again when breathing has stopped. Heart massage is a series of chest compressions to help restart a heart that has stopped beating.

Before performing CPR, it's important to make sure the dog really needs it. Performing CPR on a dog that is still breathing or whose heart is beating can cause further injury. To check for breathing, see if the dog's chest is rising and falling–the chest movement may be very shallow. You can also hold a mirror to the dog's mouth to see if breath causes the mirror to fog.

Feel for a pulse to see if the heart is beating. Place your fingers on the femoral artery in the groin area (the inside of the hind leg). If the dog's heart is beating, you'll feel a pulse. If the dog has a pulse but isn't breathing, perform artificial respiration. If the dog is breathing, but doesn't have a pulse, perform chest compressions.

When the dog isn't breathing and doesn't have a pulse, you can perform CPR.

CPR is most effective when two people can work on the dog: one to perform rescue breathing and one to perform chest compressions. Emergencies that might call for the use of CPR include choking, electrical shock, or a traumatic injury that causes the heart and lungs to stop.

Rescue Breathing

Place your Lab on a flat surface, right side down. Open his mouth and pull his tongue forward. Wearing surgical gloves, swipe your fingers through the mouth to check for any foreign bodies and remove them if possible.

Place your hand around the muzzle to prevent air from escaping, and blow gently into the nose every two to three seconds. You should see the chest rise and fall. If you don't, blow more forcefully. Continue until the dog starts breathing again on his own, or until the heart stops beating.

Performing Chest Compressions

Position the dog in the same way as for rescue breathing. Kneel behind his back, and place the heel of one hand over the widest part of the rib cage (not over the heart). Rest the heel of the other hand on top of the first. With elbows straight, push down firmly for one count, then release for one count. Try to perform eighty compressions per minute. If the dog's heart doesn't start beating within ten minutes, you're not likely to be successful.

Performing CPR

Position the dog in the same way as for rescue breathing or chest compressions. Give five compressions, followed by one breath. If you have another person helping you, give one breath after every two to three compressions. Continue for ten minutes or until the dog's breathing resumes and his pulse is steady, whichever comes first.

Never do CPR, chest compressions, or rescue breathing on a healthy dog "for practice." You could seriously injure him. Instead, sign up for one of the pet first-aid/CPR workshops offered by the American Red Cross.

How to Move an Injured Dog

As you probably learned at some point in your life, it can be dangerous to move a person with an injury. The same is true for dogs. If your Lab is injured and must be moved out of harm's way or transported to a veterinary hospital, you can take steps to minimize potential injuries from moving him.

If you must pick your dog up, keep the injured side away from your body. Lift him by placing one arm around his chest or between his front legs. Support his rear with your other arm. If a hind leg is injured, place your arm between the hind legs. Don't forget to bend your knees and lift with your legs; it's much easier on your back.

Another way to move the dog is to lay him on a blanket or a large, flat, sturdy piece of wood. This can then be used as a stretcher, but it will require two to four people to carry the dog (assuming it's a full-grown Lab). In the car, cushion the dog with pillows, towels, or rolled blankets. Keep him warm with a blanket or towel to help ward off shock.

Dealing with Emergencies

Remember that an emergency is a life-threatening situation. The purpose of first aid is to keep the dog alive until he can receive veterinary help. By dealing with it quickly and calmly, you can greatly increase your Lab's chances of survival. Here's how to recognize some common emergencies and what to do for them.

Bleeding

No matter what kind of injury your Lab has, if he's bleeding, that's what should be dealt with first. Dogs can bleed to death in a matter of minutes if blood flow isn't controlled quickly. The first thing to determine is whether the bleeding is from an artery (bright red and spurting) or from a vein (darker red and slower flowing). Arterial bleeding is most serious, but in both cases, you need to put pressure on the wound and keep it there until bleeding stops.

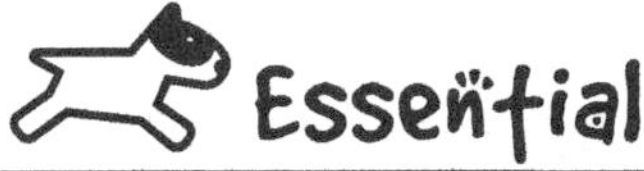

Tourniquets can do more harm than good and should be used only as a last resort. Ask your veterinarian to show you how to apply one. Never use a tourniquet on any wound that can be controlled by direct pressure.

Using sterile gauze bandages (ideally) or in a pinch any type of cloth—from a towel to a T-shirt—apply firm, consistent pressure to the wound. It may take five to ten minutes for bleeding to stop completely.

Traumatic injuries, such as being hit by a car, and certain poisons can cause internal bleeding. Signs of internal bleeding are bleeding from the nose, mouth, or rectum; coughing blood; blood in urine; pale gums; and collapse. Keep your Lab warm and get him to the veterinarian as soon as possible.

Bloat

Sometimes referred to as gastric torsion or gastric dilatation volvulus, bloat occurs when the stomach fills up with gas and fluids and then twists. It's sort of like blowing up a balloon and tying it off. Bloat usually affects large, deep-chested dogs, including Labrador Retrievers.

Alert!

You can help prevent bloat by feeding your Lab three times a day instead of once or twice. Restrict access to water immediately before and after meals, and limit the amount of water he drinks at one time. Strenuous exercise directly after eating can lead to bloat, so put your Lab in his crate for a nap after every meal.

The trapped gases and fluids cause abdominal pain, signaled by shallow breathing or a dull, vacant, or pained expression. The stomach looks stretched out and sounds hollow like a drum if thumped. Other signs of bloat include pacing restlessly, sluggish behavior, gagging, drooling, and unsuccessful attempts to throw up. Because the stomach is tied off, a dog with bloat is unable to vomit or belch. As the condition worsens, the pulse weakens, the gums become pale, and the dog collapses.

Bloat is not a condition where you want to take a wait-and-see attitude. If you even suspect it's a possibility, take your Lab to the veterinarian or to the emergency hospital if it's in the middle of the night. The earlier bloat is recognized and treated, the better chance your Lab has of surviving.

The veterinarian will pass a long plastic or rubber tube through the mouth and into the stomach, allowing air and fluid to escape. X-rays can determine whether the stomach is twisted, a condition that requires emergency surgery to return the stomach and spleen to their correct positions. Suturing the wall of the stomach to the abdominal wall helps prevent bloat from recurring.

Broken Bones

Your Lab might break a bone from a bad fall or from being hit by a car. Assume that a bone is broken if your Lab can't stand on a leg, if a bone is protruding through the skin, or if the dog can't move (a spinal injury, perhaps). Immediate veterinary care is a priority, but first you need to stabilize the dog.

After muzzling him for safety, pad a movable flat surface, such as a board or tarp with blankets or towels. Lay the dog on it and secure him so he doesn't fall off. If the break has caused an open wound, cover it with sterile gauze pads or a clean cloth, wrapping the cover loosely with a bandage to keep it on. Don't try to set a broken leg. It's most important to keep the dog warm and get him to a veterinarian quickly. After treatment, broken bones take eight to twelve weeks to heal.

Choking

Your Lab can choke if something gets caught in his throat, such as a piece of rawhide. Suspect an obstruction if your Lab is pawing at his mouth, gagging or retching, or having difficulty breathing. If coughing doesn't dislodge the object and your Lab is conscious, get him to the veterinarian to have it removed. Trying to get your fingers around it to pull it out can push it further into the throat.

If your Lab loses consciousness because he can't breathe, lay him on his side, open his mouth, pull his tongue forward, and sweep your fingers through the mouth to see if you can grasp the object and remove it. Then perform rescue breathing or CPR if necessary. If it doesn't come out easily, move on to the Heimlich maneuver.

If the Heimlich maneuver doesn't work, try holding the dog's hind legs in the air and thumping his back between the shoulder blades with the heel of your hand. When the object is dislodged, perform rescue breathing or CPR as needed. Take the dog to the veterinarian for an exam to make sure he's okay.

To perform the Heimlich maneuver on a dog, hold him with his back against your chest and your arms around his waist. With your hands at the dog's upper midabdomen (just behind the last rib), make a fist with one hand and grasp it with the other hand. Quickly thrust up and in with the fist four or five times. This forces a burst of air through the larynx, which should dislodge the object.

Deep Cuts or Lacerations

Stop bleeding as described above. When bleeding has stopped, clean the area around the wound with povidone iodine or chlorhexidine to reduce the risk of tetanus or other infection. Be sure not to touch the wound with either product, as they can sting and irritate the skin. Then flush the wound with tap water until it looks clean. Don't rub the wound with anything—not even a gauze pad—or you could start the bleeding again. When the edges of a wound gape open or when cuts or lacerations are more than ½ inch long, the veterinarian should close the wound with stitches.

Electrocution

Chomping into a plugged-in electric cord or coming into contact with downed wires can cause burns or even death from electric shock. If you find your Lab unconscious near an electrical outlet, never touch the dog. Shut off the main power and pull the plug. Then administer rescue breathing or CPR as needed. If CPR is effective, take the dog to the veterinarian as soon as possible for further treatment.

Dogs that are shocked but don't lose consciousness may cough, have difficulty breathing, drool, or have a strange odor in the mouth from electrical burns. Take them to the veterinarian. Mouth burns from electrical shock can heal on their own, but some dogs develop an ulcer at the burn site. If the ulcer doesn't heal, it may need to be removed surgically.

Fishhooks

Labs were originally fishermen's dogs, and they still enjoy being out on boats and around water. If you enjoy fishing with your Lab, there's a chance that he may one day have a sharp encounter with a fishhook. Keep a pair of wire cutters handy for just such an eventuality.

A fishhook stuck in the skin must be pushed all the way through in the direction the barb is going. Don't try to pull it out. When the barb is visible, you can then cut it off with the wire cutters and pull the rest of the hook through. Treat the resulting puncture wound as described on page 257.

If your Lab swallows a fishhook or has the hook embedded in his mouth, don't try to remove it on your own. Get the dog to the veterinarian as soon as possible. To prevent such an injury, keep fishhooks well out of reach, and pay attention to the surroundings any time you're walking your Lab around a lake or other area where fishing is common.

Heatstroke

Too much activity on a hot, humid day can lay your Lab low with heatstroke. Supervise your Lab's activity level in the dog days of summer, and make sure he always has plenty of fresh water and access to shade if he's outdoors. Never leave your Lab shut up in a car or truck on a hot or even a sunny day. Even if the windows are cracked and the car is parked in the shade, temperatures can reach dangerous levels in a matter of minutes.

Signs of heatstroke are heavy panting and difficulty breathing. The tongue and mucous membranes appear bright red. Your Lab may drool thick saliva or start vomiting. Body temperature can rise to 104°F or higher. If left untreated, the dog goes into shock, collapses, and dies. Never let the situation become this dire.

At the first signs of heatstroke, move the dog into an air-conditioned area if possible and begin cooling him with cold water. Bathe him with wet towels or use a spray bottle to wet him down. You can also place the wet dog in front of a fan to help lower his temperature. Take the dog's temperature every ten minutes. When the temperature falls below 103°F, you can stop cooling the dog and dry him off.

Take the dog to the veterinarian as soon as possible. Heatstroke is associated with breathing problems, seizures, and other serious conditions, which can develop hours after the dog has seemingly recovered.

Hypothermia and Frostbite

Just as heatstroke is caused by extreme heat, hypothermia and frostbite result from extreme cold. Hypothermia is excessively low body temperature. Frostbite, which often accompanies hypothermia, occurs when a part of the body—usually an extremity such as a paw or ear—freezes.

The Lab's double coat helps protect it from hypothermia. Nonetheless, puppies and old dogs, dogs submerged in cold water for long periods, and Labs without the correct double coat can fall victim to this condition. Signs of hypothermia include shivering, lethargy, and a body temperature below 95°F (remember that a dog's normal temperature range is 100 to 102.5°F). To treat hypothermia, warm the dog by wrapping it in blankets. Dry wet dogs thoroughly. Call the veterinarian if the dog's temperature is below 95°F.

Suspect frostbite if your Lab's skin looks pale white or blue. Apply warm compresses to the frostbitten area until the tissue begins to regain color. Take the dog to the veterinarian as soon as possible. You may have heard that it's a good idea to massage frostbitten areas or to rub them with snow or ice, but that's not true and can cause further damage.

Insect Bites and Stings

Bees, wasps, and other insects can inflict stings or bites that cause allergic reactions. These reactions can include hives (raised circular areas on the skin), swelling, rashes, itching, and watery eyes. Minor reactions, such as a rash or itching can be treated with calamine lotion or a paste made of baking soda. Ice packs help reduce pain and swelling.

A bite or sting on the face or neck can cause dangerous swelling that closes off the dog's airway. Anaphylactic shock is a systemwide reaction characterized by agitation, diarrhea, vomiting, difficulty breathing, and collapse. Any time your Lab has these signs, take him to the veterinarian immediately.

Poisoning

Labs will eat just about anything on the off chance that it might be food, and poisons are no exception. Snail bait, putrefying animals, garbage, drugs, rodent poisons, antifreeze, household medications, plants, and insecticides are all sources that can poison your Lab. Here's what to do if your best efforts at Lab-proofing your home and yard fail.

If you see your Lab eat something that you know or suspect is toxic, the first thing to do is to confirm what its ingredients are. Look on the label or call the National Animal Poison Control Center (contact information listed in Appendix A). Depending on the substance, you may be advised to induce vomiting by giving the dog hydrogen peroxide. The usual dose is one teaspoon for every 10 pounds the dog weighs. Give the appropriate amount every twenty minutes, up to three times, until the dog throws up. After the dog vomits, give a 5-gram tablet of compressed activated charcoal from your first-aid kit. The activated charcoal prevents absorption of any remaining poison in the dog's stomach. Take your dog to the veterinarian for further treatment.

Antifreeze has a sweet taste, and antifreeze poisoning is common in dogs. Signs of antifreeze poisoning are depression, vomiting, and seizures. The dog may have an uncoordinated walk, as if it's drunk. If you see these signs, take your dog to the vet immediately.

Do not induce vomiting in the following instances:

- When the dog has already thrown up.
- When the dog is unconscious, convulsing, or having problems breathing.
- When the dog has swallowed an acid, alkali, cleaning solution, household chemical, or petroleum product.
- When the dog has swallowed a sharp object.
- When the label on the substance advises against inducing vomiting.

Some poisons are absorbed through the skin. If your Lab comes in contact with a toxic substance, flush the area with water for thirty minutes, then bathe the dog in lukewarm water. Be sure to wear plastic or rubber gloves to protect yourself from the poison.

If your Lab gets into the garbage or eats a dead animal, he can suffer bacterial poisoning. Suspect garbage poisoning if your Lab appears to have a stomach ache, has bad breath, vomits, and has diarrhea. Garbage poisoning can be fatal, so don't hesitate to take your Lab to the vet if he shows these signs.

Signs of poisoning may not become apparent for several days. Suspect poisoning if your Lab is weak or shows signs of internal bleeding, such as nosebleeds, or bleeding from the mouth or rectum. Take him to the veterinarian immediately. If possible, bring the packaging of the suspected poison with you.

Puncture Wounds and Animal Bites

Puncture wounds are caused by sharp, pointed objects, such as nails, barbed wire, or jagged pieces of wood. Treat a puncture wound the same way you would a bite wound. As long as you clean the wound promptly, your Lab shouldn't need a tetanus shot.

If another animal bites your Lab, it's important to clean the wound as soon as possible. Bite wounds are chock full of bacteria from the other animal's mouth. If you know your dog has been bitten, stop any bleeding and then clean the wound with povidone iodine or an 0.05 percent solution of chlorhexidine, a disinfectant that's effective against bacteria, viruses, fungus, and yeast. If you suspect the animal that bit your dog was rabid, notify your veterinarian immediately. If the bite is severe, your Lab may need stitches. A course of antibiotics can help ward off any infections.

Don't attempt to treat a snakebite by sucking out the venom, making cuts over the wound, applying ice, or washing the wound. All of these actions are either dangerous to you or can make the situation worse.

Labs that spend a lot of time in the field are at risk of snakebite, as are dogs that live in areas where snakes are common. Teeth marks in the shape of a horseshoe usually indicate a bite from a nonpoisonous snake. An exception is a bite from the venomous coral snake, which also leaves a horseshoe-shaped mark. The bite of a poisonous snake leaves fang marks (one or two bleeding puncture wounds in the skin) and usually causes pain and swelling. Signs of poisoning from a snake bite include restlessness, panting, drooling, vomiting, diarrhea, an uncoordinated gait, shallow breathing, and shock. Left untreated, a bite from a poisonous snake can kill a dog.

If your Lab is bitten by a poisonous snake, keep him still to prevent the venom from spreading too rapidly. Carry the dog if you can, and get him to the veterinarian as quickly as possible for antivenin, supportive treatment, and antihistamines. Clean and care for the wound as described on page 257. Ⓔ

The Senior Labrador Retriever

No dog ever lives long enough, but Labrador owners can look forward to spending ten to thirteen years with their dogs. That's the typical Labrador life span, although some dogs may have longer or shorter lives depending on such factors as genetic heritage, nutrition, and level of care. As Labs age, their veterinary and nutritional needs change, and they may develop certain health problems associated with age. Fortunately, they can benefit from the many advances in veterinary medicine, as well as regular health testing, appropriate diet, and exercise. The following tips will help your Lab stay healthy and comfortable in his golden years.

When Is a Dog Old?

The traditional age at which dogs are considered seniors is seven years. The way Labs age is as individual as their personalities. Some Labs still act like pups at ten years of age, while others start slowing down much earlier. Signs of aging include the following physical changes:

- A graying muzzle
- A thinner coat
- Less energy
- Poor dental health
- Haziness of the eye lens
- Cataracts

- Decreased sense of smell
- Stiff or painful joints
- Less tolerance of temperature extremes

Other signs of aging include weight gain or weight loss, changes in appetite, more frequent urination caused by excessive thirst, and poor skin condition. If your Lab starts showing any of these signs, it's a good idea to schedule a geriatric exam for him. If you start screening your dog at age seven for diseases associated with aging, you and your veterinarian are more likely to catch problems while they can still be dealt with easily. There are many new diets, medications, and procedures that can help ease your Lab's transition to this new period of his life.

One of the oldest dogs on record was a black Lab named Adjutant. He lived to be twenty-seven years and three months old.

A Golden-Age Health Exam

Even if your Lab is still frisky as a pup, a geriatric screening exam, starting at age seven, establishes a basis for comparison as he grows older. The typical geriatric exam includes bloodwork or other diagnostic tests to determine the status of your Lab's organ function and body chemistry, as well as a physical exam to check dental health and skin condition. Because dogs age at a more rapid pace than humans—the equivalent of five to seven years for every chronological year that passes—changes can occur quickly. For that reason, if your Lab does develop a health problem, it's a good idea to schedule checkups every six months instead of every year.

▲ An eleven-year-old chocolate female Lab enjoys being outside.

At some point, your Lab may show behavioral changes related to aging, such as disorientation or a different sleep pattern. Don't assume that nothing can be done. Your veterinarian may recommend lifestyle changes that can help—a change in diet, an increase in exercise—or prescribe medication that can improve the situation. Simply reducing stress by providing a stable routine is also beneficial.

Nutrition

Does your Lab need a different diet as he grows older? A dog's nutritional needs do indeed change with age. Older dogs tend to be less active, so they need fewer calories to maintain an appropriate weight. They also need a food that's high in protein, because the body is able to metabolize protein less efficiently.

Many foods are available to meet the needs of older dogs. Look for a diet that contains about 25 percent protein, with a reduced concentration of fat and calories. Such diets may also be higher in fiber to further reduce caloric density. This means the food gives your Lab a feeling of fullness, without the added calories of a maintenance diet. You can do the same thing by slightly reducing the amount of dog food you give and adding plain canned pumpkin (not the sweetened kind) to your dog's meals.

You may have heard that a high-protein diet is bad for dogs because protein stresses the kidneys. Although a low-protein diet may be prescribed for dogs with kidney disease, it's not necessary to restrict protein for normal, healthy dogs, no matter what their age.

What about Supplements?

We are usually told that dogs don't need vitamin or mineral supplements as long as they're eating a balanced diet. Nonetheless, supplements can sometimes be beneficial for older dogs. For instance, your veterinarian may recommend a B-vitamin supplement if your Lab has reduced kidney function, or fatty acids, vitamin E, and zinc supplements to help dogs with dry, itchy skin. Talk to your veterinarian about whether a supplement can improve your older Lab's condition.

Decreased Appetite

You may notice that your Lab's appetite isn't as good as it once was. Sometimes this can be attributed to a decrease in his sense of smell. You can make meals more appetizing by warming food in the microwave to increase the scent—do the finger test to make sure it's not too hot—or adding some canned food or low-sodium beef or chicken broth.

When should you be concerned about your Lab's nutritional status? Rapid, unexplained weight loss is always something to be concerned about. If your Lab starts losing weight, even though he's eating the same amount of food and getting the same amount of exercise, take him to the veterinarian for a checkup. He could have a serious health problem.

◀ A 11½-year-old female yellow Lab.

Problems of Aging

Your Lab may get the best care and diet available, but age-related disorders are inevitable. The problems your Lab may face as he ages include arthritis, cancer, cognitive dysfunction syndrome, diabetes, hearing loss, hypothyroidism, kidney disease, laryngeal paralysis, and vision loss. Fortunately, veterinary medicine has many ways of dealing with these problems, especially if they're diagnosed in the early stages.

Arthritis

This painful degenerative joint disease commonly affects older dogs. Over eight million dogs in the United States have been diagnosed with arthritis, and more than 80 percent of them are aged seven years or older. Signs of arthritis include a lowered activity level; lagging on walks; reluctance to run, jump, or climb stairs; stiffness when getting up or lying down; soreness when touched; and swollen joints that seem hot or painful. Arthritis pain can also cause dogs to behave abnormally. They may snarl or snap if touched in a painful area.

There's no cure for arthritis, but you can take a number of steps to help your Lab feel more comfortable. Weight loss relieves stress on joints, and anti-inflammatory medications reduce pain and inflammation.

To help deal with arthritis, your veterinarian may prescribe a nonsteroidal anti-inflammatory drug (NSAID), such as carprofen or etodolac. While canine NSAIDs have provided excellent results for many dogs, they are not innocuous drugs and can have side effects, including vomiting, diarrhea, and liver or kidney damage. Be aware that some Labs are highly sensitive to these types of drugs, and some have even died suddenly after being given them. Be sure you understand the potential risks and side effects as explained by your veterinarian. It's a good idea to have liver and kidney values checked every three months if your Lab is taking a canine NSAID. In fact, your veterinarian will probably require it before renewing any prescription.

Supplements that contain glycosaminoglycans (GAGs) or glucosamine, chondroitin, and ester C are believed to support joint flexibility and mobility. These supplements, known as nutraceuticals, often help to relieve the pain of arthritic dogs, especially in mild cases. The advantage of nutraceuticals is that they rarely cause side effects. Occasionally, a dog given nutraceuticals will have vomiting or diarrhea, which is treated by slightly reducing the dose. Glucosamine can also cause a dog to drink more water than usual and sometimes prolongs bleeding time, which means the blood doesn't clot as well. These side effects are unusual, though. Be aware that nutraceuticals aren't a quick fix. It can take up to two months to see results.

Ibuprofen, acetaminophen, and other nonsteroidal anti-inflammatory drugs (NSAIDs) are great for relieving pain in people, but they can be toxic to dogs. Never give your Lab ibuprofen or any similar anti-inflammatory. Your veterinarian may prescribe aspirin in small doses to relieve pain, but you should never give it without checking with your vet first, so you don't give too much.

Cancer

Cancer occurs when cells grow uncontrollably on or inside the body. These uncontrolled growths may remain in a single area or spread to other parts of the body. Labs as a breed aren't particularly prone to cancer, but all dogs run a higher risk of developing cancer as they age. Common types of cancer seen in dogs are mamary (breast) cancer, skin tumors (see Chapter 18), testicular tumors (in dogs that haven't been neutered), cancers of the mouth or nose, and lymphoma.

The good news is that treatment for cancer is better than ever, especially if it's diagnosed in the early stages. Most forms of cancer are diagnosed through a biopsy, the removal and examination of a section of tissue. Blood tests, x-rays, and physical signs can also help in obtaining a diagnosis. Physical signs of cancer include the following:

- Abnormal swellings that don't go away or that grow larger
- Sores that don't heal
- Unusual or excessive weight loss
- Lack of appetite for any length of time

- Bleeding or discharge from any body opening
- Unusual and bad-smelling odors
- Difficulty eating or swallowing
- Loss of energy
- Persistent lameness or stiffness
- Difficulty breathing, urinating, or defecating

Cognitive Dysfunction Syndrome (CDS)

More commonly referred to as senility, this newly recognized disorder in dogs is defined as any age-related mental decline that can't be attributed to another cause, such as hearing or vision loss, a tumor, or organ failure. Dogs with cognitive dysfunction syndrome (CDS) may seem disoriented or confused. They sometimes wander aimlessly, stare into space, or appear lost in their own home. They interact less with family members or show changes in sleep and activity patterns. Sometimes they break housetraining. The acronym DISH can help you remember the signs of CDS:

- **D**isorientation
- **I**nteraction changes
- **S**leep or activity changes
- **H**ousetraining is forgotten

Signs of CDS can occur as early as eight years of age. If your Lab shows signs of CDS, talk to your veterinarian. Certain health problems such as kidney, thyroid, or adrenal gland disease can resemble CDS, so a definite diagnosis is essential. If CDS is the problem, medication has been developed that can help. Possible side effects of the medication include vomiting, diarrhea, hyperactivity, or restlessness.

Choline supplements may help increase mental alertness. They're available from holistic veterinarians or pet supply stores.

Diabetes

This disorder of the pancreas gland is a common disease in older Labs. It's seen most often in female dogs that are six to nine years old. Contributing factors include obesity and genetic predisposition.

What causes diabetes? The pancreas produces a hormone called insulin, which the body uses to drive glucose (blood sugar) into the cells. Diabetes occurs when the pancreas doesn't produce enough insulin or stops producing insulin altogether. Glucose levels build up in the bloodstream, causing high blood sugar.

Dogs with diabetes drink unusually large amounts of water, which in turn causes them to urinate frequently. They may even start having accidents in the house because they have to go so often. They also eat ravenously, yet still lose weight. Sudden blindness is another sign of the disease. If your Lab develops any of these signs, take him to the veterinarian. A urinalysis and blood tests are needed to diagnose diabetes.

There's no cure for diabetes, but it can be managed successfully. Your Lab will need insulin injections once or twice a day. Your veterinarian will show you how to administer the injection. Once you've had a little practice, it's quite easy, even if you're needle-phobic. Most dogs don't seem to mind the insulin injection, especially if they're given a treat or a meal immediately afterward. Weight loss through exercise and dietary control is another factor in successfully managing diabetes.

Hearing Loss

Just as with people, a dog's hearing tends to become less acute as he ages. This is usually caused by degenerative changes in the dog's inner ear. Your Lab may be able to hear only certain sounds, or he may suffer total hearing loss.

Fortunately, dogs can get along well even with diminished hearing. They simply make better use of their other senses, such as sight and smell. To let your hearing-impaired Lab know you're in the vicinity, make it a habit to stomp your foot when you're behind him, so he can feel the vibrations and know where you are.

Teaching a dog hand signals when he's young makes it easier to communicate with him later on if he loses his hearing.

Hypothyroidism

Hypothyroidism, the most common hormonal disease in dogs, is a failure of the thyroid gland. When the level of thyroid hormones falls below normal, many different body systems are affected. Signs of the disease include rough, scaly skin; hair loss, and unexplained weight gain. Dogs with hypothyroidism may also develop skin infections, allergies, and chronic ear infections. Hypothyroidism is common in middle-aged and older dogs, and Labs are among the breeds in which it is seen most frequently.

Hypothyroidism is managed with a daily dose of thyroid hormone replacement. The amount given is determined by the dog's weight. Your veterinarian will recommend blood testing every six months to ensure that the amount of medication being given is still appropriate.

Kidney Disease

The kidneys remove waste products from the body. They also help the body maintain appropriate levels of water, minerals, and vitamin B. As dogs age, however, kidney function can begin to deteriorate. A sign of this is increased water consumption and urination.

As part of caring for your older Lab, your veterinarian will recommend routine screening tests (bloodwork) to make sure the kidneys are functioning adequately. In the past, kidney dysfunction didn't show up in blood tests until 75 percent of the kidney's function was destroyed. Now, however, a new early renal disease (ERD) test detects microscopic levels of albumen (a type of protein) in the urine, a clear indication of damage to the kidney's filtration unit.

While the ERD test doesn't tell veterinarians how much of the kidney is still functional, it is known that significantly more of it is still functional when the ERD test becomes positive than when a blood test becomes positive. This allows your veterinarian to put your Lab on a special low-protein diet much earlier in the disease's progression, which can greatly lengthen his life.

Laryngeal Paralysis

This dysfunction of the larynx (voicebox) is common in older Labradors. The larynx fails to open properly as the dog inhales, causing obstruction of the airway. Usually the cause is unknown, although the condition sometimes develops as a result of injury to the larynx or laryngeal nerves. Signs of laryngeal paralysis include gagging or coughing during eating or drinking, noisy breathing, difficulty breathing, bluish gums, lack of energy, and fainting. Take your Lab to the vet right away if he shows any of these signs.

Laryngeal paralysis is diagnosed through a physical exam, chest x-rays, and examination of the larynx while the dog is lightly anesthetized. The veterinarian may also run thyroid gland function tests to rule out hypothyroidism. Mild cases can be treated by controlling the dog's weight, limiting activity (especially on hot days), and avoiding stressful situations. Sedatives or tranquilizers can sometimes help by keeping the dog calm, as can walking the dog with a harness instead of a neck collar. More severe cases require surgery to remove the part of the larynx that's obstructing the airway or to suture part of the larynx in an open position out of the flow of the airway.

Vision Loss

One of the most visible signs of aging in dogs is nuclear sclerosis, a condition in which the nucleus, or center, of the eye's lens becomes hazy and gray. This is caused when new fibers form at the edge of the lens and push inward toward the center, a normal aging process of the lens. It does not significantly affect the dog's vision, although it can cause some difficulty with close-up focus on objects.

Labs can also acquire cataracts as they age. These acquired cataracts are not the same as the juvenile cataracts that can affect younger Labs. They can occur as early as six years of age, and are a consequence of aging, or, in some cases, a side effect of diabetes. They begin at the center of the lens and spread outward toward the edge. Eventually, the lens becomes entirely opaque and the dog can no longer see.

Most dogs get along well without their sight, using their senses of smell and hearing to navigate familiar areas. As long as you don't move the furniture around, your Lab with cataracts should do just fine. If necessary, however, cataracts can be removed surgically.

Keeping Your Old Lab Comfortable

A Lab's golden years are a special time. Your Lab has always been one to go for the gusto, but as he ages and starts to slow down, he will appreciate anything you can do to make his life more comfortable. Here are some ways you can help:

- Provide soft bedding.
- Consider purchasing a heated bed to warm and soothe achy, arthritic bones.
- Provide a stepstool or ramp for getting on furniture or into the car.
- Allow extra opportunities to go outside to eliminate.

- Help him stay active with short walks and gentle games of fetch.
- Brush his teeth and schedule regular veterinary cleanings.
- Groom him weekly and check for lumps, bumps, or sores that may indicate a problem.

When to Say Goodbye

This is the most difficult decision a dog owner will ever make. Someday—far in the future, it's to be hoped—your Lab will be very old or sick and no longer enjoying life. As a dedicated caregiver, it is your duty to decide when it's time to give your Lab a peaceful release from life. Because you know your dog best, only you can make this decision, based on your Lab's quality of life. Factors to consider include appetite, attitude, activity level, elimination habits, comfort, and interaction with family members.

If you decide the time has come to say goodbye to your Lab, bring him to the vet. Euthanasia is painless. Your Lab will receive an injection of a drug that stops the heart and breathing muscles.

We all wish our dogs could go quietly in their sleep, dreaming of birds, but this happens only for a lucky few. When your Lab is no longer interested in eating, finds it difficult to move around, loses control of his bladder and bowels, and no longer enjoys being petted or interacting with family members, it's time to consider letting him go. Questions to ask yourself include whether your Lab has more good days than bad, whether he can still do his favorite things, and whether he acts as if he's in pain. The answers will help you get through the sadness when you finally must make that call to the veterinarian to set up an appointment for euthanasia. Remember the good times, and cherish your Lab forever in your heart and memories.

Appendix A

Resources

Associations, Breed Clubs, Foundations, and Registries

American Animal Hospital Association
12575 W. Bayaud Ave.
Lakewood, CO 80228
303-986-2800
www.aahanet.org

American Kennel Club (Operations Center)
5580 Centerview Dr.
Raleigh, NC 27606-3390
919-233-9767
www.akc.org

AKC Canine Health Foundation
251 W. Garfield Rd., Ste. 160
Aurora, OH 44202-8856
888-682-9696
www.akcchf.org

ASPCA Animal Poison Control Center
1717 S. Philo, Ste. 36
Urbana, IL 61802
888-426-4435
www.napcc.aspca.org

Association of Pet Dog Trainers
17000 Commerce Pkwy., Ste. C
Mt. Laurel, NJ 08054
800-738-3647
www.apdt.com

Canine Backpackers Association
P.O. Box 934
Conifer, CO 80433
www.caninebackpackers.org

Canine Companions for Independence
2965 Dutton Ave.
P.O. Box 446
Santa Rosa, CA 95402-0446
800-572-2275
www.caninecompanions.org

Canine Eye Registry Foundation
Purdue University - CERF/Lynn Hall
625 Harrison St.
West Lafayette, IN 47907-2026
765-494-8179
www.vet.purdue.edu/~yshen/cerf.html

Delta Society
580 Naches Avenue SW Suite 101
Renton, WA 98055-1329
425-226-7357
www.deltasociety.org

Foundation for Pet Provided Therapy (Love on a Leash)
P.O. Box 6308
Oceanside, CA 92058
760-740-2326
www.loveonaleash.org

Labrador Retriever Club (Membership)
Betty Dunlap
4650 Shifman Road
Goorich, MI 48438
810-797-4184
www.thelabradorclub.com

LABMED
73 White Bridge Road #103-166
Nashville, TN 37205
972-208-2470
www.labmed.org

Morris Animal Foundation
45 Inverness Dr. E.
Englewood, CO 80112-5480
800-243-2345
www.morrisanimalfoundation.org

National Association of Dog Obedience Instructors
PMB #369
729 Grapevine Hwy.
Hurst, TX 76054-2085
www.nadoi.org

National Association of Professional Pet Sitters
17000 Commerce Pkwy., Ste. C
Mt. Laurel, NJ 08054
800-296-7387
www.petsitters.org

National Dog Registry
Box 116
Woodstock, NY 12498
800-637-3647
www.natldogregistry.com

North American Dog Agility Council
11522 South Hwy. 3
Cataldo, ID 83810
www.nadac.com

North American Flyball Association
1400 W. Devon Ave. #512
Chicago, IL 60600
800-318-6312
www.flyball.org

Orthopedic Foundation for Animals
2300 E. Nifong Blvd.
Columbia, MO 65201
573-442-0418
www.offa.org

PetCare Insurance
3315 E. Algonquin Rd., Ste. 450
Rolling Meadows, IL 60008
866-275-7387
www.petcareinsurance.com

Pet Sitters International
201 E. King St.
King, NC 27021-9161
336-983-9222
www.petsit.com

Therapy Dogs, Inc.
PO Box 5868
Cheyenne, WY 82003
877-843-7364
www.therapydogs.com

Therapy Dogs International
88 Bartley Rd.
Flanders, NJ 07836
973-252-9800
www.tdi-dog.org

United Kennel Club
100 East Kilgore Rd.
Kalamazoo, MI 49002-5584
269-343-9020
www.ukcdogs.com

United States Dog Agility Association
P.O. Box 850955
Richardson, TX 75085-0955
972-487-2200
888-244-5489 (information line)
www.usdaa.com

Veterinary Pet Insurance
P.O. Box 2344
Brea, CA 92822-2344
800-872-7387
www.petinsurance.com

World Canine Freestyle Organization
P.O. Box 350122
Brooklyn, NY 11235-2525
718-332-8336
www.worldcaninefreestyle.org

Books

Activities

A Guide to Backpacking with Your Dog, by Charlene LaBelle (Loveland, CO: Alpine, 1998).

Hiking with Dogs, by Linda B. Mullally (Globe Pequot Press, 1999).

Introduction to Dog Agility, by Margaret H. Bonham (Hauppauge, NY: Barron's Educational Series, Incorporated, 2000).

Show Me!, by D. Caroline Coile (Hauppauge, NY: Barron's Educational Series, Incorporated, 1997).

The Simple Guide to Getting Active with Your Dog, by Margaret H. Bonham (Neptune City, NJ: TFH Publications, 2002).

Tracking Dog: Theory & Methods, 4th ed., by Glen R. Johnson (Mechanicsburg, PA: Barkleigh Productions, Inc., 1999).

Volunteering with Your Pet: How to Get Involved in Animal-Assisted Therapy with Any Kind of Pet, by Mary R. Burch and Aaron Honori Katcher (Hungry Minds, 1996).

Adoption and Rescue

The Adoption Option, by Eliza Rubenstein, Shari Kalina (Howell Book House, 1996).

Save That Dog!, by Liz Palika (Howell Book House, 1997).

Behavior, Intelligence, and Training

All Dogs Need Some Training, by Liz Palika (Howell Book House, 1997).

Dog Behavior: A Guide to a Happy, Healthy Pet, by Ian Dunbar (Howell Book House, 1998).

Getting Started: Clicker Training for Dogs, by Karen Pryor (Sunshine Books, 2002).

How to Teach a New Dog Old Tricks, 3rd ed., by Ian Dunbar (James & Kenneth Publishers, 1998).

The Intelligence of Dogs: A Guide to the Thoughts, Emotions, and Inner Lives of Our Canine Companions, by Stanley Coren (Bantam Books, 1995).

The Trick Is in the Training: 25 Fun Tricks to Teach Your Dog, by Stephanie Taunton and Cheryl S. Smith (Barron's Educational Series, Incorporated, 1998).

Dogs (Fiction and Nonfiction)

Betty and Rita Go to Paris, by Judith E. Hughes (Chronicle Books, 1999).

The Incredible Journey, by Sheila Burnford and Carl Burger (Laurel Leaf, 1996).

Jake: A Labrador Puppy at Work and Play, by Robert F. Jones and Bill Eppiridge (Sunburst, 1994).

Just Labs, by Steve Smith (Minocqua, WI: Willow Creek Press, 1995).

The Lost History of the Canine Race, by Mary Elizabeth Thurston (Avon, 1997).

My Dog's Brain, by Stephen Huneck (Penguin Studio, 2001).

Sally Goes to the Beach, by Stephen Huneck (Harry N. Abrams, 2000).

Upland Passage: A Field Dog's Education, by Robert F. Jones (Noonday Press, 1997).

Health

The Dog Owner's Home Veterinary Handbook, by James M. Giffin, M.D., and Liisa D. Carlson, D.V.M. (Howell Book House, 1999).

Hands-On Dog Care, by Sue M. Copeland and John M. Hamil, D.V.M. (Doral Publishing, 2000).

UC Davis Book of Dogs: The Complete Medical Reference Guide for Dogs and Puppies, by Mordecai Siegal (Harper Resource, 1995).

Travel

The Dog Lover's Companion, series (Avalon Travel Publishing).

Take Your Pet USA, by Arthur Frank (Artco Publishing).

Traveling with Your Pet, The AAA Petbook, edited by Greg Weeks (American Automobile Association).

Magazines

AKC Family Dog
American Kennel Club
260 Madison Ave.
New York, NY 10016

AKC Gazette
American Kennel Club
260 Madison Ave.
New York, NY 10016

Dog Fancy
Fancy Publications
P.O. Box 6050
Mission Viejo, CA 92690

Dogs USA
Fancy Publications
P.O. Box 6050
Mission Viejo, CA 92690

Dog World
Fancy Publications
P.O. Box 6050
Mission Viejo, CA 92690

Popular Dogs: Labrador Retrievers
Fancy Publications
P.O. Box 6050
Mission Viejo, CA 92690

APPENDIX 

Guidelines to Finding a Breeder

Qualities of a Reputable Breeder

A reputable breeder is someone who has been involved with the breed for several years and knows everything about it. Here are some characteristics of a reputable breeder:

- A good breeder shows his dogs in conformation classes or competes with them in field trials so their conformation and working ability can be evaluated by breed judges.
- A good breeder is knowledgeable about the breed's history and health, genetics, and breed type.
- A good breeder doesn't breed his dogs until they're physically mature—at least two years old.
- A good breeder tests his breeding stock to ensure that they're free of hereditary diseases before breeding, and submits the results to health registries.
- A good breeder monitors his dogs' health through hip evaluations, eye exams, and other observable expressions of genetic conditions.
- When he breeds a litter, a good breeder handles pups frequently and accustoms them to the sights and sounds surrounding them.

Questions to Ask

Your interview with the breeder should give you a good idea of how committed she is to Labradors and how long she has been in the breed. If she's a reputable breeder, she'll be impressed that you've done your homework. Be wary of someone who ignores your questions or is offended by them. Questions you should ask include the following:

- How long have you been involved with Labradors?
- What got you interested in the breed?
- Do you show your dogs or compete with them in field trials?
- What titles have your dogs earned?
- What breed clubs do you belong to?
- What's the goal of your breeding program?
- Do you screen your breeding stock for heritable diseases?
- Can I see the health certifications for this puppy's parents and grandparents?
- How old are the puppy's parents?
- Do you provide a health guarantee?
- Are you willing to take this dog back for any reason?

Questions to Answer

Before you make an appointment with a breeder, be aware that the interview process is a two-way street. The breeder will want to know just as much about you as you want to know about him. Be prepared to answer all kinds of questions such as:

- Why do you want a Labrador?
- Where will the dog live?
- How do you plan to exercise the dog?
- Is anyone home during the day?
- Have you owned a dog before? What happened to it?
- Who will train the dog?
- Do you have a fenced yard?

Index

C

D

E

F

G

H

I

K

L

M

S

T

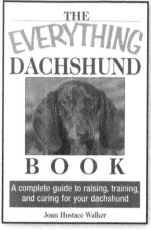

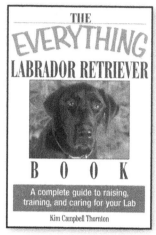

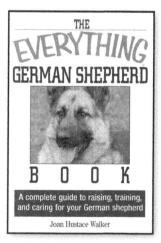

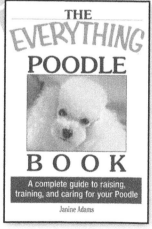